MW00719760

CASE

*Using Software
Development Tools*

Related titles of interest from John Wiley & Sons:

Expert Systems: Tools and Applications, Harmon, Maus, and Morrissey

Expert Systems: Artificial Intelligence in Business, Harmon and King

Putting Artificial Intelligence to Work: Evaluating and Implementing Business Applications, Schoen and Sykes

New Techniques in Software Project Management, Simpson

Artificial Intelligence Programming with Turbo Prolog, Weiskamp and Hengl

CASE

Using Software Development Tools

Alan S. Fisher

WILEY

John Wiley & Sons, Inc.
New York • Chichester • Brisbane • Toronto • Singapore

Publisher: Stephen Kippur
Editor: Therese A. Zak
Managing Editor: Ruth Greif
Editing, Design, and Production: Publishers Network

This publication is designed to provide accurate and authoritative information in regard to the subject matter covered. It is sold with the understanding that the publisher is not engaged in rendering legal, accounting, or other professional service. If legal advice or other expert assistance is required, the services of a competent professional person should be sought. FROM A DECLARATION OF PRINCIPLES JOINTLY ADOPTED BY A COMMITTEE OF THE AMERICAN BAR ASSOCIATION AND A COMMITTEE OF PUBLISHERS.

Copyright © 1988 by John Wiley & Sons, Inc.

All rights reserved. Published simultaneously in Canada.

Reproduction or translation of any part of this work beyond that permitted by section 107 or 108 of the 1976 United States Copyright Act without the permission of the copyright owner is unlawful. Requests for permission or further information should be addressed to the Permission Department, John Wiley & Sons, Inc.

Library of Congress Cataloging-in-Publication Data

Fisher.
   CASE: using the newest tools in software development/Alan S. Fisher.
      p.   cm.
   Bibliography: p. 281
   ISBN 0-471-63747-5 (pbk.)
   1. Computer software—Development. I. Title.   99-10142
QA76.76.D47F57   1988   CIP
005.1—dc19

Printed in the United States of America

88 89 10 9 8 7 6 5 4

To
Ann and Janis

Trademarks

Accolade is a trademark of Computer Corporation of America.

Ada is a registered trademark of the Department of Defense, Ada Joint Program Office.

Apple Lisa, Apple Macintosh, HyperCard, MacDraw, and MacWrite are registered trademarks of Apple Computer, Inc.

Altos, Dorado, and Star are registered trademarks of the Xerox Corporation.

APS Development Center is a trademark of Sage Software, Inc.

AutoCAD is a registered trademark of Autodesk, Inc.

Brackets is a trademark of TLA Systems and Education, Ltd.

CASE 2000 and DesignAid are trademarks of Nastec Corporation.

Cortex and CorVision are trademarks of Cortex Corporation.

dBASE, dBASE II, and dBASE III are registered trademarks of the Ashton-Tate Corporation.

DEC is a registered trademark of Digital Equipment Corporation.

DESIGN/2.0 is a trademark of Meta Software Corporation.

DSSD, DocumentOrr, and STRUCTURE(S) are registered trademarks and DesignMachine is a trademark of Ken Orr & Associates.

DIALOG is a registered service mark of Dialog Information Services, Inc.

Entity-Relationship Diagrammer, Data Flow Diagrammer, and Action Diagrammer are trademarks of KnowledgeWare, Inc.

Excelerator and XL/Interface Micro Focus are trademarks of Index Technology Corporation.

IBM, IBM PC, ISPF, MVS, VM, and VM/CMS are registered trademarks of International Business Machines Corp.

IDMS/Architect is a trademark of Cullinet Software, Inc.

Information Engineering Facility is a trademark of Texas Instruments, Inc.

Interleaf is a trademark of Interleaf, Inc.

Kolinar and SQL/MENU are trademarks of Kolinar Corporation.

Lotus and 1-2-3 are registered trademarks of Lotus Development Corporation.

MacBubbles is a trademark of StarSys, Inc.

Micro Focus and VS COBOL Workbench are trademarks of Micro Focus, Inc.

Microsoft and MS-DOS are a registered trademarks of Microsoft Corporation.

Netron and Netron/CAP are trademarks of Netron Inc.

Panel is a trademark of Roundhill Computer Systems.

PostScript is a registered trademark of Adobe Systems, Inc.

PowerTools and PRISM are registered trademarks of Iconix Software Engineering, Inc.

ProMod is a registered trademark of Promod, Inc.

PSL/PSA and Structured Architect are registered trademarks of Meta Systems, Inc.

Scribe is a registered trademark of Unilogic, Inc.

Software through Pictures is a trademark of Interactive Development Environments, Inc.

Statemate1 and AD CAD are trademarks of of AD CAD, Inc.

TAGS and IORL are registered trademarks of Teledyne Brown Engineering.

Teamwork is a registered trademark of Cadre Technologies, Inc.

Teletype is a registered trademark of the Teletype Corporation.

Telon is a trademark of Pansophic Systems, Inc.

ThinkTank is a trademark of Living Videotext, Inc.

UNIX is a registered trademark of AT&T Bell Laboratories, Inc.

VisiCalc is a registered trademark of VisiCorp.

Windows for Data is a trademark of Vermont Creative Software, Inc.

WordStar is a registered trademark of MicroPro International Corporation.

Preface

Welcome to the fast-paced, rapidly growing field of computer-aided software engineering! As software projects in many fields grow to monumental size and complexity, the need for computer-aided software analysis and generation is more pressing than ever. Put simply, CASE tools help software engineers and data processing professionals *specify* and *design* software. Some CASE tools go one step further by automatically generating software based on this specification and design.

Unfortunately, there is no formal or well-accepted definition of computer-aided software engineering, although there is a general consensus that CASE deals with the requirements analysis and design specification stages of software development. Computer-aided software engineering is a somewhat nebulous term, much like "artificial intelligence." As soon as a technique or technology becomes more fully understood, it is no longer artificially intelligent, but is just another implement in the software developer's arsenal. Computer-aided software engineering is the same. Undoubtedly, when certain CASE methodologies become commonplace in software tools, they will no longer be "computer-aided."

This book presents an overview of computer-aided software engineering technologies and commercially available CASE tools. It is a practical book for practicing project managers and software engineers, addressing the issues of managing software projects using CASE in addition to its technical underpinnings. Most CASE methodologies evolved from structured systems methodologies developed in the 1960s and 1970s, and this book emphasizes those that have achieved *commercial* acceptance. There is so much depth and diversity in this area alone that entire books can be written (and have been) about each of the CASE methodologies.

This book is intended as an overview of computer-aided software engineering, and as such, presents only a moderate level of technical detail. Many illustrations and examples are included to explain the concepts and fundamentals. Readers interested in pursuing topics in more depth are invited to review the annotated bibliography at the end of this book. There are many fine works on structured systems methodologies employed in commercially available CASE tools, as well as others that are too new to have yet attracted a large following. However, ample detail is presented to develop a firm understanding of the underlying technology. As a technical overview, this book is segmented into four parts, each appealing to a different audience:

Part 1: Introduction to CASE. This introductory section is targeted at project managers and other individuals responsible for directing a software project, but who do not necessarily participate in the project's day-to-day activities. These chapters describe the types of computer-aided software engineering tools and practices and how they reduce a software development project's cost, length, and risk. An overview of the software development process is presented with an eye toward where computer-aided software engineering can leverage existing efforts. Three different tool categories are described: requirements and design specification tools, data modeling tools, and user interface design tools.

As a justification for computer-aided software engineering, this section articulates the failure points in the traditional software development process and examines where CASE can remedy or altogether circumvent these obstacles. The evolution of software tools and techniques is traced, leading to present-day CASE tools.

Part 2: CASE Technologies and Methodologies. This section is more technically detailed than the first and is intended for those wanting to understand the underlying methodologies and techniques used in the different types of CASE tools. This material is appropriate for practicing software developers and project managers active in building software systems. Throughout the 1960s and 1970s, different structured systems design methodologies were developed to aid analysts and software engineers in their requirements analysis and design efforts. Many of these methodologies are in use in today's CASE tools, ranging from the popular Yourdon/DeMarco Structured Analysis methodology to data modeling to user interface design. These chapters explore the popular structured systems methodologies used by vendors as the nucleus of their software products.

Part 3: Specific CASE Tools.   Also for the technically inclined, this section describes ten different CASE tools in detail, leading the reader through a series of examples executed with the respective tools. Tools for requirements analysis and design specification are presented, as well as tools for user interface design. All are commercially available.

This section will interest both software project managers and practicing software engineers responsible for selecting a CASE tool for use in a project. While the CASE tool market is still embryonic, many vendors are exploring different technologies in hope of better leveraging their customers' development efforts. These chapters highlight the differences between similar tools.

As the most technically detailed of the four sections, *"Specific CASE Tools"* can be skimmed by scanning only the screen shots and illustrations, since this information is most useful to those interested in the specifics of certain CASE tools. For the project manager, the screen shots will convey the "look and feel" of typical CASE tools. Understanding these practicalities is important in deciding how tools mesh with your particular development practices and engineering staff.

Part 4: Managing CASE Technology.   The final section will appeal to those interested in making a CASE tool purchasing decision in which the strength of the vendor and the company's support policies weigh heavily. The likely directions and future advances in computer-aided software engineering are described, as well as the technical challenges facing today's technology. These chapters address the issues of instituting a CASE tool program in your organization, including selecting an appropriate first software project for CASE technology, the software team structure, and the equipment resources required for a successful software project. This section will also appeal to those interested in investing in CASE tool vendors.

Do not feel obligated to read all four parts of this book. In fact, each of the parts has a different audience in mind. Sections that appear uninteresting or too detailed can be skimmed or ignored. Frequently, this type of cursory examination can unearth the concepts more quickly than a detailed reading of the text. There are many illustrations, tables, and screen shots throughout this book, and most of the high-level concepts can be gleaned from just perusing the diagrams and reading the captions.

CASE tool technology will rapidly unfold during the next five years as the software community learns more about large software projects and automatic software generation. More and more software development organizations are beginning the technology assimilation process. Software professionals are rapidly homing in on concepts like *zero defect software* and *the software factory*. CASE technology is part of this convergence, and those organizations which ignore it will be left behind to suffer reduced software development productivity and increased development costs.

Acknowledgments

Of all the individuals lending their valuable assistance to this project, David King of Price Waterhouse deserves the foremost acknowledgment. He successfully navigated me around the many tar pits inherent in authoring a book from proposal to successful completion. His careful and guiding hand made writing this book a very straightforward and smooth endeavor. And, whenever I needed inspiration, David's book *Expert Systems* (co-authored with Paul Harmon), served as an excellent model replete with good organizational and structural ideas.

I also extend my appreciation to Jonathan King of Teknowledge, Inc. and Mitch Shapiro of Texas Instruments for scrutinizing various parts of this manuscript and for providing honest feedback on many of my ideas. A very special thanks goes to Eleonore Johnson of Teknowledge for meticulously proofreading this manuscript. Her thorough copy editing helped purge my idiosyncratic, and sometimes murky, prose. My wife Ann also deserves credit for scrutinizing the various manuscript drafts and locating many inconsistencies. Her efforts contributed a nonengineering perspective to this book's development.

One group in particular—the CASE tool vendors—deserves a special mention. Without their help, cooperation, and more than one Federal Express shipment, this book would have lacked the realism galvanized by highlighting specific packages rather than simply concepts. Many individuals and organizations helped compile technical information on the different CASE tools, and their efforts made this book as technically accurate as possible. In particular, I would like to thank Karen Chiacu at CADRE Technologies; Doug Rosenberg and Jolene McClenaghan at Iconix Software Engineering; Judith Van Der Kay at Index Technology; Karen Elkind at JYACC; Cathy Van Horn at Nastec Corporation; Cheryl Israel at Optima, Inc.; Thomas Scott at Promod; and Melonie Fischer at Teledyne Brown Engineering. I would like to especially thank Dr. Dave Brown of Auburn University for contributing his very lucid description of Teledyne Brown Engineering's TAGS system.

Finally, Teri Zak, my editor at John Wiley & Sons, deserves praise for shepherding this book through the review and production process. Her behind-the-scenes work made this all appear very transparent to me, much like a good CASE tool does with software.

Contents

Part 1

Introduction to CASE

Chapter 1

The Case for CASE

This book is about Computer-Aided Software Engineering (CASE) tools and how they are revolutionizing the world of software development. Only fifteen years ago a computer with 64,000 bytes (64K) of main memory—referred to as "core"—was considered a large computer. "Huge" programs could be stored in 64K. Even as recently as 1978, with the introduction of the early personal computers, 64K was considered the upper limit on what a large application program would consume. Almost all serious programming was done in assembly language, which simultaneously provides the best in execution performance and yet limits the size of a program because of the difficulty in constructing very large assembly programs.

In September 1981, IBM introduced its IBM PC personal computer with a memory capacity of 640,000 bytes—ten times larger than the previous generation of personal computers only three years before. Yet many application programs have since grown in size to challenge even the boundaries of this once vast amount of memory. These application programs, now written in higher level languages, such as C, Pascal, and Lisp, are even more complex and sophisticated than before.

Software developers on all hardware platforms, from personal computers to mainframes strove harder and harder to please their end-users with increasingly more intelligent, robust, and powerful software. Typically, this translates into more sophisticated end-user interfaces, allowing expanded end-user interaction.

However, as software projects grow larger and more complex, they become prone to unpredictable behavior and outright failure. These problems stem directly from the vast

A man's got to know his limitations.
— Dirty Harry in Magnum Force

3

amounts of software that must be written for many applications being built today—literally hundreds of thousands of lines of code for projects ranging from digital switching systems to space shuttle control software to complex payroll and accounting packages. Even "personal computer" software programs contain upwards of 40,000 to 50,000 lines of code.

In programs of this magnitude, it is almost impossible to achieve 100 percent reliability. There is bound to be at least one bug! While old-time mainframe users may be willing to tolerate a few "irregularities," today's fifteen million relatively unsophisticated personal computer users will not.

Unfortunately, many of these large software applications are critical to the success and orderly operation of commercial enterprises and to the reliable operation of national defense systems. A study done in 1980 by TRW estimated that 64 percent of software errors arose from the requirements analysis and design phases, and only 30 percent of these design errors were being detected before the software

Figure 1.1 Most software errors originate in the requirements analysis and design specification phases of the software development process. Unfortunately, less than one-third of these design errors are caught before acceptance testing begins. (From *"CASE Makes Strides Toward Automated Software Development,"* Computer Design, January 1, 1987.)

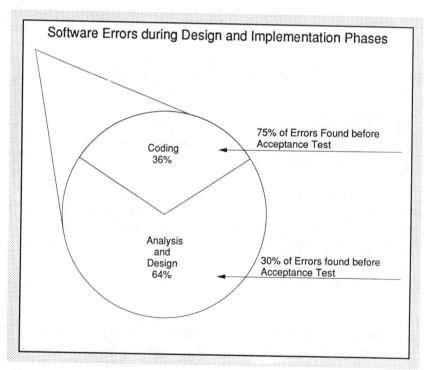

was delivered for acceptance testing (Figure 1.1). This underscores the need to "design it right the first time."

In contrast, only 36 percent of a program's errors originated in the implementation phases of the project, and a full 75 percent of these coding errors were found before acceptance testing began.

What is CASE Software?

Computer-aided software engineering tools substantially reduce or eliminate many of the design and development problems inherent in medium to large software projects by automatically generating most of the software based on designs specified by the software architect. Figure 1.2 shows how CASE tools allow the software designer to focus on the systems architecture rather than on the actual implementation (the coding).

The ultimate goal of CASE technology is to separate the application program's design from the program's code implementation. Generally, the more detached the design process is from the actual code generation, the better. Many organizations and individual programmers have recognized this basic software planning and structuring principle for a long time. Over the course of the last fifteen years, several *structured methodologies* have been developed and

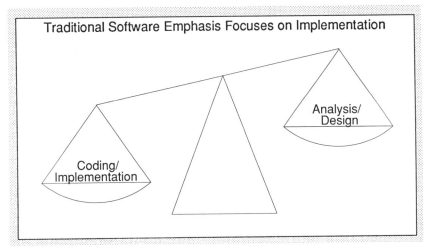

Figure 1.2 Traditional software development practices emphasize implementation, coding, and debugging. Computer-aided software engineering focuses on requirements analysis and design specification.

introduced to large numbers of programmers. These structured methodologies provided a design framework and a set of formalisms and practices upon which to conduct software development work.

Although not perfect and largely relying on the thoroughness of the individual practitioner, these methodologies have allowed software developers to build more complex systems. Usually, these methodologies function by decomposing large software systems into sets of smaller, more tractable modules. Typically, the interfaces between these modules are well-designed by the software architect, allowing individual programmers to independently construct and test their respective assigned modules. Then during the final stages of the software development process, all of the modules are collected and *integrated* to form the final program.

Many of today's CASE tools implement structured systems methodologies developed in the 1960s and 1970s.

In many respects, CASE tools are a direct development of these early paper-based structured methodologies. Now many of those same structured methodologies and organizational techniques are being implemented as software programs themselves, instead of relying on the individual programmers and software engineers to religiously practice the methodologies.

One definition of computer-aided software engineering is the use of *tools that provide leverage at any point in the software project development cycle.* This definition would include most tools that software engineers are acquainted with today, including compilers, debuggers, performance profilers, and source code control systems. Compilers, after all, provide value by translating higher level languages, such as C, COBOL, and FORTRAN, into lower level machine code, directly executable by the computer; and writing in C is far superior to writing in assembly language or machine code!

A more restrictive but operationally better definition for computer-aided software engineering is the use of *tools that provide leverage in the software project **requirements analysis** and **design specification** phases, and those tools which, potentially, generate code **automatically** from the* *software design specification.* This more restrictive definition will be used in order to focus on the higher leverage design and automatic code generation tools now being introduced by a number of CASE tool vendors.

Requirements analysis and design specification packages are examples of CASE tools that allow the software designer to display and graphically edit a software *schematic.* Interactive graphics editing is certainly less time intensive, not to mention more enjoyable, than regenerating paper-based designs. Furthermore, these design specification tools provide *consistency checking* features, verifying that all software modules interface properly and all data structures are fully specified.

Other CASE tools are more highly focused than the design specification tools. An example of a focused tool is a *user interface generator.* Examples of this class of CASE tools are interactive form design and generation packages which allow the software designer to develop and specify a form-based user interface for an application program. These tools usually operate in a what-you-see-is-what-you-get fashion.

Before CASE tools can be discussed in detail, the software development process should be fully understood. CASE tools provide leverage by exploiting the design and development process, generally in the early stages, to yield implementation benefits later in the project.

The Software Development Process

The software development process consists of several well defined steps which, if properly followed, lead to well-designed, very maintainable software. In some respects, the software development process is simple common sense. Yet most software development organizations fail to follow one or more of the steps, usually because of time or budget constraints. More often than not, long-term quality and maintainability goals yield to the short-term pressures of "getting something out the door." The important requirements analysis and design specification steps fall by the wayside in favor of immediately starting the code implementation.

Never time to do it right, always time to do it twice! As software professionals, many of us have had to deal with code written under such conditions.

It is more instructive to think of software development not as a linear process but as a *cycle*, as illustrated by Figure 1.3. Processes typically have ends, but software development, in many circumstances, does not. Almost always, a software program will require ongoing maintenance activity, and if the program is successful, continued development may be required to expand the program's capabilities. An active and supportive user community will see to that! Continued development mandates good up-front end-user requirements analysis and design specification practices, leading to maintainable and extendible software.

Each phase of the software development cycle is defined briefly in the following list. Although generally executed in a linear, step-by-step fashion, "feedback loops" exist, usually in the requirements analysis and design specification phases. This is especially true in the development of

Figure 1.3 Although many view software development as a linear process, it is actually a cycle consisting of several well defined phases. Requirements Analysis and Design Specification are the two most demanding phases and largely determine the success or failure of the development effort.

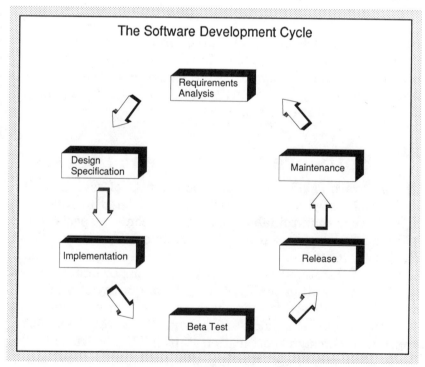

The Software Development Cycle

Requirements Analysis

Design Specification

Maintenance

Implementation

Release

Beta Test

custom software where design prototypes built during the design specification phase may unearth hidden end-user requirements.

Requirements Analysis
Analyzing and articulating end-user requirements to produce a *requirements specification*. Requirements specifications include functionality requirements, machine environment constraints, user interface designs, and performance goals.

Design Specification
Composing a software blueprint, showing what to build and how to build it. Design specifications include module decompositions, data structure definitions, file format definitions, and important algorithm descriptions.

Implementation
Coding, testing, and debugging each module designed in the design specification. Code walk-throughs are held to ensure quality and reliability in the implementation.

Unit Test and Integration
Testing each module built during the implementation phase, then integrating the modules into a single program structure. The program as a whole is then tested to make sure the modules fit together and perform as designed.

Beta Test Release
Sending early copies of the software to actual end-users. Beta test releases identify trouble spots, performance problems, and bugs. Active end-user polling is conducted to provide maximum feedback to the development team.

Final Release
Acting on the beta testing information, repairing the software, and readying it for final release to the general end-user community.

Maintenance
Fixing any bugs or problems found by users of the released version. The maintenance team is responsible for releasing minor upgrade versions of the software to

accommodate bug fixes as necessary. Enhancement suggestions are collected for use in continued rounds of development.

This process works best when different *specialists* are responsible for the different phases. When the same group of individuals, such as a project team, perform all the steps in the cycle, they tend to take short cuts. The same group loses perspective as the project progresses, finding it more difficult to stand back and objectively look at the project's overall goals and requirements. The end result of these short cuts is lower quality, less reliable software. Software development is an engineering task serving practical purposes, not an art form!

Although the software development process is represented as a cycle, it is not continuous. Time gaps and lags exist between the various phases. Some gaps occur because sign-offs or acceptance procedures are required, such as the contracting organization accepting a requirements specification. Other gaps occur as different specialist crews transition in to work on certain phases. Usually, several months or even several years exist between the maintenance phase and the next requirements analysis phase. This normal lag allows users to install and use the software. But once the software becomes assimilated into routine use, the end-users will begin to formulate (even clamor for) enhancement requests. For software products the time gap between maintenance and the next generation requirements analysis may be zero. Even as one version of the software is being beta tested and readied for release, the next version is being planned and designed.

The software development cycle concept is not just something fabricated to look good in books on software engineering. Rather, this cycle has been developed and refined over the years by thousands of practicing software professionals. In a slightly more primitive form, the development cycle diagram is referred to as the "waterfall diagram" because of the series of boxes describing each stage, one after another descending on the page in a cascading fashion. The chief difference is that the waterfall model, as shown in Figure

1.4, treats the software development process like a factory with the raw materials coming in one end and a finished product moving out the other. The "cyclic" model, Figure 1.3, views software development as a continuous process with software releases like photo snapshots at particular points in time.

The relative importance of the different phases varies in terms of level of effort and calendar time. The earlier phases demand more engineering effort but consume less calendar time, while the later stages are less effort-intensive but take longer. The requirements analysis and design specification phases require substantial interaction among systems engineers and end-users. The beta testing and maintenance phases are "reactive," awaiting commentary and feedback from the end-users on the application's behavior. For example, a beta test typically consumes 20% of a project's life span but only 5% of its technical effort. These estimates are only approximate and actual results will depend on the nature and scope of the individual project. But since calendar time is generally a scarcer commodity than the development resource (programmers), computer-aided software engineering's goal is to develop tools that maximize

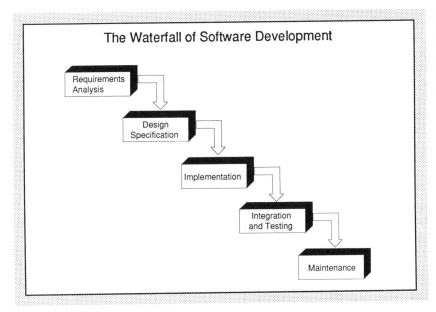

Figure 1.4 The "waterfall" model of software development is the traditional model followed by most software professionals.

the software designer's impact in the early project phases in order to reduce the amount of calendar time spent on the later phases.

CASE technology is equally valuable when programmers are scarce, as is common in most data processing departments. Application programming backlogs occur because of the time it takes to implement an application, as well as the difficulty involved in recruiting qualified programming talent. CASE technology helps reduce this backlog by making each programmer-hour more productive.

For example, if a CASE design tool automatically generates code (or at least part of it), two benefits are accured. First, since the tool is automatically generating part of the code, implementation time will substantially drop, maybe down to zero. Secondly, you might feel more confident about the generated code's quality because it was automatically produced by a software tool which itself has been thoroughly debugged and tested. So time is saved in both the unit test and integration phases. Although today's CASE technology does not support automatic code generation for general software, automatic code generation has been achieved in a number of focused areas, such as automatic user interface code generation and data base schema design and access code generation.

Each phase in the software development cycle has a specific set of checkpoints and deliverables designed to ensure maximum quality and reduce the need for redesign at a later time. The checkpoints are specification, design, and code walk-throughs. The deliverables are items such as design documents or interim software releases. Figure 1.5 illustrates several of these deliverables and checkpoints. The checkpoints are depicted using the standard flow-charting "conditional" diamond to indicate that the deliverables must be received in good order before progressing to the next development phase. A development phase is not complete until the deliverables are received and the milestones have been met. Project teams ignoring these formal checkpoints run the risk of uncovering major errors or omissions substantially later than need be.

The documents and walk-throughs shown in Figure 1.5 are not cast in concrete, however. Different projects have different quality goals and requirements. Smaller projects may not need formal code walk-throughs but large projects most assuredly will. What is important is that software managers decide what is acceptable during the planning stages *before* a project begins. Methodology and quality assurance should be considered at the outset of a project, not once it is partially completed. Both project management and the contracting organization must decide the project's level of effort and the cost of a potential error once the software is in the field. If the software is destined to be part of a "mission

Figure 1.5 Each stage in the software development process ends with a review or checkpoint that produces a specific deliverable, such as a design document or reviewed code. Computer-aided software engineering can help designers write requirements and design documents. Some tools automatically generate code, reducing the time spent in the implementation and testing phases.

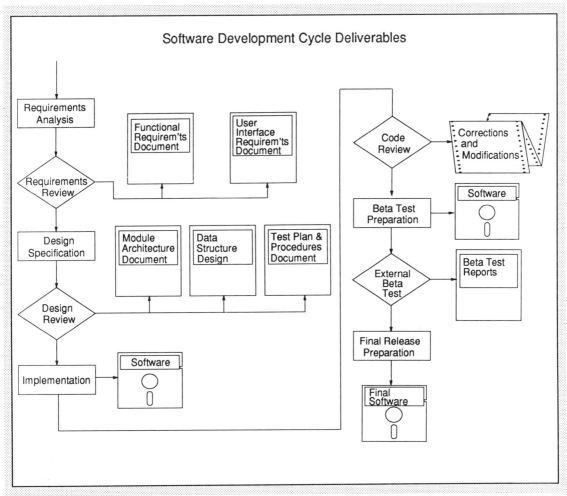

critical" application, such as jet engine control or commercial cash trading management, then failure due to a design flaw or a programming error is very costly. On the other hand, failure in a simple utility or reporting program might be more of a nuisance than anything else.

Software development is an involved and complex process. The reader must develop a reasonable understanding of what happens during each phase and where CASE tools can provide assistance. The essence of computer-aided software engineering is providing leverage during the early development phases to save effort and expense in the later phases.

Why the Software Development Process Breaks Down

During the software development cycle, any number of failures can occur. Most failures, however, result from poor planning, insufficient requirements analysis, and ill-conceived design specifications. A sure indicator of improper requirements analysis or design specification is the implementation phase dragging on for much longer than originally planned. The more thought and effort invested in the requirements definition and detailed software design, the lower the risk of a protracted or failed implementation.

Figure 1.6 itemizes common problems and their symptoms occurring at different points in the software development cycle.

Many blame software development failures on poor project planning. However, detailed requirements specifications and system designs are necessary before a project plan can be written and the milestone and completion dates accurately cast. By analogy, a building project cannot be completely estimated until the blueprints are finalized. Thorough and complete project plans are the result of specifications and design, and it makes little sense to gauge the size of the implementation and fielding tasks without them.

Software Development Analysis	Failure Symptom
Requirements Analysis	No written requirements Incompletely specified requirements No user interface mock-up No end-user involvement
Design Specification	Lack of, or insufficient, design documents Poorly specified data structures and file formats Infrequent or no design reviews
Implementation	Lack of, or insufficient, coding standards Infrequent or no code reviews Poor in-line code documentation
Unit Test & Integration	Insufficient module testing Lack of proper or complete test suite Lack of an independent quality assurance group
Beta Test Release	Complete lack of a beta test Insufficient duration for beta test Insufficient number of beta testers Wrong beta testers selected
Maintenance	Too many bug reports Fixing one bug introduces new bugs

Several major themes underlie software project failures:

- **Lack of complete requirements definition.** If you lack a firm idea of what you are building, it is very difficult to built it right! Although plain common sense, this is often the most overlooked part of software development—identifying the system's requirements.

- **No development methodology.** Once you know exactly what you are going to build, you need to select design techniques and establish implementation procedures. Following a formal methodology—a set of design techniques, development procedures, coding standards, checkpoints, and work rules—helps ensure software design completeness and implementation quality.

Figure 1.6 Failure points in software development. Software projects can easily go awry. This table illustrates several of the common symptoms found during a project's different stages.

■ **Improper design partitioning.** An incomplete requirements specification leads to the development of the wrong software, but an improper design leads to low quality implementation. Designs should be partitioned into manageable components and modules with formal pathways for importing and exporting data. Poorly partitioned designs lead to nightmarish code!

Where Can CASE Help?   If the cause of most implementation shortfalls and reliability problems stem from improper or insufficient requirements analysis and design specification, what is the remedy? During the 1960s and 1970s, several *structured methodologies* were developed to impose rigid structures on the requirements analysis and design specification phases of the software development cycle. These methodologies presented a straightforward, cookbook style approach to software development which, by following the methodologies, would greatly reduce the risks caused by requirements and design error.

Several of these methodologies are Yourdon/DeMarco Structured Analysis (data flow diagrams) for requirements analysis, Hierarchical plus Input and Output (HIPO) charts for software module structuring, and Warnier-Orr and Entity-Relationship Diagrams for data modeling. These methodologies all attack different parts of the requirements analysis and design specification process. The knowledgeable software manager maintains these methodologies in his technological arsenal and knows when and how to employ them. He realizes that several different methodologies will frequently be used on the same software project, each for its own speciality.

These formal, structured methodologies are the backbone of computer-aided software engineering. These methodologies provide the rigorous framework necessary to thoroughly specify and design software applications.

Does CASE Stifle Creativity?

As in all software undertakings, there are human factors to be considered. Most software professionals consider themselves to be craftsmen: skilled artisans that have endured the painstaking rigors of learning the art and practice of software development. We place ourselves among the ranks of skilled surgeons and attorneys rather than with work-a-day laborers. Indeed, many of us learned our trade as apprentices to highly skilled masters who meted out their specialized knowledge to us as our skills and aptitude developed. CASE technology will not replace true talent and ingenuity.

Yet, at least superficially, CASE technology seems to diminish our aura of craftsmanship by giving us tools that encourage following a strict regime for software development. Will CASE tools restrict or mute our programming creativity? Indeed, can mechanical aids turn art into engineering? In the larger software development organizations where the usage of particular tools is often mandated, this issue becomes paramount.

To address the creativity issue, we must identify the well-spring of programmer creativity. What is it that makes our skills nonmechanical, and which components of application development inherently require thought and cannot be automatically duplicated by a CASE tool? Most software professionals believe that software engineering creativity is the essence of program architecture and of designing a well-crafted software solution that meets an end-user group's needs. In fact, many software designers would agree with Frank Lloyd Wright's notion that "form follows function." That is, first and foremost, a software application must meet end-user needs. Only when the functional needs are met does the "look and feel" of the program—its form—demonstrate the individual programmer's craftsmanship.

True craftsmanship resides in the layout of the user interface and in the organization of the internal data structures. Although the physical construction of software—the coding—does provide the programmer opportunity to demonstrate individual skill by writing succinct, "minimalist" code, the true genius of an individual programmer is in how well the end-users are served with the best, easiest to use, software solution.

CASE tools will not banish our creativity; rather they will provide us with tools to better demonstrate it.

CASE tools give us power equipment to compliment our hand tools. CASE tools enhance our creativity by enabling us to construct more thoughtful designs in a shorter amount of time. A data flow diagramming tool eliminates the drudgery of hand drawing, allowing the software analyst more freedom to pursue alternate architectures. A user interface layout program permits the software engineer to focus on the human factors of interface design, letting the tool regenerate a new working implementation for each end-user feedback cycle.

There will still be a need for "hand crafted" modules in many situations, and we should certainly not abandon our hand tools. CASE technology is not nearly at the stage where 100 percent of an application's code can be automatically generated. Yet the technology can provide leverage in many situations, making it a powerful amplifier of programmer creativity.

Summary

This chapter presented the shortcomings of traditional software development practices and how problems in the early development phases can snowball into failure later in the project. Next we examine how CASE tools can remedy software development bottlenecks and reduce the risk of project failure. Chapter 2, *"Where CASE Fits In,"* discusses the different types of commercially available CASE tools and how they augment existing development technology. Chapter 2 traces the historical development of CASE technology and contrasts CASE tools with traditional software development tools, such as compilers and fourth generation languages.

Chapter 2

Where CASE Fits In

Over the years, software tools have evolved to meet the ever-increasing demands of the system software and application programs. When assembly language became too cumbersome for the majority of software developers to use, COBOL and FORTRAN language compilers were developed. As developers realized how efficient it was to reuse code written for one application in others, standardized off-the-shelf subroutine packages were developed covering a wide range of areas. As the size of applications grew too large for one individual or a small group of individuals to manage, source code control systems were created to orchestrate the access, modification, and installation of software code files and modules.

Yet even with these *implementation-oriented* software tools, today's application programs are becoming so large and complex that no single individual can fully specify the application's functional requirements or its underlying architecture and design. When applications were fairly straightforward, even large systems could be modified with reasonable ease. However, applications are so complex—many requiring over one million lines of code—that a clean, coherent design is an absolute necessity. No longer can the design be developed or modified during the project's implementation phase.

The Evolution of Software Tools

Computer software development tools are currently undergoing another revolution as CASE tools are forged to fortify the *requirements analysis* and d*esign specification* phases of the software development cycle. Today, all software analysts and programmers are familiar with and use programming language compilers, symbolic debuggers, and commercially available subroutine packages. A large percentage of these professionals are acquainted with source code control systems

What one programmer can do in a year, two programmers can also do in a year.
— Conventional software wisdom

for managing and organizing large bodies of source code. Today, many are being introduced to computer-aided software engineering tools: tools that help the program analyst and software engineer specify the application's requirements and design. Several years hence, automatic source code generation, which many still consider to be the province of academic computer science departments and industrial research laboratories, will become commonplace. (Figure 2.1)

Over the next decade, the software industry will migrate away from legions of programmers proficient in one programming language (usually COBOL, ADA, or C) and who participate in all phases of the software development cycle. The industry will favor smaller groups of software designers and programmers, each highly skilled in one particular phase of the software development cycle. This division of responsibility is common in mainframe application development, which has traditionally distinguished between analysts, systems programmers, and applications programmers. Analysts are responsible for writing the requirements and design specification documents. Specialized data base analysts develop data base schema designs for new information management applications. Finally, application programmers write the actual

Figure 2.1 CASE tools are a natural outgrowth of existing software tools. Most current tools—compilers, debuggers, and profilers—focus on the implementation, testing, and release (configuration management) phases of software development. CASE tools extend this coverage by helping analysts and engineers with the requirements analysis and design specification phases. Next generation CASE tools will generate working code directly from the design, an increasingly prevalent trend.

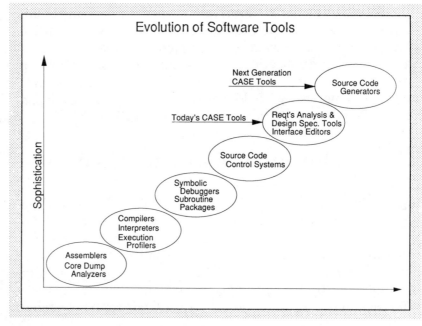

code based on the design specifications and data base designs. This trend is one of specialization. Other industries, such as the construction industry, have undergone this process as they mature.

The advent of the personal computer elevated the need for better, more visual user interfaces as more and more white-collar professionals began using computers. So now the software industry has a need for user interface specialists with the cognitive psychology skills necessary to design understandable man-machine interfaces. The Structured Analysis methodology, described in detail in Chapter 4, models the underlying business process being implemented in software. Requirements analysis, also known as systems engineering, is becoming a profession in its own right. In the software design stage, designers specializing in data modeling and structured design methodologies are responsible for transforming the requirements specification into a buildable software architecture. Figure 2.2 illustrates the different types of specialized tools each group will use.

The Benefits of CASE Tools

For many software development organizations, the qualitative benefits of CASE tools outweigh the quantitative benefits. Design and development times will almost always be reduced by using CASE tools, but perhaps their most

Development Phase	Specialized Tools
Requirements Analysis	User Interface Prototyping Tools Structured Analysis Tools Information Modeling Tools
Design Specification	Data Modeling Tools Design Specification Tools
Implementation Maintenance	Compilers Assemblers Symbolic Debuggers Smart Text Editors Execution Profilers Source Code Control Systems

Figure 2.2 Software development tools. Tools for software development are becoming increasingly more specialized. CASE tools leverage the requirements analysis and design specification phases of the software development cycle while more traditional tools assist in the implementation and maintenance phases.

satisfying benefit comes in the form of insurance, or peace of mind, that the job is being done properly, on schedule, and to the user's specification. CASE tools yield a tremendous benefit in revealing many requirements (and surprises) *before* the implementation begins. (CASE tools are definitely not for adventure seekers!) This section describes many of the benefits of CASE technology. However, you should realize that much of the actual value received from computer-aided software engineering largely depends on how well it is integrated into the software development organization, as is discussed in Chapter 13, *"Introducing CASE Into Your Organization."*

Complete Requirements Specifications.   Most software engineers have witnessed the failure of a software application out in the field because what they built was not what the end-users wanted. Encouraging the software designer to completely specify the system's requirements is the goal of *requirements analysis and specification* CASE tools. Most specification methodologies enforce end-user involvement because it is impossible to complete the specification without developing a model of the end-user's process or business function. Although the risk of creating an Edsel still exists, despite the best efforts of all involved, the probability of doing so is greatly diminished with complete, detailed, and accurate requirements specifications.

Accurate Design Specifications.   There is nothing more frightening for a novice software engineer to face than the task of maintaining a large software system with incomplete, inaccurate, or nonexistent design documentation. Rarely is in-line software documentation sufficient to communicate the system's architectural design without embroiling the reader in unnecessary detail. Furthermore, we have all seen designs that violate sound design practices: designs that expose unnecessary detail, encourage "spaghetti code," and ignore the "separation of concerns" doctrine. ("Separation of concerns" is a software design principal that advocates organizing software programs into groups of modules, each with well-defined inputs and outputs. Each module is treated as a black box whose internal structure is not publicly known. Only the input and output parameters are visible to the other modules.)

Often development teams say "we'll write the design specifications after the code has stabilized." A home purchaser contracting to build a custom new home would never let a contractor build the house first and then draw up the blueprint. As a software project manager, you *should never* let a software development team write the code first and then draw up the design specifications unless the project is considered a throw-away prototype aimed at uncovering new end-user requirements.

Current Design Specifications. Perhaps worse than incomplete design specifications are inaccurate design specifications that have not been kept up-to-date relative to modifications made to the source code base. Many futile hours can be wasted trying to understand a system's architecture from pouring over the design specification but not being able to reconcile it against the actual implementation.

CASE design tools can help maintain synchronization with the code implementation. Many of these tools actually attach the code to the specification, so that as the specification changes, so does the underlying code. Other CASE tools, most notably user interface design tools, automatically generate code. There is no need to maintain synchronization because you never touch the underlying code; only the design is edited!

Reduced Development Time. Completely specifying the software architecture substantially reduces, if not eliminates, *waste* from unnecessary or thrown-away code. Reducing such waste translates directly into reduced implementation time. Many software professionals feel most productive when they are sitting in front of a screen actually writing code. The constant gratification of a compile and run cycle is tremendously appealing to most of us, a trait which most likely stems from our homework assignments in overburdened undergraduate programming courses where good program design skills are rarely emphasized. The immediacy of homework project deadlines compel junior programmers to start writing code without considering its design.

Software professionals must feel they are being as productive in the requirements analysis and design specification phases as they feel when writing code during the implementation

---

CASE tools are design tools, not after-the-fact documentation tools.

CASE tools provide facilities to keep design specifications up-to-date in the face of ongoing software maintenance, redesigns, enhancements, and code evolution.

As design specification aids, CASE tools should be so compelling to use that software architects, systems analysts, and software engineers inherently want to use them before beginning implementation.

phase. Because of the highly interactive, graphical orientation of most CASE tools, using a CASE tool seduces many software engineers into believing they are writing code (and hence being productive) when in fact they are really designing software architectures. Time spent designing is repaid manifold during the implementation, testing, and release phases.

Highly Extensible/Maintainable Code.   Any successful software project will never really be finished. End-users will either demand (strongly suggest) functional improvements or will identify bugs in the software's operation, mandating some form of continuing development or maintenance work on the software. This becomes particularly acute when the software application is an actual product for sale to end-users. It is much easier to develop a design specification when embarking on a new software project or a major rewrite of an existing system; it is much more difficult to keep the design specification synchronized with *evolutionary* maintenance and enhancement work.

Although each minor enhancement or bug fix may not warrant an update to the design specification, the aggregation of several modifications will. It is difficult to enforce the discipline of making periodic design specification updates under these conditions, especially when the maintenance has been left to a skeleton crew (typically one or two people).

It is difficult even for CASE tools to provide assistance in maintaining design specifications if the software built from those specifications is handwritten. But those CASE tools that *automatically* generate software from design specifications are not encumbered by this problem. In fact, this trend predominates in areas where software can be automatically generated, such as user interface design and database access design.

To summarize, high-quality CASE tools:

- Are more compelling to use than writing code.
- Help design rather than document.
- Maintain synchronization with the source code base.
- Reduce the risk of failure and surprise.
- Reduce total development time.

A Taxonomy of CASE Tools

In this section we turn our attention away from software engineering practices and focus on computer-aided software engineering tools themselves. The technological underpinnings of computer-aided software engineering are nothing new. Most CASE tools implement pencil and paper structured design technologies developed during the 1960s and 1970s as shown in Figure 2.3. These methodologies were popularized in many commercial data processing shops as a way to manage their application backlogs by reducing technical development risk. During the 1980s, these analysis and design methodologies migrated into CASE tools as graphical workstations and personal computers became widely available. This migration is accelerating as the complexity of the design task grows beyond what can reasonably be accomplished on paper using a pencil and paper methodology.

Figure 2.3 There are many structured design and modeling methodologies, each with a slightly different focus. Many of these methodologies are being popularized by CASE tool implementations. Selecting the right methodology for the job requires careful consideration.

Computer-aided software engineering technologies are not revolutionary, they are *evolutionary*. As structured design methodologies are refined to meet today's needs, they are being reborn in software form. These techniques and methodologies are more compelling to use than their pencil and paper ancestors, which helps increase their popularity.

No single CASE tool or methodology can perform the entire specification and design job. Certainly several complimentary methodologies are required to handle all facets of the software development job, from data structure design through user interface specification. Although there is a trend toward combining complimentary methodologies into "integrated tool environments," the universal tool still lives in the future.

Data Base Fourth Generation Languages.   Many software professionals consider data base fourth generation

Figure 2.4   CASE tools automate existing software development methodologies that have been practiced since the 1960s and 1970s. These new tools make structured methodologies, data modeling, and design specification techniques available to many more software developers and remove much of the pencil and paper drudgery.

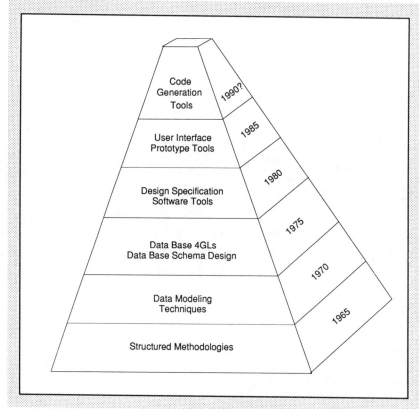

languages (4GLs) to be a form of computer-aided software engineering. Briefly, fourth generation languages are high-level languages which provide data base access facilities. They are much easier to use than languages traditionally used for programmatic data base access, such as COBOL and C. The goal is to remove the burden of tedious data base access code by replacing it with a much smaller amount of code written in a higher-level 4GL specifically designed for data base access. Many 4GLs provide form layout and design capabilities using common text editors and were the first technology demonstrating the leverage of focused tools over coding from scratch.

With a 4GL, the application programmer can declare the input/output screen forms presented to application program end-users. These forms are declared as sets of fields with well-defined properties, such as data input type checking (e.g. integer range validation and legal data verification) and protected field display. The application programmer also specifies data base access queries in the 4GL, allowing retrieved data to be displayed on the form and information input via the form to be added to the data base.

Deciding whether 4GLs are CASE tools is difficult. From this book's perspective, 4GLs are not CASE tools because they do not add leverage to the design process. Rather, they are higher-level, focused, compiled languages for the data base world. This, however, does not negate their importance as a software development tool. Data base 4GLs are a very valuable and time-saving technology.

Data Modeling Tools.   In data base applications, a single data base is frequently shared by many different applications, each of which adds or extracts information. Before establishing a data base for multiple applications and populating it with data, careful thought must be given to its content and architecture. Because data base applications constitute a large proportion of commercial software applications, data modeling techniques were developed to help data base designers architect a data base to be as versatile yet, at the same time, as efficient as possible.

CASE tools for data modeling help the data base designer model this information flow throughout the firm and construct appropriate viewpoints for the various organizations requiring access. A well-designed, efficient data base saves countless hours of application programming time as new applications are written to access the data base.

Data modeling tools assist the data base designer by modeling the organization's flow of information. A good example is order entry transaction processing. The sales force receives orders for a firm's products (data flows from account representatives to data entry clerks). These orders are entered into a data base and posted against individual customer accounts to generate billing invoices. From there, the manufacturing organization receives notice to manufacture the goods that have been sold and move the goods to the shipping department. The shipping department accesses the data base for the shipping address and to record notification that the goods have been shipped and by what carrier.

Throughout this example, several organizations within the firm have had to access the central data base for information regarding the order: data entry clerks, the accounting department, the manufacturing department, and the shipping department. Each organization needs to see different pieces of information. These different organizations also have to be protected from each other so one cannot accidentally or intentionally alter data that another has the sole responsibility for creating or updating.

Analysis and Design Specification Tools.   Design specification tools generally use the Structured Analysis and Structured Design methodologies pioneered by Tom DeMarco and Edward Yourdon. These general-purpose specification and design tools can be used to specify and design almost any piece of software. Analysis and design tools usually implement data flow diagramming and structure charting techniques, and they are excellent for graphically depicting information flow between computational processes.

Many design specification tools have extensions for specifying real-time systems prevalent in defense-related software projects. Many of these tools provide or assist in composing the DOD-STD-2167 specification documents required on defense-related *mission critical* software projects. (More about DOD-STD-2167 in Chapter 14.)

Design Specification tools are an excellent fit for the portions of an application where a focused tool doesn't make sense, such as internal calculation or "kernel" routines. The software designer must, of course, judge when a more focused tool, such as a user interface design tool, is called for and when a general-purpose design specification tool is appropriate.

User Interface Prototyping Tools.   For many commercial applications, the user interface is the largest single component of the application program. User interfaces vary greatly in style and content. Some are designed for ease of use by unsophisticated users, such as automated teller machines, but other interfaces are built for high-volume processing, such as word processors.

> Focused CASE tools, such as user interface editors, are easily integrated into your software development practices.

Whatever the application, the user interface deserves special attention. We have all seen examples of failed user interfaces that have fallen short of their goal. Often, they differ only slightly from an interface regarded as highly successful. What differentiates a winning interface from a losing interface? Frequently, it is the time spent prototyping the interface and securing feedback from the end-user community that distinguishes the high-quality interface. Quality user interface development is still an art, and there is little formal methodology for designing user interfaces. Frederick Brooks' adage, *"plan to throw one away,"* (The Mythical Man-Month) still applies to interface development.

Prototyping can be a long and laborious process, and there is always the strong temptation to use the prototype as the final implementation, rather than redesigning based on end-user feedback. Fortunately, CASE tools for user interface are appearing in the commercial marketplace.

This type of rapid prototyping offers the leverage needed for highly productive and successful software projects. Often, just being able to display screen mock-up sequences is enough to open the communication channel between end-user and software designer. If the software designer has the capability to mock up interfaces rapidly, even nonfunctional ones, he has a vehicle for valuable feedback from the end-user community.

Although user interface tool vendors may not consider themselves CASE tool vendors, they are in fact producing CASE tools. User interface CASE tools add value to the software development process during the requirements analysis and design specification stages. These tools leverage the designer by reducing implementation risk and greatly enhancing end-user acceptance.

User interface tools are primarily oriented toward specific hardware (and sometimes operating system) platforms such as the IBM Personal Computer and certain popular mini-computers. This orientation is by necessity. Hardware platforms vary greatly in terms of display technology, making it difficult to field the same user interface development tool on several radically different hardware platforms. An acceptable user interface on the IBM PC is quite different from an acceptable interface on an IBM 3278 mainframe terminal.

For several years, forms generation packages, such as ISPF for IBM mainframes and Panel for the IBM PC, have helped software professionals design specialized form-filling interfaces for a variety of applications. Form-filling interfaces are among the most straightforward and widely accepted interface styles available. In their inception, many of these packages began as subroutine libraries, *not* as CASE tools. However, they evolved into CASE tools when their vendors added graphically oriented editors which allow the software designer to visually lay out a screen and then automatically generate software for that layout.

Code Generation Tools.   Automatic code generation is the ultimate goal of most CASE tool vendors and certainly of all CASE tool users. Code generation is the ability to automatically generate working or compileable software directly from a design specification. Ultimately, the software designer's time is much better invested in fleshing out application specifications and architectures rather than in coding and debugging. Unfortunately, truly generalized code generation is not available in any of today's general-purpose tools or so called application generator products. But code geration is available in a variety of focused tools, especially in user interface design tools.

In the past, CASE technology focused on general purpose requirements analysis and design specification. Now new developments in CASE technology are emphasizing *specialty development tools*. Specialty development tools focus on one particular type of software, such as database access and user interface development. For example, there are a growing number of forms generation packages appearing in the marketplace, ranging in sophistication, price, and delivery environment (PC to mainframe). Future tools will attack the more general problem of automatic code generation. *Automatic programming* is a difficult problem and is still largely considered a research topic. Still, each new tool makes small innovations in this area, and eventually, code generation will be commonplace.

A simple taxonomy of CASE tools might pigeonhole individual tools dictated by the software development cycle phase where they add leverage, such as requirements analysis, design specification, or implementation. However, most of the general-purpose tools span several development cycle phases, usually the requirements analysis and design specification phases. These tools, which typically implement the Yourdon/DeMarco Structured Analysis methodology (see Chapter 4), are able to transform data flow diagrams and mini-specifications into structured designs including data structure definitions and module hierarchies.

As with all developing technologies, certain parts of computer-aided software engineering are more advanced than others. This makes it difficult to summarize today's state of the art. However, as Figure 2.5 illustrates, there is a general trend emerging of tools being built to cover the entire software development cycle, including automatic code generation.

Many of today's tool vendors are recognizing that their tool implementations cannot focus on just one or two facets of the development process, such as analysis and design

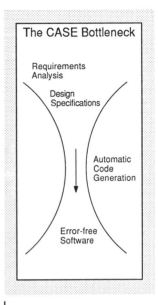

Figure 2.5 The fundamental bottleneck in CASE technology is the ability to automatically generate working software directly from design specifications and user interface layouts. Many of today's successful tool vendors are recognizing this problem and working toward its solution.

specification or user interface layout. Rather, tomorrow's successful tools must deal with all phases of the development cycle and tackle the fundamentally difficult problem of automatically generating error-free software directly from design specifications. This barrier is beginning to crumble with innovations being made in many of today's CASE tools and will further diminish during the next decade as tool vendors advance CASE technology, expand the scope of their tools, and develop standards.

General Characteristics. Fundamentally, CASE tools must meet several criteria in order to be successfully adopted as part of a software developer's tool kit. Meeting these criteria is essential to the tool's acceptance into the development organization's standard practices. CASE tools must perform the following tasks:

- **Break down complexity.** A major goal of CASE technology is to decompose requirements and designs into manageable components. Their function is to simplify, explain, and reduce.

- **Presentable to several audiences.** CASE tools for the requirements and design phases of the software cycle serve several masters. On one hand, their output must be understandable by the end-users and the contracting organization paying for the software development. On the other hand, the tool must provide real value to the developers themselves; otherwise, using the tool is a wasted exercise.

- **Cheaper than building the real thing.** Using a CASE tool should be cheaper and more efficient in the long run than building the software system using traditional methods. CASE tools should substantially reduce implementation and maintenance efforts by yielding higher-quality specifications and designs.

- **Quantitative and Verifiable.** The specifications and designs generated by CASE tools must accurately and concisely articulate the software features and components to be built. Each requirement in the software implementation must be verifiable and traceable back to the requirements document. Performance criteria, boundaries, and error conditions must be established as part of the design.

- **Maintainable.** Specifications and designs produced by or built using a CASE tool must be adaptable as the requirements and design goals of the project change. A design document that falls out of synchronization with the underlying code becomes useless and may actually cause developers to waste time in future enhancements to the software.

- **Graphically oriented.** Good CASE tools present specification and design information visually. CASE tools are to software engineering what CAD (Computer-Aided Design) programs are to schematic design and layout. For end-users and developers alike, it is much easier to comprehend a graphic illustration than to read several pages of text description.

These past few sections have dealt with the evolution and development of computer-aided software engineering technology and with its benefits in building large, complex software systems. The next section discusses the human side of CASE technology and how it can help smaller, one- and two-person projects.

CASE and the Lone Programmer

Many software professionals advocate the idea that good software is produced by small groups of developers. Frederick Brooks supported this notion in his book, *The Mythical Man-Month*, which recounts his experiences in managing large programming projects at IBM. Most software professionals agree that software designed and developed by large teams (committees) tends to be of mediocre design and questionable quality.

Most software projects are too big to build alone, but they are not too big to *design* alone.

One concept underlying CASE technology is the ability to leverage the analysis and design skills of the software professional during the requirements and design phases—the times when the most creative skill is needed. The goal is to free the lone designer, or the most skilled team member, allowing this person to concentrate fully on developing the requirements and design specifications.

Unfortunately, as frequently happens, the cobbler's children, in this case the software development community, are often the last to get new shoes; so it is with CASE technology. CASE tools do cost money and require effort in learning. Money and time are scarce commodities among individual software contractors and product authors. Nevertheless, it is fairly easy for individual software developers to "ease" into CASE, and the learning costs are relatively small.

Individual programmers working on smaller projects are aided by CASE tools as well, although little time may be saved using a CASE tool on a small, one-man project, there is a tremendous benefit in the improved code quality and accompanying design documentation. These benefits are generally well worth the investment because of the reduced maintenance costs.

Summary

This chapter presented an overview of computer-aided software engineering, the benefits of using CASE tools, and the different types of CASE tools. Effectively using computer-aided software engineering technology necessarily means understanding the software development process. Investment in requirements analysis and design specification pays ample returns later during the implementation and testing phases. The next chapter, *"CASE in the Software Development Process,"* explores the workings of each software development phase, emphasizing where CASE tools can help by reducing development risk and accelerating the development process.

Most software projects are too big to build alone, but they are not too big to design alone.

Chapter 3

CASE in the Software Development Process

The software development process must be fully understood before computer-aided software engineering technology can be truly appreciated. In many respects, you must have traveled the software development road at least once to know the washed-out bridges, potholes, and sharp drop-offs in order to fully appreciate the eight-lane interstate highways introduced by CASE technology.

By this book's definition, CASE tools primarily provide leverage in the first two software development phases—functional requirements analysis and design specification—to substantially reduce the effort spent in the later implementation and unit testing stages. For this reason, more discussion is devoted to these first two phases than the others.

Functional Requirements Analysis

The first step in the software development process is constructing a requirements specification for the intended software application. In the requirements specification stage, members of both the contracting organization and the end-user community are interviewed by an *analyst* or a *systems engineer*. (There is little difference between an analyst and a systems engineer. The term "analyst" originated in commercial data processing, while the term "system engineer" originated in the scientific software and computer science worlds. Although a system engineer generally has formal university training in computer science while an analyst may not, these terms are used interchangeably throughout this book.) From these interviews, the analyst synthesizes a set of requirements. For software product development, the marketing group, the end-users, and the software engineering group all participate in this process. Building a requirements specification is a process of negotiation and fact-finding as the mandatory features are distilled from the less important.

No problem is so big or so complicated that it can't be run away from.
—Linus, in Peanuts®

During the requirements analysis stage, a lot of give and take occurs between the various organizations involved as they collectively refine the set of software deliverables; that is, the exact tasks the application will perform. Defining the functional requirements involves modeling the end-user's existing policies in order to develop an understanding of the business role or function the software is intended to handle. Skilled analysts and systems engineers expect this process to be *iterative*, requiring substantial interaction with the contracting organization and end-user group. This process can be exhausting and at times frustrating, but the end result is always worth the trouble. Remember, contracting organizations and end-users usually start with real, but vaguely articulated, requirements.

The task of the systems analyst is to define, explore, probe, and refine those requirements into a workable specification. Many CASE tools are nothing more than requirements and design specification editors. They eliminate the drudgery of drawing and redrawing data flow diagrams, module hierarchies, Warnier-Orr diagrams, and entity-relationship diagrams. With CASE technology, undertaking these iterative analysis and design processes becomes less of a chore, allowing the analyst and designer to concentrate on the work they know best—building requirements specifications and designing software modules. This is why CASE tools can be so beneficial.

Functional requirements documents are often cast in very specific, predefined formats that articulate and identify each and every requirement down to a very fine detail. The formats can be specific to an individual company or can be one of several industry standard formats. For example, for mission critical weapons software, the Department of Defense has mandated the use of DOD-STD-2167 as a requirements specification documentation format. There is also an IEEE (Institute of Electrical and Electronic Engineers) format for software requirements specifications. If the software contains a visual user interface component, the interface should be mocked up, either in a "story board" format on the delivery computer system or on paper with artist's drawings.

The functional requirements specification in Figure 3.1 is a portion of the functional product requirements document for

3 Schedule Print Screen

The following fields will be present on the **Print** screen:

3.1 Vertical Grid On Printed Schedules
A vertical grid will be superimposed on printed schedules to make viewing task bar start and end dates easy to read.

3.2 Vertical Grid Field On Print Screen
A *Vertical Grid* form field will be present on the Print screen with the values of YES and NO, making the vertical grid an optional printing feature. Users can select between the two values by using the left and right arrow keys to switch values.

3.3 Start Print Date
A *Start Print Date* field will be present on the **Print** screen specifying the starting date of the schedule to be printed. This will give the user control over the amount of the project schedule being printed.

3.4 End Print Date
An *End Print Date* field will be present on the **Print** screen specifying the ending date of the schedule to be printed. This will give the user control over the amount of the project schedule being printed.

Figure 3.1 Partial Functional Requirements Document. Each requirement in a functional requirements document should be clearly articulated and separately enumerated. This makes it easier to trace individual requirements to the implemented code and back again from the code to the requirements document.

Quick Schedule, a project scheduling program for the IBM Personal Computer. (Quick Schedule is an easy-to-learn and use project scheduling tool whose major benefit is its ability to generate small schedules in much less time than the more sophisticated, high-end project management packages. Quick Schedule is marketed by Channelmark Corporation, 2929 Campus Drive, San Mateo, CA 94403. (800) 851-2917, in California (800) 223-1479.) This requirements specification document is structured much like a book, organized into chapters and broken into sections and subsections. The first chapter describes the overall purpose of the Quick Schedule product, its intended audience, use, and focus. The second chapter defines the complete set of screens that the user can access.

The third and subsequent chapters detail the individual requirements for each screen. Notice that a *user-oriented* approach was taken; that is, the software requirements are described from the user's viewpoint rather than from the software designer's perspective. The requirements specification's job is to articulate the behavior of the software, not describe its structure or suggested implementation.

In Figure 3.1, each requirement in the requirements specification is defined by a separate section in the document. Each individual field on the "Print" screen is carefully described so the implementation team can reference very specific, unquestionable requirements. Not shown, but also accompanying the Quick Schedule requirements specification, is a set of screen mock-ups illustrating screen layout and showing how typical project schedules should look in Quick Schedule.

The requirements specification contains more than an enumeration of the program's features, however. It contains the specification for the complete software *system*, including components such as:

- **Features and capabilities definition.** This is a straightforward listing of the program's features and capabilities and is the easiest part of the requirements specification to draft. Forming a coherent package out of a feature grab bag is somewhat more difficult. Nevertheless, if all other components are omitted, this is the one to keep. At least the software development team will have an idea of what to build!

- **User interface screen and form designs.** This crucial specification component is often the most difficult to reach a consensus on. Countless iterations and end-user feedback sessions are the norm, but the end result is well worth the effort, as the project team will be rewarded with reduced design and implementation times. Most important is developing a *user interaction model* which describes how the end-user interacts with the application. What are the typical usage patterns? It is important to specify the user interface to streamline and simplify operation wherever possible. Are novices expected to grow into the program, learning new features as they progress? If so, are there on-line help facilities?

- **Performance criteria.** Establish quantifiable and measurable performance metrics for programs with response-time goals. While establishing performance criteria is a very difficult task, this is especially important for systems that rely on data base or file access as an integral part of their operation.

- **Target hardware software environment.** The hardware platform executing the program must be specified up front as this can greatly affect the program's design. Equally important is the choice of operating system, data base system, and so on. All too often, these crucial decisions are delayed until the beta test phase and left as a "simple porting exercise" while the contracting organization makes up its mind.

The *requirements review* culminates the requirements analysis process. This is the first of many scheduled review steps during the software development cycle, all oriented toward maintaining high quality, reliable software. The contracting organization and end-user group must be amply represented during this meeting: customer satisfaction is of paramount importance for a systems analyst. An independent party should act as the review meeting's arbiter to ensure there are no communication gaps or misunderstandings between the contracting organization and the system analysts. Any discrepancies should be itemized and resolved before beginning the next phase, design specification. After all, the system cannot be adequately designed based on incomplete requirements.

Building a complete, thorough requirements specification is the step most often omitted or left partially completed. There is quite often a compulsion to go on "gut instinct," with the software team or the marketing group second guessing the end-user. Only after the functional requirements stage has been completed can an accurate development schedule and milestone table be built.

Design Specifications

Design specification, the second step in the software development cycle, translates the requirements specification document into an architectural blueprint detailing the proposed *software implementation*. This architectural blueprint generally identifies the major modules to be constructed, the data communication paths between modules, the major subroutines within each module, data structure definitions, and the file format specifications. Frequently, a design specification will include algorithmic detail at the pseudocode level for the key processes. The output of the design phase is a software engineering "blueprint" or detailed architecture that the programming team can use to generate code.

The design specification phase is the second most likely phase to be shortchanged after the requirements analysis phase. Software professionals are more likely to see the logic in developing a design specification than a requirements specification. All too often, though, major components of the software design are synthesized during the implementation phase, causing costly time delays and cost overruns. The design phase sometimes consumes as much time as the actual software implementation phase, but the more refined and detailed the design specification, the lower the implementation cost and maintenance risk.

The sequence of steps best followed for building a design specification is:

1. Segregate the specified functionality into a set of 10 to 50 modules.
2. Organize the modules hierarchically, with higher-level modules calling the lower-level modules.
3. Define the data paths between the modules.
4. Define the external data file formats.
5. Define the access paths to the external data files.
6. Define the data structures that flow between the modules along the data paths.
7. Design the key algorithms.
8. Define the subroutines within each module.

The first step, segregating the specified functionality into a set of modules, is the most significant and the most difficult step. This is the major design hurdle that separates the senior software engineer from the junior programmer. Segregating software functionality requires the designer to abstract the functionality delineated in the requirements specification and somehow decide what software modules need to be built. The designer must decide what to put where, and this requires experience for which there is little substitute. This decomposition of the whole into logically separable components requires the designer to have the experience, for example, to realize that the twenty different screens identified in the requirements specification can all be handled by a centralized screen manager (or that a CASE tool can create them!).

Good software is organized as a set of *independent* modules, each of which can be designed, built, and tested separately. Each module views the others as black boxes with well-defined sets of inputs and outputs. Each module is accessed only through these inputs and outputs. This *separation of concerns* doctrine (a logical segregation of functionality) makes it easier to independently change the underlying design of a single module without affecting the operation of the others. As long as the black box view is maintained for each module, the goal of functionally independent modules is achieved. Figure 3.2 illustrates the Quick Schedule module structure.

Several structured systems methodologies help the designer organize systems into individual modules. Structured Analysis, discussed in detail in Chapter 4, provides a method for translating requirements specifications using data flow diagrams into module definitions. Jackson Structured Programming is another popular design methodology. Most of these methodologies are amenable to implementation in CASE tools, as is discussed shortly.

Associated with each module are the data structures used or modified by the module. Some data structures may be strictly local to a particular module; that is, they are not used or referenced outside of that module. Other data structures are

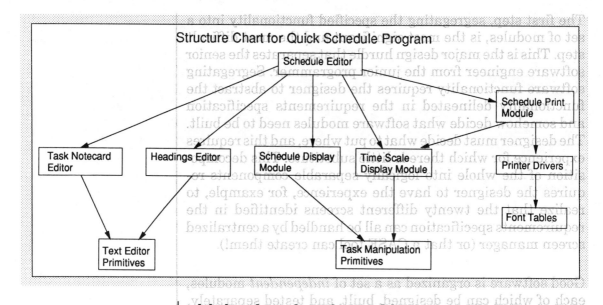

Structure Chart for Quick Schedule Program

Figure 3.2 Structure Chart for Quick Schedule Program. Each module is completely separable from the others with clearly defined data paths connecting the modules. Notice that modules tend to call vertically and not horizontally. This is a good organizational principle of structured design.

global and can be referenced by one or more modules and passed between modules. Data structure design is perhaps the most crucial part of the design specification phase. Data structures, after all, represent the substance of what the program manipulates. Intelligent data structure design pays off immensely in clarity, separation of program modules, and algorithm design.

In the Quick Schedule data structure definitions of Figure 3.3, the TASK RECORD structure is used strictly by the Task Primitives module. Each task in a Quick Schedule schedule is represented by a record of this format, and only the Task Primitives module can directly modify these task records. No other module is allowed to directly access task records except by using the Task Primitive functions. This partitioning makes it very easy to change the underlying TASK RECORD data structure definition in future versions of the product, because such a modification only affects a small group of subroutine functions.

The data structures in Figure 3.3 are easily translatable into actual C language data structures. For many designs, specifying the data structures in the target language is sufficient. For larger, more complex designs, more formal mechanisms are required. Two excellent techniques, Warnier-Orr Diagrams and Entity-Relationship Diagrams, are discussed in

```
    /* TASK RECORD
     * Information for each individual task is stored in a Task Record.
     * A Task Record, except for the task's note card, completely defines
     * a schedule task.  The task's note card, if present, is pointed
     * to from the Task Record.
     */

    TASK_RECORD::
          Description:char 35 +            /* Task description text.          */
          TASK_POSITION +                  /* Row & Column of task.           */
          TASK_DURATION +                  /* Length in days/minutes.         */
          NOTECARD_INFO +                  /* Detailed task notes/info.       */
          TASK_START +                     /* Task starting date.             */
          TASK_COMPLETION;                 /* Amount of Task completed.       */


    TASK_POSITION::
          Row:integer +                    /* Starting screen row.            */
          Col:integer ;                    /* Starting screen column.         */


    NOTECARD_INFO::
          NoteCardText:char 250 +          /* Detailed task note text.        */
          MaxCardLen:integer +             /* Notecard lines allocated.       */
          NoteCardWidth:integer +          /* Width of notecard lines.        */
          NoteCardLen:integer ;            /* # notecard lines used.          */


    TASK_START::
          AnchorFlg:bit field +            /* Task anchored @ date?           */
          AbsStartDay:integer +            /* Start day from 1/1/87.          */
          RelStartDay:integer +            /* Work day since Start Date.      */
          AbsStartMin:integer ;            /* Minute since start of day.      */


    TASK_COMPLETION::
          CompDays:integer +               /* Completed days in task.         */
          CompMins:integer ;               /* Completed minutes in task.      */
```

Chapter 7. Like other structured methodologies that trace their origins to pencil, paper, and drawing templates, Warnier-Orr Diagrams and Entity-Relationship Diagrams have been implemented in CASE tools.

Once the data structures have been identified and specified, the software designer turns to designing the individual subroutines around the data structures. At this level, each module is fleshed out with individual subroutines, specifying their calling and returning parameters. Good data modeling

Figure 3.3 Quick Schedule Data Structure Definitions. Data structure definition is a very important component of software design. Once the data structures and file formats are defined, the code tends to "write itself" because the data manipulation activities are obvious.

practices create data structures that strongly suggest the individual subroutines needed to use the data structures. In other words, with a set of well-defined data structures, the code practically writes itself! Figure 3.4 illustrates several of the Task Primitive subroutines that manipulate the individual TASK RECORD data structures.

For each routine, the designer should define the following:

- Purpose and function

- Data structures used (inputs and outputs)

- Return or error codes

- Side effects

A crucial factor in producing high-quality, maintainable software is the *design review*. It is mandatory that design reviews be held for each major component of the software before implementation begins. Well-designed software will be much easier to maintain once released, and extending the software with planned or unplanned features will be much easier if the software was structured in a flexible manner. Design reviews do not present a difficult obstacle for most organizations in which several designers contribute to a design. While design by committee is generally ill-advised, two or three designers achieve a certain degree of synergy.

Typically, each module will require one or two two-hour design review sessions. The review meeting should consist of the analysts or systems engineers responsible for writing the requirements specification, as well as those responsible for building the design specification. As in the construction-crew approach, an impartial outside "software building inspector" should preside over all design reviews and have the final say as to whether a design is approved for the next project phase, implementation. The design review is the final step in building design specifications. Mistakes up to this point are easily corrected, but once implementation begins, correcting errors becomes rapidly more difficult.

NAME
    taskMake(Timep, Pos)

PURPOSE
    Create a new task at a specified row and column.

INPUTS
    TIMEREC_PTR Timep   Current date/time settings.
    POSITION Pos   Row & Column position of task.

RETURN CODES
    Index   Task identification handle >= 0.
    -1   Error while creating task; maximum # tasks reached.

NAME
    taskDelete(Index)

PURPOSE
    Delete a specified task.

INPUTS
    int Index   Task identifier.

RETURN CODES
    1   Successful task deletion.
    -1   Illegal task identifier; identifier out of bounds.

NAME
    taskIncLen(Timep, Index, Amount)

PURPOSE
    Increment the length of a specified task.

INPUTS
    TIMEREC_PTR Timep   Current date/time settings.
    int Index   Task identifier.
    int Amount   # days/minutes to increment by.

RETURN CODES
    1   Successful increment of task's length.
    -1   Illegal task identifier; identifier out of bounds.

NAME
    taskShift(Timep, Index, Amount)

PURPOSE
    Shift all tasks on a row to the right.

INPUTS
    TIMEREC_PTR Timep   Current date/time settings.
    int Index   Task identifier.
    int Amount   # days/minutes to increment by.

RETURN CODES
    1   Task successfully shifted.
    0   No need to shift task; task not shifted.
    -1   Illegal task identifier; identifier out of bounds.

Figure 3.4 Quick Schedule Task Primitives. Each task primitive design lists its purpose and function, the data structures imported and exported, the return and error codes, and any side effects. A design review is held before the implementation actually begins to ensure design correctness and completeness.

Implementation and Coding

Finally the software writing begins. Coding should strictly follow the software design blueprint developed in the design specification phase. Depending on the design's structure and organization, many of the modules may be built in parallel. This parallelism is the hallmark of a good design. The component parts have been segregated by function so that there are few module interdependencies. Each module should be designed to be treated like a black box with a well-articulated set of inputs and outputs. For testing and debugging purposes, other modules can be "stubbed out," or simulated, by testing harnesses (see "Unit Test and Integration" in this chapter).

Coding Standards. It is quite common for implementation teams to have established a set of *coding standards and guidelines* dictating the style and feel of the software. Coding standards typically specify the documentation format for subroutine headers, the indentation style of nested blocks, and nomenclature for specifying variable and subroutine names. Strictly enforced coding standards enhance a program's readability and maintainability by those other than the original development team. In addition, consistent coding practices make code reviews go much more easily (Figure 3.5).

Software developers are sometimes tempted to postpone code documentation as a clean-up chore. How often have we heard, "I'm all done except for the documentation"? When asked why the code was not documented during its implementation, the response is usually, "Why document the code when it changes during development?" This response is indicative of either bad software design (why should the design change during implementation?), or a second-rate programmer, and frequently both! Code reviewers should insist the reviewed code be amply documented.

Unfortunately, there are no CASE tools available to help enforce consistent coding practices. However, certain types of focused CASE tools, such as user interface tools, will automatically generate code based on the design specification. This method of code generation eliminates the need to enforce coding standards or even review the generated code unless it is modified for some reason after being generated.

4. Naming Conventions

Apply the following standards when naming subroutine functions, variables and macros:

- Restrict name length to less than 32 characters long, since some C compilers can recognize only up to 31 characters.

- Capitalize each word in a function's name. For example, *SeeEachPart()*.

- Use common capitalized prefixes to name an entire family of functions or variables. An underscore should separate the prefix name from the routine name. For example, *IO_PutString()* and *IO_PutInteger()*.

- Macro names should be entirely in upper case. For example, *TOKEN(p)*.

- Flag (Boolean) variable names should end with a **Flg** suffix. For example, *AbortFlg*.

- Pointer variable names should end with a **PTR** suffix. For example, *NextTokenPtr*.

Figure 3.5 Code Standards Document. A consistent set of coding standards and practices makes it easier for review panels to conduct quality assurance walk-throughs of completed code. This consistency in implementation style enhances the software's maintainability and reliability.

Code Reviews and Walk-throughs. Frequent *code reviews* and *structured walk-throughs* should be held among team members to ensure quality standards. High-quality software implementations are strict in their attention to detail, such as error recovery, code documentation, and maintainability. It is all too common to ignore issues such as error recovery until the end of the implementation. Such inattention can lead to unexpected recoding efforts when a subroutine's structure becomes too complex as the developers attempt to retrofit in a reasonable error-recovery mechanism.

Code walk-throughs should be oriented toward a small, narrow objective and should evaluate the software against documented design and quality standards. Walk-throughs should be structured according to a preset agenda and led by the implementor of the module being reviewed. Also, walk-throughs should not last for more than two hours to avoid a decline in the group's productivity. It is not the objective of a code walk-through to fix bugs and errors, only to locate them. The outcome of the code walk-through can be one of three things:

1. Accept the code as is.

2. Conditionally accept the code pending revisions.

3. The code should be revised and another walk-through scheduled.

Code walk-throughs are held when a module has been completed, not while it is still under construction. They most certainly are not design sessions. If a module needs to be reviewed in *progress*, then the module is probably too large and should be further decomposed into smaller, more manageable modules. Remember, code walk-throughs are for finding errors. They are *not* fault-finding or finger-pointing sessions nor should they attempt to be error-correcting sessions. Walk-throughs are designed to protect the programmer's ego without sacrificing quality. Programming staff should be considered competent to correct their own mistakes once they are isolated.

Finally, if major modules are separable and can be individually demonstrated without the others, the implementation team should take the opportunity to preview the software to interested parties. This is usually the case with user interface software. Collecting feedback from the end-user community will add an extra measure of insurance that the final product will be successfully accepted.

Unit Test and Integration

Once the major modules have been completed and debugged, "stress testing" can begin on the system as a whole. During this development phase, each module should be thoroughly tested on its own, generally using special *testing harnesses* designed to supply inputs and validate outputs to and from the module. Testing harnesses are programs that submit data to the module being tested and then examine the returned data. Generally, one or more testing harnesses are constructed for each module. Often, more than the returned data must be validated, such as printouts (reports) and data base access.

Test harnesses are commonly built by a separate quality assurance group in the development organization, although on smaller projects such work is done by the development team itself. Performing the unit testing and the final testing outside the development team in a separate quality assurance group is advantageous, for such groups have far fewer biases than the development organization. As more naive users, they are tempted to test the system in areas the development team might have neglected.

Once the individual modules have been tested, they are integrated into the final, whole executable system. Then the system is tested further with a *test suite* of cases designed to test the boundaries of the system. This portion of the system assembly is sometimes called an *alpha test*. The alpha test release is distributed to internal testers and local end-users to expose any bugs or errors before a beta test version is released to external testers and end-users.

During the unit test and integration phase, attention is given to module and system performance. Frequently, bottlenecks occur which must, of course, be remedied. Tools such as code profilers (or performance monitors) are employed to uncover performance critical sections of code, which, once identified, may be rewritten to provide better performance. Although there are no CASE tools to assist in the unit test and integration phase, the previously described requirements analysis and design specification CASE tools are designed to substantially reduce the amount of testing that must be performed. Reducing the testing and debugging time necessary to produce high-quality software is of paramount importance. (Figure 3.6)

However, there is no substitute for good design during the design phase of the software project. Major problems uncovered during the unit test and integration phase are usually the result of poor requirements specification or software design and are not due to a poor implementation. One such indicator of poor design is the appearance of performance problems. Unit test and integration is the development phase where performance monitoring and tuning takes place, and certain "inner loops" will need tightening in every system. But if reengineering is required, then a flawed design is indicated.

Another important facet of the unit test and integration phase is *configuration management*. Configuration management is the process of assembling the individual software components into a final releasable module. When software is under development, there may be several versions of each source code file and module (group of files) in existence. Although only one copy of each file can, in actuality, be modified (worked on) at

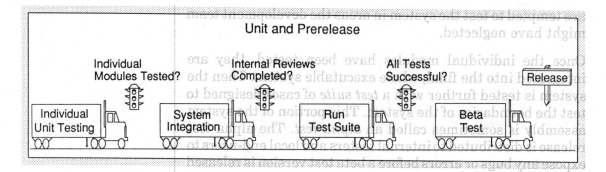

Figure 3.6 Integrating, testing, and releasing a software system requires several distinct check-points, each designed to ensure software quality and reliability.

any one time by any single programmer, other copies may be in use by other project team members in their own personal versions of the code. This is always the case when the other team members need stable versions of the code in order to adequately test and validate their own work.

The configuration management process ensures that only the correct and approved version of each file and module is included in the final released software package. Configuration management tools maintain a complete inventory for each program component, file, and module comprising a particular configuration, or version, of a project. Because the development life cycle includes several software releases—unit test and integration, beta test, and the final release—it is necessary to enforce stringent version control. In many circumstances, the configuration manager allows backtracking to a previous version of a file or module to verify that a suspected bug was introduced in a particular release (configuration), or whether it has been latent all along.

Several good configuration management tools are available under different operating system environments. Under the Unix environment, for example, SCCS (Source Code Control System) and RCS (Revision Control System) are valuable additions to the project team's tool kit. Under MS-DOS on the IBM PC is a version control facility by Polytron Systems.

Stand-alone configuration management tools are not considered CASE tools by the definition used in this book because they do not directly enhance the requirements and design activities in the software development cycle. However, these tools are essential components in a software engineering environment for medium to large projects. Relying on them to automatically build and configure software releases can save a tremendous amount of grief. Some CASE tools, such as the TAGS system from Teledyne Brown Engineering (illustrated in Chapter 10) include a configuration management facility. This trend of "vertically integrating" facilities that help in all phases of software development is becoming increasingly prevalent.

Beta Test Release

Now that the system has been fully integrated, debugged, and stress-tested for any performance problems, the system is ready for release to a small group of end-users in a preintroduction field test called a *beta test*. The number of end-users selected for a beta test varies, depending on the type of system being deployed, and can range from one, for very specialized software, up to several hundred, for consumer software applications.

In all cases, beta testers should be carefully selected and should include a diverse mix of individuals ranging from very naive to very sophisticated users. This diversity ensures the software system will be tested under the widest possible range of conditions. It is crucial that the beta test have a definite ending point when the beta testers submit detailed reports to the software development group. Without this enforced deadline, the beta testers will be lax in submitting their reports, rendering the entire beta test effort worthless. Remember, the purpose of the beta test is to acquire meaningful feedback and take corrective action based on that feedback *before* the software is released to the end-user community.

The following are several goals and criteria for ensuring a good beta test:

- **Select beta testers that will actually use the software!** Actual end-users are best. After all, they are the ones slated to use the software on a daily basis. Your best friend probably is not a good candidate.

- **Select beta testers you know.** Do not select random people to test your software. Select individuals and organizations you know will provide a clear and detailed analysis of the software package.

- **Select an adequate number of beta testers.**   Software developers frequently err in enlisting either too few or too many beta testers. Selecting too few testers generally results in too little feedback in addition to the normal biases of a small sample size. Selecting too many beta testers makes a beta test program too large and unwieldy to manage. Too often, software product developers indiscriminately send beta test copies to their friends and associates, more as a courtesy than as part of a meaningful beta test program.

- **The beta test period must be of sufficient duration.**   Give the beta tester time to unpack the software, install it, and give the package thorough testing. Generally, a minimum of three months is required for an adequate shakedown. Anything shorter and the time, effort, and resources expended on the beta test may be wasted.

- **Supply adequate documentation with the beta test software.**   The beta test should also stress test the software's documentation. Although very little will be mentioned about software documentation in this book, documentation constitutes an integral component of the entire software product/package and is possibly more crucial than the software itself. If you expect end-users to rely on the documentation, then it should be an integral part of the beta test.

- **Provide training, if necessary, to the beta testers.**   If training is a normal component of the delivered software package, then training must be provided to the beta testers. Lack of proper training could severely shortchange the beta test process. This may mean conducting a training course, either in your offices or at the customer's site.

- **Poll beta testers regularly.**   Periodically checking the beta testers ensures they are using the software as well as communicating genuine interest in their feedback. For software products, call each beta tester two to three weeks after shipping the package to the test site to verify that the package was received in good order and to prompt the test site to install the software if they have not already. Then every three to four weeks, calls should be placed inquiring about questions, problems, or enhancement requests.

Beta test report forms are the primary formal feedback conduit to the development team and should always be sent with the software (or announcement of installation). What constitutes a beta test form depends on the information gathered. Are execution speeds and response times important? Are the interface commands and keystroke sequences properly organized and presented? Are the data entry forms clear and understandable? Is the right data base information accessed? There should be some mechanism for polling the beta testers during the beta test to verify that they are indeed using the software and are not encountering any immediate problems. All too often, beta tests are conducted with no formal beta test reporting mechanism, resulting in a useless expenditure of time and effort. Beta testers must be rigorously polled to ensure the critical test information is reaching the development team.

Final Release Preparation

Following the beta test is a period of time spent correcting any problems reported by the beta testers in preparation for the final release. This requires that the software program be recertified by the quality assurance group to verify that the corrections suggested by the beta testers did not introduce further bugs in the software. This is rarely a problem in well-designed and highly modular software. In poorly designed software, however, where many modules depend on many others, these corrective and maintenance activities can become a nightmare.

The release preparation steps are:

1. Correct bugs and nits identified during beta test.
2. Rerun test suite on corrected software.

3. Correct any documentation problems identified during beta test.

4. Package software, documentation, and release notes.

5. Distribute to end-users.

Sending out a final release requires the composition of detailed installation instructions and perhaps training individuals in the end-user organization. During the final release preparation stages, end-user documentation, if any, is packaged with the software.

Maintenance

This is an often-overlooked phase of the software development cycle, for any successful software application will always be under development. If the application is eminently useful, there will be frequent suggestions for improvements; a lack of suggestions indicates the application probably isn't being used.

The responsible group should institute a formalized request-tracking mechanism. These responsibilities extend beyond the usual *software problem report* (i.e., bug report) cataloging and should separate problems from suggestions. User suggestions are frequently the basis for the next major update to the application and should always be reviewed closely.

In an ideal, fully integrated CASE environment, the maintenance problem of introducing one bug while fixing another would disappear altogether. Maintenance itself is not the problem. Rather, it is the potential change to the underlying requirements or design specifications that makes maintenance a difficult process. The goal is for the software problem report to become a "software enhancement request" submitted by end-users. Maintenance is then redefined as adjusting the requirements specification and/or design specification followed by an automatic regeneration of the code. This process is already possible in a variety of business application oriented (screen painters, report layout editors, etc.) CASE environments. This idealized CASE environment without coding or maintenance is discussed in Chapter 15.

Software Problem Report

Reference #:	
Name:	
Organization:	
Date:	
Software Program:	
Software Version:	
Operating System:	
Hardware Configuration:	
Test Data Attached?	
Is Problem Repeatable?	
Problem Description:	

Figure 3.7 Bugs and enhancements identified after the software is released constitute an important information source for both the maintenance and subsequent requirements analysis phases of the software development cycle. Successful software applications are never completed; an active and supportive end-user community will see to that.

Part 2 of this book, "CASE Technologies and Methodologies," describes in detail the underlying technologies, techniques, and methodologies used in most of today's commercially available CASE tools. Some of these are well-known methodologies such as Structured Analysis and Warnier-Orr diagrams. Others are relatively new and less-understood technologies, such as user interface design. Part 3, "Specific CASE Tools," presents tools representative of these respective CASE technologies.

Part 2

CASE Technologies and Methodologies

CASE Technologies and Methodologies

Chapter 4

The Structured Analysis Methodology

Many of the general-purpose analysis and design CASE tools emphasize the *Structured Analysis* methodology. Structured techniques in general emphasize diagrammatic and schematic designs, enhancing communications between the organization writing the requirements specification and the development team commissioned with building the software. Just as a photograph or blueprint of a building is infinitely more expressive than a written description, a structured diagram is a more easily understood mechanism for partitioning complex problems. All project members can then visualize the abstract ideas that exist in the minds of the designers.

Traditional written specifications are usually long and repetitious, making them boring to read and difficult to comprehend. Their length and complexity make written specifications difficult to modify quickly as requirements change. Consequently, the resulting written specifications are seldom updated to reflect changes in requirements.

The benefit of graphically oriented structured techniques is a sharper definition of the resulting software application, a reduced risk of false starts, and a higher probability that the program will actually implement its intended function. Without structured techniques, rapidly changing requirements can become problematic. Even if a project starts with well-defined goals and requirements, new opportunities or other technical considerations can cause a shift in the requirements. These changes inevitably exact a premium in time, due to delayed project schedules and adjusted deliverables, as well as money and development resources.

Structured Analysis Overview: Yourdon/DeMarco

Structured Analysis was developed by Edward Yourdon and Tom DeMarco to provide a method for focusing on an

Make things as simple as possible but no simpler.
— Albert Einstein

application's data flow rather than the control flow advocated by more traditional, top-down specification methods. The goal of Structured Analysis is to produce a *structured specification*, which is a type of functional requirements document. Structured specifications differ from traditional functional requirements documents in that the traditional documents are largely text based, while structured specifications are largely graphics based.

Structured Analysis cannot preclude shifting requirements, but it can accommodate these changes and minimize their impact by helping to organize the software modules in a functionally separate and maintainable manner. Over the years, the Structured Analysis methodology has evolved into three complementary techniques: data flow diagrams, data models, and control specifications. Generally, a structured specification will include all three of these components, although different applications will stress one more heavily than the others.

Control Specification: State Transition Diagrams, Decision Trees, Flow Charts. Many types of systems are characterized by their dependence on certain activities happening at certain times. These *real-time* systems interact directly with a changing physical environment. Examples of real-time systems are avionics control systems in aircraft or cruise control systems in automobiles. These systems must continuously respond to events or conditions in an external environment, since the timing and sequencing of events are critical.

Functional Design: Data Flow Diagrams. Complex systems contain large numbers of discrete functions and processes. These functions process data as it flows through the system. Data flow diagrams depict the world from the data's perspective. This is typically how the user community already thinks about the system for which the software application is being designed. A one-to-one correspondence often exists between the data elements flowing between processes and the physical pieces of paper and job functions already existing. Data flow diagrams constitute a key part of the functional requirements document. (Figure 4.1)

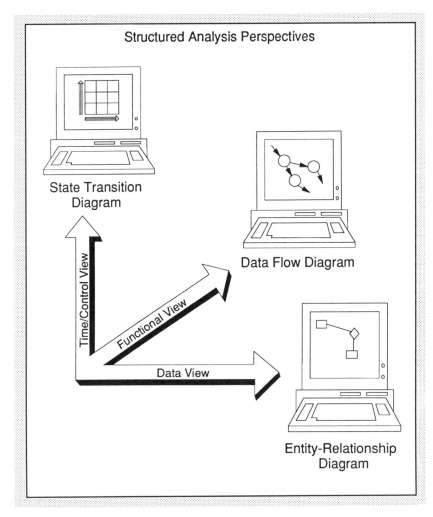

Figure 4.1 The Structured Analysis methodology encompasses several technologies with differing functions. The central technique—the data flow diagram—models a system's function from the data's viewpoint. Data dictionaries and entity-relationship diagrams specify the composition of the individual data flows. State transition diagrams, decision trees, and program design languages describe how the processes in the data flow diagram transform the data.

Data Modeling: Entity-Relationship Diagrams. Since all software applications contain and use data, data structure design, data base design, and file format specification form an integral part of the application design process. Consequently, it is important to graphically model data in the data base and its various uses by the individual application programs. Structured Analysis enlists the help of a *data dictionary* to organize the various data elements in an application's design.

The Structured Specification

Because of its graphical orientation, a structured specification is one of the best methods of bridging the gap between data processing professionals, who are focusing on *how* to build the software, and the end-users, who are focusing on *what* is being built. It is easy to give a definition of Structured Analysis because it is really a simple set of tools whose use produces a structured specification. Those tools are:

- **Data flow diagrams.** A graphic depiction of the different data items in a system and their movement from process to process. Data flow diagrams depict a system from the data's viewpoint rather than the control flow's viewpoint. Data flow diagrams reveal only data flow, not control flow.

- **Data dictionaries.** A catalog of all data items found in the data flow diagram. Each data element, no matter how small or how large, is cataloged in the data dictionary.

- **Process Specifications.** Also called mini-specifications. Process specifications document the data transformations occurring in a data flow diagram. These specifications delineate how the data elements flowing into the individual processes are transformed into the outgoing data elements. Decision tables, decision trees, Structured English, and pseudocode are among the many process specification techniques.

Structured specifications, built using Structured Analysis techniques, give the software developer and the end-user a common communication vehicle both can use to iron out any discrepancies in deciding the application's function. If a piece of data or a process is absent from or misplaced on the data flow diagram, then it stands out.

The Structured Analysis process, as shown in Figure 4.2, is identical to the traditional software development process, except that the bulk of the requirements specification is constructed from data flow diagrams and process specifications (mini-specifications). In Figure 4.2, the "Structured Analysis" box is really the requirements analysis phase, and the "Structured Design" box is the design specification stage (see Chapter 3). The user interface design is also part of the requirements analysis, but is expressly not included as part of Structured Analysis, although user interaction may be modeled as a set of input and output transactions (data flows).

The Structured Analysis methodology has evolved with time. Tom DeMarco, in his classic *Structured Analysis and System Specification*, devotes very little attention to user interface specification. Visual interfaces, as discussed in Chapter 8, are a relatively new phenomenon, elevated to importance by the personal computer boom which introduced millions of people to computers. Data flow diagrams built using Structured Analysis do model the end-user inputs and outputs very well; the traditional Structured Analysis methodology doesn't encompass the data's presentation to end-users. From the Structured Analysis perspective, once these inputs and outputs, called *data flows* (more about these in the next section), are identified, then an end-user interface can be designed. This end-user interface masks much of the underlying processing detail.

To reiterate the point made earlier, no single specification technique encompasses the entire requirements analysis stage. The skilled software analyst must select appropriate tools for each different component in the structured specification.

Data Flow Diagrams

Simply put, data flow diagrams depict a software application's operation from the data's viewpoint. Data elements flow from process node to process node where they are modified. There is no notion of control flow in a data flow diagram, and for this reason, the data flow diagram best depicts the system as the end-user views it.

Data flow diagrams consist of only four graphical components, as shown in Figure 4.3:

- **Data flows.** Data flows are the individual data items (data structures) that are transmitted and received by processes. They are represented by labeled vectors on the data flow diagram. The direction of the arrow indicates the direction of data flow.

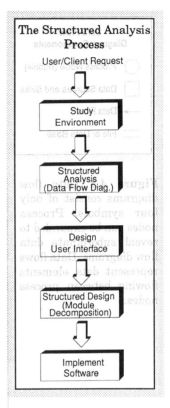

The Structured Analysis Process

User/Client Request

Study Environment

Structured Analysis (Data Flow Diag.)

Design User Interface

Structured Design (Module Decomposition)

Implement Software

Figure 4.2 Structured Analysis is a requirements analysis methodology, focusing on modeling data and information flow. Data flow diagrams produced by the Structured Analysis process can be translated into module hierarchies through a structured design process.

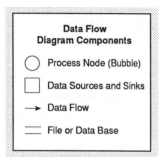

Figure 4.3 Data flow diagrams consist of only four symbols. Process nodes can be expanded to reveal subordinate data flow diagrams. Data flows represent data elements flowing between process nodes.

■ **Processes.** Data flows flow into and out of individual processes. Processes, represented as bubbles on the data flow diagram, manipulate (transform) the incoming data flows into outgoing data flows. A variety of techniques for describing the transformation processes are discussed in the next chapter.

■ **Data sources and sinks.** Sources and sinks are external originators and receivers of data flows. People and machinery are examples of data sources and sinks. Sources and sinks are represented as square boxes on the data flow diagram.

■ **Files and data bases.** Individual processes may require data from files and data bases to perform their operations. Data may be extracted or deposited into files and data bases, which are represented as horizontal bars or sometimes as "cylinders" on the data flow diagram.

Figure 4.4 illustrates a typical data flow diagram for an order entry processing application. Notice that the process nodes tend to resemble the physical entities processing the "paperwork," and the data flows represent the paperwork "transactions" actually sent between the processing entities. Frequently, drawing a system's data flow diagram will reveal inherent simplifications that can be made to the system. In many cases, data flow diagramming is nothing more than process modeling, a technique long used by industrial engineers and business managers. Nevertheless, it is extremely important to model a system's behavior before beginning a software implementation. Data flow diagrams are a communication vehicle between system engineer and end-user, and the Structured Analysis-based CASE tools make their composition and editing very quick, simple, and straightforward.

Think of the data flow diagram as a road map. The data flows (arrows) are the roads connecting the cities (process nodes). Data elements (cars) flow along the data flows as they travel from process node to process node. Along the way, the process nodes transform the incoming data elements into outgoing data elements. The order entry and collections system for the mail-order company in Figure 4.4 illustrates a typical data flow diagram. It starts with the receipt of a telephone call signifying an order. This order is taken by the order entry clerk, initiating a series of other transactions between processes. Customer-billing invoices must be generated along with shipment of the actual products ordered. This can trigger out-of-stock flags, alerting the Purchasing Department, which in turn transmits stock-ordering information to the Accounting Department.

At the data flow diagram level, we are not concerned with the underlying processing occurring in the process nodes. Our only concern is identifying the processes and the data elements flowing between them. Ultimately, a process specification will be attached to the lowest level process nodes. These process specifications describe how input data flows are transformed into output data flows.

Study Figure 4.4 in detail for a moment. A quick observation indicates there is a tremendous traffic congestion around the Accounting process bubble. This bubble is a good candidate for further refinement, possibly suggesting the Accounting process be decomposed into several discrete accounting functions (bubbles). The accounting function appears to be involved in customer billing and collection, inventory stock order and payment, and management reporting. Also, the Customer data source box on the left is probably not the same as the Customer data sink on the right. Usually, the customer's purchasing department places the order, and the customer's receiving department receives the order. The systems engineer or analyst should have no problem working through and refining this model with help from the operations group personnel.

> Inconsistencies and poor system modeling are difficult to hide on data flow diagrams.

Data Flow Diagrams are Hierarchical. Each process node in a data flow diagram may be expanded or "opened up" to show a lower-level data flow diagram. This technique lends itself well to a graphical software implementation where the system designer can point to a process node (with a mouse, cursor keys, or other pointing device) and "explode" the process node to reveal a lower-level data flow diagram.

This "roll up" feature is unique to data flow diagrams and provides an extremely useful mechanism for abstracting

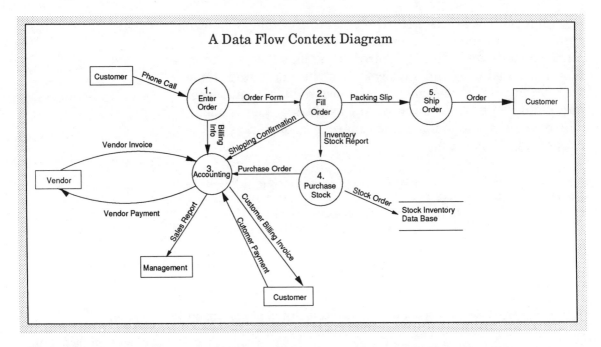

Figure 4.4 The topmost data flow diagram is called the *context diagram*. The context diagram shows all of the input and output data flows entering and exiting the entire software system. Rectangular boxes indicate data sources and sinks external to the software system.

arbitrary levels of detail. Flowcharts and other *control-oriented* structuring methodologies do not have this property, which is analogous to a book outline showing successive levels of refinement.

The "top-level" data flow diagram is called a *context diagram*. All data sources and sinks flowing into and out of the data flow diagram are shown on the context diagram; there are no other sources and sinks hidden in lower-level data flow diagrams. The context diagram permits the entire underlying structure—the lower-level data flow diagrams—to be treated as a black box. This important design concept provides a powerful structuring mechanism allowing a separation, or segregation, of functionality.

Data flow diagrams use a consistent numbering convention to indicate level. This numbering scheme augments the process names given each node. The top-level process nodes are sequentially numbered with integers, as in Figure 4.5. The second level and lower nodes are numbered like subsections in a book. For example, the data flow diagram underneath process node 2 in the context diagram has process nodes numbered 2.1, 2.2, 2.3, and so forth. The data flow diagram

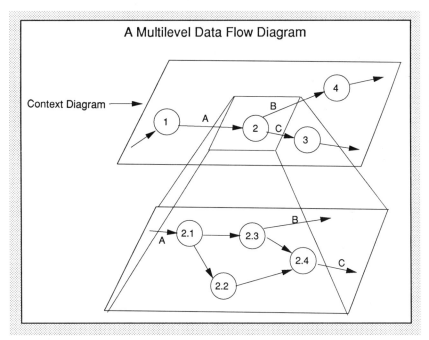

Figure 4.5 Data flow diagrams are multi-leveled. CASE tools implementing the Structured Analysis methodology allow the analyst to position a cursor over a process node and "explode" open to the next lower level.

underneath process node 2.2 has process nodes numbered 2.2.1, 2.2.2, 2.2.3, and so on.

The numbers do *not* indicate any type of sequencing information, such as flow information. They are only for enumeration, identification, and level indication purposes. In data flow diagrams for large systems with many hundreds of process nodes, identifying a particular node only by its symbolic name becomes prohibitively difficult, so the node's numerical identifier is frequently used. This greatly reduces confusion, and the node's numerical identifier immediately conveys a sense of the node's "degree of detail," as depth information is contained in the enumeration scheme.

In practice, data flow diagrams do not nest more than five or six levels deep, although there is a wide variance on this depth. Smaller systems tend to be shallower while larger systems are deeper. Usually, the data flow diagram under a particular process node is limited to ten or twelve subordinate process nodes—the amount comfortably fitting on one page of paper or on one graphics display screen. Once this number of nodes (lower-level data flow diagrams) is exceeded, there is usually too much detail to represent at that level and further

Figure 4.6 Process nodes are numbered hierarchically to indicate their ancestry in multilevel data flow diagrams. The data flow diagram's capability to "roll up" and "explode" successive layers of detail in a stepwise refinement fashion is an important structuring property.

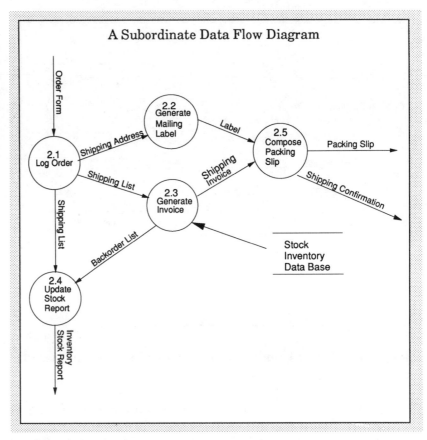

A Subordinate Data Flow Diagram

subordination is required. This is easy, because most Structured Analysis CASE tools allow the analyst to simply "pop open" a diagram underneath the indicated process node bubble where the subordinate data flow diagram can be drawn.

Leveled Data Flow Diagrams.   The process of subdividing processes into lower-level data flow diagrams is called *leveling*. The data flow diagram generated by displaying all of the lowest-level process nodes, or primitives, is called the *leveled set*. The leveled set is important because there must be a *process specification*, or algorithmic description, for each process node in the leveled set. Figure 4.7 shows a process specification, also called a mini-specification, attached to the Generate Invoice process of Figure 4.6. The leveled set will usually contain process nodes from several different levels in the aggregate data flow diagram because not all process nodes will be decomposed to the same depth. There is absolutely no requirement that the leveled set of process nodes come from the same level in the data flow diagram.

It is not always easy to determine when a particular process node has been sufficiently decomposed. One general rule is that each process node should break down into a single subordinate data flow diagram of about one page in size or one screen in size when using a CASE tool providing Structured Analysis (data flow diagram) facilities. Data flow diagrams larger than one or two pages probably indicate a system that is not properly structured, while data flow diagrams with only two or three nodes indicate that no further decomposition is possible.

Another method for determining the bottom-level process node is when the process node has a single input data element and a single output data element with a clean and easily described transformation between them. This rule also applies to situations where there are one-to-many and many-to-one data transformations. (Figure 4.8)

Consistency Checking. All CASE tools implementing the Structured Analysis methodology (data flow diagrams) provide a consistency-checking mechanism. Some tools allow the designer to invoke this consistency checker at will, but others disallow the creation of any process, data flow label, or other object that is inconsistent with the rest of the data flow diagram. In general, this checking scrutinizes the data flow diagram for such inconsistencies as:

- Unnamed or unconnected data flows, processes, or data stores.

- Data sources or sinks appearing only on the context diagram.

- No data stores appearing on the context diagram.

- Processes lacking at least one input and output.

- Unbalanced data flows between parent and child diagrams.

Because vendors enhance the Structured Analysis methodology with their own proprietary extensions, the complete set of

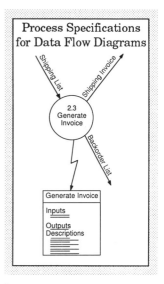

Figure 4.7 The lowest-level (primitive) process nodes constitute the data flow diagram's leveled set. Individual proces specifications, also called mini-specifications, are attached to each node in the leveled set. These process specifications articulate the process's operation—the transformation between input and output data flows.

Figure 4.8 Data Flow Diagram Leveling Criteria. Leveling is the process of subdividing higher-level data flow diagrams into lower-level ones.

Context Diagram	Single-page depiction of all top-level process nodes, input and output data flows, and data sources and sinks.
Mid-level data flow diagram	Process nodes can be decomposed into page-sized subordinate data flow diagrams.
Bottom-level process node	Single input, single output data flows; One-to-many input to output transformation; Many-to-one input to output transformation.

consistency checks vary from tool to tool. The important concept is that CASE tools *automate* the consistency-checking process, an extremely tedious procedure when done by hand.

Summary

In summary, data flow diagrams:

- Are graphical specifications.
- Are hierarchical and multileveled.
- Emphasize the flow of data, not the flow of control.
- Specify requirements, not software designs.

Data Dictionaries

Data dictionaries form the underpinnings of data flow diagrams. Data dictionaries are catalogs, or data bases, of all the data elements found in a data flow diagram. This includes the individual data flows and the process nodes. All of the attributes of any particular piece of data can be found in the data dictionary. Each data flow element is really just a data structure. Data flows can be atomic data types, such as integers, real numbers, and strings; or they can be more complex data structures comprising several lower-level data structures. When this is the case, the data dictionary contains the component data structure definitions.

Datum	Elements
Customer-Invoice	Customer-Info
	Invoice-Info
	List-of-Goods
Customer-Info	Customer-Name
	Customer-Address
Invoice-Info	Invoice-Number
	Salesman-Name
	Customer-Account-Number
	Invoice-Date
List-of-Goods	Product-Code
	Quantity-Ordered
	Description
	Product-Price

Figure 4.9 An Example Data Dictionary. Data dictionaries contain descriptions of all data elements in a data flow diagram. This example shows how lower-level data structures comprise the *Costumer-Invoice* datum.

Structured Analysis CASE tools automatically maintain the data dictionary. When you create a new data flow or process node, it is automatically added to the data dictionary. When a data flow is edited, the data dictionary is updated to reflect the change. Sometimes, several queries into the data dictionary may be required to flesh out the details on a particular data element because individual data elements can be composed of other, lower-level data elements. Figure 4.9 shows the data dictionary entries composing a high-level data element called *Customer Invoice*.

Data dictionaries look conspicuously like BNF (Backus-Naur Form) *production rules* hidden in relational data base clothing. In fact, this is how many CASE tools portray (and allow the designer to edit) data dictionaries, as shown in Figure 4.10. Data dictionaries share many of the properties of BNF diagrams. Like BNF diagrams, data dictionary elements can share lower-level elements. But unlike BNF diagrams, there is no top-level production rule that expands into other production rules. In a data dictionary there are many individual data elements (sets of individual productions) that expand into lower-level data structures (productions).

Figure 4.10 Data dictionaries are very similar to Backus-Naur Form production rules for formal grammars. Many CASE tools allow designers to edit data dictionary entries using a BNF syntax.

Customer-Invoice =	Customer-Infor + Invoice-Info + List-of-Goods.
Customer-Info =	Customer-Name + Customer-Address.
Invoice-Info =	Invoice-Number + Salesman-Name + Customer-Account-Number + Invoice-Date.
List-of-Goods =	Product-Code + Quantity-Ordered + Description + Product-Price.

In CASE tools that support interactive data flow diagram editing, the central data dictionary is constantly updated, modified, and appended to as new process bubbles are created and new data flows defined. Several of the more sophisticated CASE tools provide access to the data dictionary, allowing software developers to "tap into" the data dictionary to extract information. Typically, this type of information is extracted so that some or all of the code generation process can be automated, making the CASE tool truly powerful indeed! At a minimum, this automates the data structure definition process. Many data dictionaries also have a "data flow from-to" field that specifies, for the appropriate dictionary entries, the process nodes being linked by the data flow element.

Consistency Checking. Most CASE tools implementing the Structured Analysis methodology (data flow diagrams) have facilities for performing data dictionary consistency checking much like data flow diagram consistency checking. These tools check for:

- Syntactically correct definitions.

- Undefined entries (entries on the data flow diagram but not cataloged in the data dictionary).

■   Circular definitions.

■   Self-defining terms (terms used in another definition which are not defined).

■   Aliases (multiple entries with equivalent definitions).

Once the data flow diagrams are complete and the data flow elements defined, it is time to move one step closer to implementation. The next chapter, *"Minispecification Techniques,"* introduces the process specification, or mini-specification. Mini-specifications add the substance to the primitive process bubbles in the data flow diagram and are called mini-specifications because they specify only one single process bubble. As you will see, there is a variety of minispecification techniques, each with its own unique set of trade-offs.

Chapter 5

Mini-Specification Techniques

It's a funny thing about life; if you refuse to accept anything but the best, you very often get it.
— W. Somerset Maugham

Mini-specifications are an important part of the data flow diagram. They are called *mini*-specifications because each mini-specification describes only one single primitive (lowest-level) process bubble in the data flow diagram. That is, they document one single process or data transformation function, and as such, they are intended to be fairly simple and straightforward.

There are many different ways to write a mini-specification, depending on the type of data transformation occurring in the process and the nature of the software application itself. There is no "correct" way to write a mini-specification. However, a methodically written set of mini-specifications makes the software implementor's job much easier, and code generated based on the mini-specifications will reflect the maturity of the design by being highly reliable and maintainable.

This chapter presents a spectrum of mini-specification techniques ranging from easy-to-read Structured English to very explicit program design languages. At the end of this chapter is a table summarizing the pros and cons of each mini-specification technique and the situations in which each technique is best employed.

What are Mini-Specifications?

Mini-specifications, commonly called *mini-specs*, are algorithmic descriptions of the task performed by a single, bottom-level process node in a data flow diagram (the leveled set). They are called *mini-spec*ifications because they document only one single process in the entire data flow diagram. They do not document anything more than that one process node. The collection of all mini-specs in a data flow diagram forms

The number of mini-specs in the aggregate data flow diagram will equal the number of bottom-level (primitive) process nodes.

the complete specification of the system. Each process node in the data flow diagram's leveled set will have a mini-specification.

Since a mini-specification documents only one process node, it is typically quite small, usually under one page in length (Figure 5.1). This makes the mini-specification very easy to modify as the data flow diagram is edited to reflect user requirements as they are defined and refined during the project's requirements analysis phase. If the mini-specification is larger than one page, then the process node is a good candidate for further decomposition into a lower-level data flow diagram. Lengthy mini-specifications are not appropriate.

Mini-specs can be written in a variety of forms, but they all have several common components:

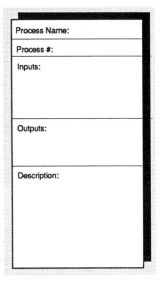

| Process Name: |
| Process #: |
| Inputs: |
| Outputs: |
| Description: |

Figure 5.1 Many Structured Analysis CASE tools use a template format to present mini-specifications to application designers. Most tools fill in default values for the process name and number. The input and output lists are automatically derived from the data flow diagram, leaving only the description slot to be filled in by the designer.

Process Name and Number. Each mini-specification has a name, usually the name of its process node. In many CASE tools, however, a subroutine function name is used, streamlining the automatic conversion from mini-specification to actual compilable code. Most CASE tools use the process name as part of a cross-reference listing generated from the mini-specs.

Input Data List. The input data list itemizes the incoming data flows (data elements) flowing into the process node. The input data list can be conveniently thought of as the input parameters to a subroutine function.

Output Data List. Like the input data list, the output data list itemizes the outgoing data flows (data elements) flowing out of the process node and into another node in the data flow diagram. The output data list is conveniently thought of as the returned (output) parameters from a subroutine function.

Body or Description. The body specifies the algorithm or operation that transforms the input data flows into the output data flows. Again, the subroutine function analogy works very well, and many CASE tools treat mini-specs as subroutine specifications.

There is no single accepted means for articulating a mini-specification's algorithm. In a true structured specification, each mini-specification will describe only the underlying policy for transforming the input data flows into the output data flows; no method for *implementing* the policy is stated. However, in practice it is difficult to adhere to this rigorous definition, and the specification methods vary from very loose, textual descriptions of the process node's operation to actual executable code.

The most common methods of specifying the body of a mini-specification are:

- Flow chart.
- Pseudocode/Structured English.
- Program design language.
- Visual program design language.
- Formal computer language.
- Decision table/State transition matrix.
- Decision tree.

Each of these mini-specification techniques is discussed below because all are commonly used in Structured Analysis CASE tools (Figure 5.2). Obviously, different vendors emphasize different techniques, although many tools support several of these mini-specification techniques. Determining the best mini-specification technique largely depends on the type of software application being built and the facilities provided by the CASE tool being used. Some CASE tools supply a mechanism for automatically translating pseudocode specifications into actual compilable source code in one of several supported programming languages, a tricky process given the current state of the art in CASE technology. Other tools stop short of code generation and focus on building better, more complete requirements and design documents.

Pseudocode/Structured English

Pseudocode, also called *Structured English*, is the purest form for stating the transformations between input data flows and output data flows. Pseudocode is a cross between a textual English language description and an exacting procedural

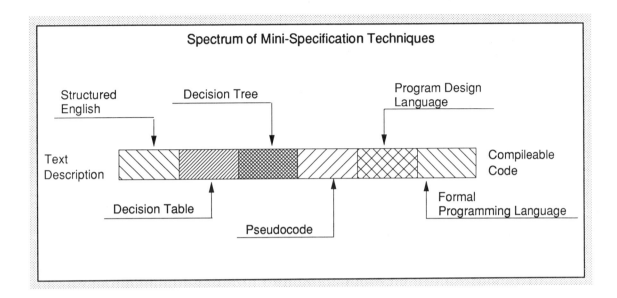

computer language rendition of the algorithm. Pseudocode specifications are structured and show an abstract level of implementation. In recent years, pseudocode has largely supplanted flow charts as a means for specifying algorithms and processes. Pseudocode is very versatile, allowing a wide range of detail ranging from free-form text notes to highly detailed structured English that resembles program code.

Figure 5.3 illustrates the mini-specification for the Generate Invoice Process (process 2.3) shown in Figure 4.6. In this case, the mini-specification is very straightforward; it involves building a shipping invoice for an order based on the in-stock availability of the ordered items. Any items not in stock are added to a back-order file and are listed as "back-ordered" on the shipping invoice. This is an example of where Structured Analysis is used to flesh out the details of a business operation. For example, in a back-order situation, are all available units shipped to the customer and the unfilled balance put on back-order; or is the entire balance put on back-order and the units shipped only when there is sufficient quantity to fill the entire order? Structured Analysis forces the analyst to specify these types of details.

The pseudocode/structured English representation of the mini-specification illustrates how the actual software

Figure 5.2 A wide spectrum of mini-specification techniques are available. Different CASE tools emphasize certain techniques over others. The system engineer must carefully select the technique(s) most appropriate for the application being built. This depends on such factors as nature of the application and its end-users.

Figure 5.3 Pseudo-code Mini-Specification. Pseudocode specifications resemble Structured English as one might use in writing an algorithm or process. Pseudocode is excellent for communicating process specifications to end-users without confusing them with language syntax.

For each item in the Shipping List, do the following:

1. Search the Stock Inventory Data Base for the item and the available quantity.
2. If the item is in stock in sufficient quantity:

    1. add it to the Shipping Invoice.

    2. decrement the Stock Inventory Data Base accordingly

3. If the item is not in stock in sufficient quantity:

    1. add the item to the Back-order List.

    2. add the item to the Shipping Invoice and label it "Back-ordered."

When all items in the Shipping List have been processed:

1. Send the completed Shipping Invoice to be shipped.

The chief advantage of pseudocode mini-specifications is the ability to specify a process in enough detail to communicate with the end-user community while not belaboring the specification with unnecessary detail.

implementation can be easily generated, either by hand or automatically, if the CASE tool provides facilities to assist in the implementation. Notice, however, nothing is mentioned in the pseudocode mini-specification about the underlying data structures, the data flows, or the routines needed to access the data base files. Furthermore, the details of the data base and shipping list searches are not completely and rigorously specified. Because the pseudocode mini-specification is only specification and not a detailed design, this level of detail is usually omitted.

Pseudocode can be handed directly to the design team for conversion into a design specification. Unlike the more formal program design languages discussed later in this chapter, pseudocode is not automatically translatable into compilable code.

Flow Charts

Flow charts have been used for years in the data processing community as a graphical means for describing an algorithm and its control flow. Flow charts focus almost entirely on control flow instead of the data flow diagram's bias toward data flow. Flow charts usually say very little about data structures, in contrast to data flow diagrams which say quite a lot. So control-flow-oriented flow charts can compliment a data-oriented data flow diagram as a mini-specification technique.

Figure 5.4 illustrates the flow chart rendition of the Generate Invoice mini-specification (process 2.3) shown in Figure 4.6. Notice the flow chart's detail suggesting a direct mapping into some underlying programming language. This flow chart, and the others from the leveled set of process nodes in the data flow diagram, could be handed directly to an implementation crew for coding. The only details left to the imagination are the data structures corresponding to the data flows and the access primitives needed to read and write the files. If the data structures already exist in the design's data dictionary, only the file access routines are left to design.

Flow charts are currently out of favor among most data processing and software engineering professionals, largely due to the drudgery of editing flow charts by hand. Flow charts document a process at a very low level—almost too low to be useful. Virtually each flow chart symbol maps directly into a specific line of code in the resulting software. Software designers find flow charts difficult to manipulate because flow charts represent the software design at a very low level, and the designer needs a higher-level schematic of the software's architecture. This makes it difficult to design a system of any size using only flow charts.

Because flow charts document the underlying software almost on a line-by-line basis, if the underlying software ever changes, even by one line, the appropriate flow chart must be religiously updated in exact correspondence to the modified code. Because of the difficulty in linking software changes to the flow chart, flow charts soon fell out of synchronization with the software, rendering them useless. Flow charting quickly earned a poor reputation as a program design methodology.

Several CASE tools use the flow chart metaphor as a mini-specification technique. These tools, like other CASE tools,

Figure 5.4 Flow charts graphically document a process one level above an underlying programming language, and they can be handed to programmers for implementation. On paper, flow charts are difficult to edit, requiring tedious redrawing. But several flow-charting CASE tools are available that eliminate much of the drawing burden.

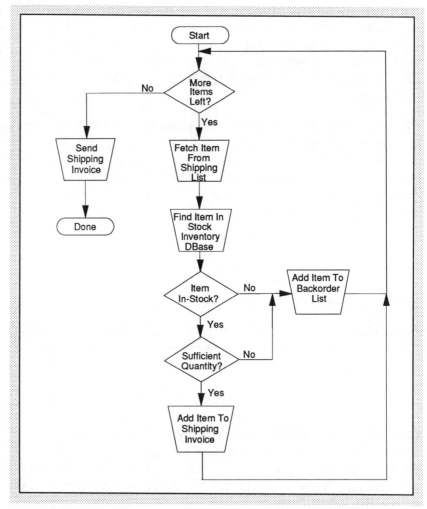

are structured graphical editors and are much easier to manipulate than the by-hand redrawing with plastic template sheets required in the past. Although this book does not discuss any specific flow-charting tools in detail, several are mentioned in Appendix A. At this writing, there are no flow-charting CASE tools directly linking the flow chart to the underlying software for any specific programming language. Such a link would enable the automatic generation of software directly from the flow chart. Several software developers have, however, implemented flow chart to code translators that transform a flow chart file into compilable code. One example is a translator built at EDS (Electronic

Data Systems, Inc. Southfield, MI) for converting Interactive Easyflow (see Appendix A) flow chart files into C language code.

Program Design Languages

Program Design Languages are the most common form of mini-specification found in CASE tools. Program Design Languages are similar to programming languages because they are formal specifications and follow a very rigid syntax, containing procedural and iterative constructs such as:

Begin-End
If-Then
Do-While
Select Case
Function Call

However, program design languages are not specific to any one programming language, such as C, COBOL, or FORTRAN. They function as generic representations that are more loosely structured than real programming languages. Analysis and design CASE tools provide built-in translators that generate compilable code for programming languages, usually Ada and C, based on the mini-specifications written in the tool's program design language. This generic representation provides an interesting flexibility: the ability to generate code in several programming languages from the generic program design language.

> The goal of a program design language is to provide the formalism and precision of an actual programming language without the overhead of strict syntax and memory allocation.

Figure 5.5 illustrates the program design language rendition of the Generate Invoice mini-specification for process 2.3 in Figure 4.6. The program design language rendition is decidedly more formal and well-defined than the pseudocode/Structured English version, but it still retains some of the looseness of pseudocode. For example, statements like *add Item to Shipping_Invoice* could easily translate into two or three pages of file access code, but this unnecessary detail is masked by the program design language. This is desirable because mini-specifications are meant to be *specifications*, not implementations.

Figure 5.5 Program Design Language Mini-Specification. Mini-specifications written with program design languages resemble subroutines in conventional programming languages. However, many of the lower-level details are omitted. Several CASE tools are capable of translating mini-specifications written in program design languages into actual program code, such as C and Ada.

```
%NAME      Generate_Invoice

%INPUTS
      Shipping_List

%OUTPUTS
      Back_order_List
      Shipping_Invoice

BEGIN
      WHILE items left in Shipping_List
      DO

            Find item in Stock_Inventory_Data_Base

            IF
                  item is in-stock AND
                  there is sufficient quantity
            THEN
                  add item to Shipping_Invoice
                  decrement Stock_Inventory_Data_Base for item
            ELSE
                  add item to Back_Order_List
                  add item to Shipping_Invoice and
                  label item "back-ordered"
            ENDIF
      END_DO
END
```

With program design languages, the inputs and outputs are clearly identified, giving each process specification the appearance of a subroutine function. As shown in Figure 5.5, the inputs and outputs are nothing more than the process node's input and output data flows. Again, the actual composition of the data flows is hidden, residing in the central data dictionary. The data dictionary can be queried to provide the underlying components of data flows like *Shipping_List* and *Back_order_List*.

The WHILE-DO looping construct suggests a subroutine body. But unlike a subroutine body, the data base lookup, *Find item in Stock_Inventory_Data_Base*, is left unspecified. In most Structured Analysis CASE tools, a program design language statement like this is treated as a function call to an unspecified subroutine.

Program design languages are influenced by the languages for which the tool will generate code. Since most of today's popular programming languages are block structured, ALGOL-like languages (which share similar concepts and structures), program design languages themselves tend to be relatively straightforward. For example, most program design languages have subroutine call constructs, conditional selection constructs like the IF-THEN, and iterative constructs like FOR-DO and REPEAT-UNTIL.

At this time there is no standard program design language used by CASE tool vendors for data flow diagram mini-specifications; this is one way for CASE tool vendors to differentiate themselves. But as the CASE industry matures, a standardized program design language will likely emerge. Although predicting the winner in such a marketing battle is always difficult, the victor tends to be the one with the widest commercial following.

Visual Program Design Languages

A unique and relatively new mini-specification technique is the *visual program design language*. Figure 5.6 illustrates the FLOWforms visual programming templates used in the PRODOC CASE tool (Intelligent Micro Systems, Inc. Narberth, PA). PRODOC uses FLOWforms much like an outline processor program, such as ThinkTank™ for the IBM PC, expanding and collapsing outline sections with a single keystroke. With PRODOC, program constructs, such as subroutines and code blocks, can be expanded on-screen to reveal the detail of each program statement; or they can be collapsed to give a coarser-grained view of the program. FLOWforms, like real programs, can be nested as deep as is desired.

Each level of detail and block of code in the visual program has an associated comment line. For example, the ...*Compare and*

Figure 5.6 Visual program design languages are a convenient way to express both pseudocode and compilable source code. This illustration shows the PRODOC FLOW-forms templates. Each basic programming construct is represented as a visual template which is filled in by the designer. Program segments can be expanded and contracted to reveal and hide successive levels of detail.

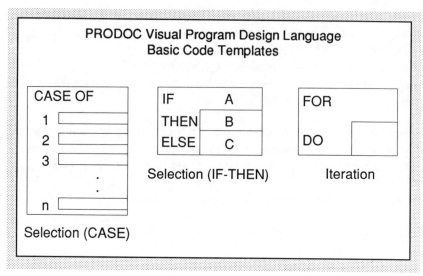

swap... comment identifies a block of code which exchanges two array elements as part of a sorting routine based on an arithmetic comparison. Nested inside the ...*Compare and swap*... block is a block called ...*Swap*... which performs the actual exchange.

Selected code blocks can be collapsed and hidden from view as shown in Figure 5.7. For example, placing the cursor on the ...*Compare and swap*... line in Figure 5.7 and pressing the "contract" key would cause the lower-level code to disappear from view. The entire data element swapping code would be represented on-screen by the single comment ...*Compare and swap*... , certainly appropriate if we are only examining the sequence of actions in the overall program rather than scrutinizing the swapping code. The reverse is also true: to view the swapping code, placing the cursor on the ...*Compare and swap*... comment and pressing the "expand" key reveals the lower-level code.

PRODOC contains code generators to produce actual compilable code in several languages, including Ada, Pascal, and C. The reverse process is also supported: existing code can be automatically converted into FLOWforms containing corresponding pseudocode and design information. PRODOC, however, is a design specification and code implementation tool and not a requirements analysis tool. PRODOC does not, for example, provide facilities for data flow diagram editing.

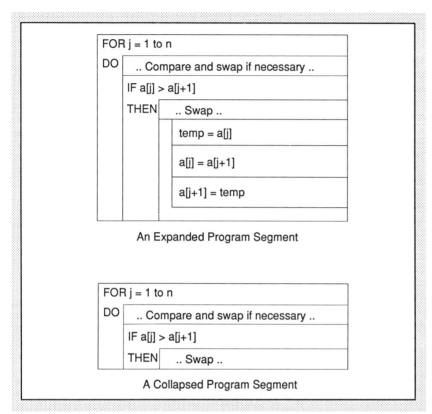

FOR j = 1 to n

DO   .. Compare and swap if necessary ..

IF a[j] > a[j+1]

THEN   .. Swap ..

temp = a[j]

a[j] = a[j+1]

a[j+1] = temp

An Expanded Program Segment

FOR j = 1 to n

DO   .. Compare and swap if necessary ..

IF a[j] > a[j+1]

THEN   .. Swap ..

A Collapsed Program Segment

Figure 5.7 Code segments can be expanded and collapsed in PRODOC to reveal and hide detail as necessary. Visual program design tools like PRODOC help organize code in a top-down, structured manner.

FLOW forms is really an amplification of *Nassi-Shneiderman* diagrams, as shown in Figure 5.8. The Nassi-Shneiderman diagram is useful for showing program organization and component breakdown. Like FLOWforms, software engineers can work with the source code at a convenient level, hiding the lower-level detail until it is needed.

X-Tools, a commercially available CASE tool from Software Design Tools, Inc., implements the Nassi-Shneiderman programming metaphor. It functions much like the PRODOC tool, allowing designers to hide or reveal program detail as necessary.

Formal Computer Languages

C, COBOL, and FORTRAN—the traditional implementation languages we have come to know and love—are examples of formal computer languages. A formal language mini-

Figure 5.8 The Nassi-Shneiderman diagram is a visual program design language used to graphically illustrate detailed control flow and code organization. This example shows an "if-then" conditional inside an iterative "for" loop.

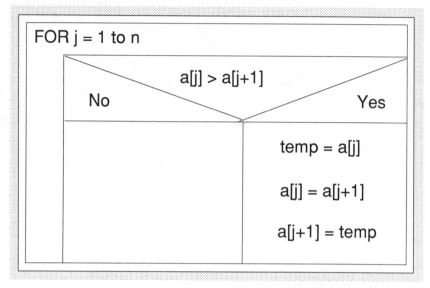

specification is the most difficult type of specification because it concentrates on implementation detail within the data flow diagram, a framework that is inherently specification-oriented. Usually, data flows are not specified to their exact atomic data types; they are typically presented as abstract data types with symbolic names. Their actual composition is described in the central data dictionary. This introduces difficulty in writing code to process the data unless the data flow diagrams are highly detailed down to the lowest level of process description.

Furthermore, once the underlying process node mini-specification is written in a formal computer language, the mini-specification quickly falls out of synchronization with the data flow diagram when the design is modified in any significant way. Then it becomes a laborious chore to edit the source code to conform to the specification. For example, adding or subtracting a single data flow to or from a process would force a reimplementation of the process specification. While this is true of any mini-specification technique, it is far more difficult with an actual programming language where the goal is writing compilable source code.

Figure 5.9 illustrates the C program language rendition of the Generate Invoice mini-specification for process 2.3 in Figure

```
Generate_Invoice()
{
        SHIP_REC                ShipRec;
        BACKORDER_REC           BackRec;
        INVOICE_REC             InvRec;
        STOCKDB_REC             StockRec;
        FILE                    *ShipListFp, *BackListFp, *InvoiceFp;
        DBID                    dbid1;

        ShipListFp = fopen("shiplist.fil", "rb");
        BackListFp = fopen("backlist.fil", "ab");
        InvoiceFp  = fopen("invoice.fil", "ab");

        db_open("stock_inventory.dbf", &dbid1);

        while (fread(&ShipRec,1,sizeof(SHIP_LIST),ShipListFp) != EOF) {

                if ((db_getnr(&dbid1,ShipRec.ItemName,&StockRec)==TRUE) &&
                    (StockRec.Quantity >= ShipRec.Quantity)) {

                        StockRec.Quantity -= ShipRec.Quantity;
                        db_modify(&DBID, &StockRec);
                        InvRec.Item             = ShipRec.Item;
                        InvRec.Quantity         = ShipRec.Quantity;
                        InvRec.Status           = STATUS_OK;
                        fwrite(&InvRec,1,sizeof(INVOICE_REC),InvoiceFp);
                }
                else {
                        BackRec.Item            = ShipRec.Item;
                        BackRec.Quantity        = ShipRec.Quantity;
                        fwrite(&BackRec,1,sizeof(BACKORDER_REC),BackListFp);
                        InvRec.Item             = ShipRec.Item;
                        InvRec.Quantity         = ShipRec.Quantity;
                        InvRec.Status           = STATUS_BACKORDERED;
                        fwrite(&InvRec,1,sizeof(INVOICE_REC),InvoiceFp);
                }
        }

        fclose(ShipListFp);
        fclose(BackListFp);
        fclose(InvoiceFp);
        db_close(&dbid1);
}
```

Figure 5.9 C Language Mini-specification. Formal programming language mini-specifications force the analyst to focus on very low-level details. Such specifications fall out of synchronization with the data flow diagram once the diagram is modified in any significant way.

4.6. Obviously, the choice of programming language depends on the language selected for the final implementation.

The C language mini-specification is very tedious to write. Mini-specification authors spend a significant amount of time focusing on the syntax details of the computer language and making sure that all the proper data elements and subroutine functions are declared and used properly. By the time they are finished with just one of the potentially hundreds or thousands of mini-specifications, they're ready to abandon CASE technology altogether as just an expensive means of writing the same code they've always written! For this reason, formal computer languages usually are not used in mini-specifications. It is far better to use a program design language that generates semicompilable code, leaving the programmers to fill in the unsupplied subroutines during the implementation phase.

Notice that the C language code in Figure 5.9 is not very robust: there is little in the way of error checking and recovery; there is no error trapping on file opening and creation, and no in-line code documentation. This illustrates one of the pitfalls of using formal programming language in mini-specifications: it is hard to balance the *specification* goals against the *design and implementation* details inherent in using a formal programming language. Facilities such as error-checking code are best left to the design specification stage, *after* the specification is complete but before the implementation stage begins.

With all these negatives, what are the benefits of using a formal computer language for process specifications? The benefit is that most of the software is written by the time the specification is complete. However, the implementation takes place at such a low level that there is no opportunity to structure the software, other than with the data flow diagram. Data flow diagrams are excellent for communicating a software specification to the end-user community while refining the specification. Unfortunately, data flow diagrams do not always provide the best software architectures and implementations. They allow the programmer little opportunity to utilize common processing functions when the same, or similar, processes occur in several different parts of the data flow diagram. Since each process node in the leveled set has its own implementation, the programmer cannot collapse and aggregate the code.

Decision Tables

Decision tables are matrices that map a set of input conditions onto a set of actions. These conditions are typically yes/no decisions, such as, "Is the item in stock?" They can also be

	RULES			
CONDITIONS	1	2	3	4
1. Item is in stock	Y	N	Y	N
2. Sufficient quantity of item available	Y	N	N	N
ACTIONS				
1. Add item to Shipping Invoice as "Included"	Y	-	N	N
2. Add item to Shipping Invoice as "Backordered"	N	-	Y	Y
3. Add item to Backorder List.	N	-	Y	Y
4. Decrement Stock Inventory Data Base	Y	-	N	N

Figure 5.10 Decision Table Mini-specification. Decision tables map unique sets of *conditions* into sets of *actions*. Decision tables are useful when there are complex interactions among several conditions. Decision tables are an excellent communication vehicle for end-users, because nonprogrammers find tables very easy to understand.

decisions with a limited set of values, such as, "Is shirt size small, medium, or large?" The actions are usually straightforward operations like, "Add the item to the back-order list." Frequently there is more than one single action for each set of condition values.

Figure 5.10 illustrates the decision table rendition of the Generate Invoice mini-specification for process 2.3 in Figure 4.6. In this example, there are only two conditions: Is the item in stock, and is there sufficient quantity of the item available to fill the order? With two conditions, there are four different ways of combining their values (yes and no):

```
4 combinations = 2 values (yes, no) * 2 values
(yes, no)
```

These four combinations are called *rules* for "rules of combination." If there were two yes/no conditions and one condition with three values (yes, no, maybe), there would be twelve possible combinations:

```
12 combinations = 2 values (yes, no) * 2 values
(yes, no) * 3 values (yes, no, maybe)
```

As shown in Figure 5.10, not all conditions in a decision table may make sense. The item cannot physically be out of stock yet have sufficient quantity available to meet the order demands. Each legal combination of decision criteria will determine one or more output actions. Some of these actions may be common to several decision combinations, and others may not.

Decision tables specify the *policies* for transforming process inputs into outputs, rather than the *operational* characteristics of the algorithm underlying this transformation. Decision tables focus on conditions and outcomes, while and other mini-specification methods, such as pseudocode and flow charts, focus on the procedural implementation of the policy.

Decision tables are very useful in explaining mini-specifications to an end-user. They are great for untangling webs of confusing rules and policies. It is also common for a decision table representation to reveal discrepancies or gaps in existing policies and procedures. People inherently like simple two-dimensional tables because they are easy to understand and are unambiguous. Think about how often we use tables—calendars, spreadsheets, airline schedules, and price charts. If there is a missing condition or action, the decision table will highlight its absence. If the conditions and actions can be simplified, the decision table presents a concise perspective that is more convenient to alter than other mini-specification techniques. The skillful requirements analyst should take advantage of this characteristic when selecting an appropriate mini-specification technique.

> Use a decision table when selection of an action depends on combinations of conditions.

Many CASE tools provide several mini-specification alternatives, including decision tables. Probably the two most common techniques supported are program design languages and decision tables, although most provide text editing facilities for pseudocode and ordinary textual descriptions.

Decision table mini-specifications are easy for programmers to follow when implementing code. Most programming languages provide array or table constructs that directly map from decision table to program array. The table "indices" are the decision table conditions, and the table's output is a set of actions, possibly represented as a set of flags or a set of values.

Decision Trees

A variant of the decision table is the decision tree, which affords a schematic view of the conditional selection process

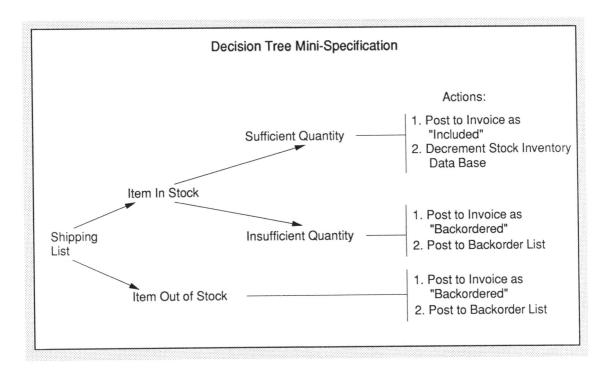

Figure 5.11 The decision tree is a graphical version of the decision table. Decision trees are useful when the selection logic consists of straightforward discriminating conditions that can quickly prune the set of possible actions. End-users find this graphical representation easy to understand.

used to derive a set of actions. Decision trees can be thought of as nested decision tables: a series of simple decision tables leading to an eventual action or conclusion. Decision trees are a more visual representation of the input to output data flow mapping. Because decisions are arranged hierarchically in a tree, there are no ambiguous, or undefined, input values.

Figure 5.11 illustrates the decision tree version of the Generate Invoice mini-specification for process 2.3 in Figure 4.6. The ambiguous condition of an item being out of stock but having sufficient quantity to fill the order has been removed. This illustrates an important point about decision trees: the high-order, most important decision points are toward the top (left for sideways-drawn trees) of the decision tree. Lower-order decision points, the less important discriminators, gravitate toward the bottom of the decision tree. Ordering the priority of the decision criteria is a task the analyst usually finds to be straightforward.

Like the decision table, the decision tree may specify multiple actions for each leaf in the tree. Also like decision tables, decision trees are not restricted to binary, yes/no decisions, as

Figure 5.12 Decision tree decision points can be multivalued.

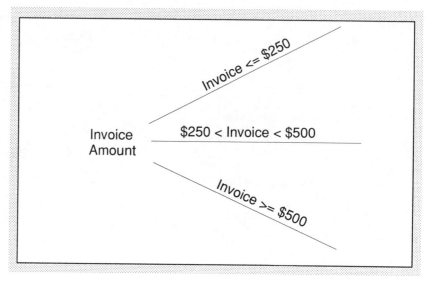

illustrated in Figure 5.12. Each decision point in the decision tree can have several outcomes or paths, depending on the condition. For example, the condition "is the shirt size small, medium, or large?" has three values and would produce three branches emanating from the decision point. Similarly, ranges might be used, such as "is the invoice amount less than $250, between $250 and $500, or greater than $500?"

Decision trees are fairly simple to modify as the specification evolves. The most difficult task is organizing the decision criteria so that each "test" occurs only once in the tree. But once accomplished, adding new test conditions and updating the tree is easy. Decision tree mini-specifications are easy for programmers to follow; the program's branching logic is already drawn out in diagrammatical form.

Mini-Specification Summary

Selecting an appropriate Structured Analysis mini-specification technique is not easy. On large projects, the analyst may select several, depending on the capabilities of the Structured Analysis CASE tool. Almost all Structured Analysis tools provide text editors for creating pseudocode and program design language mini-specifications. The more complete tools support decision tables or decision trees as well. Others

Mini-Specification Technique	Pros	Cons
Pseudocode/Structured English	Appropriate when detail not completely known. Quick and easy. Good for communicating algorithms to end-users.	Not suitable for highly detailed procedures or policies. English may ambiguous translated into compatible code. Cannot be automatically translated into compatible code.
Flow Chart	Close correspondence with underlying code. Good for procedural specifications	Difficult to modify if specification details changes. Difficult to modify if underlying code changes.
Program Design Language	Can be translated into actual program code. Quickly determines whether further task decomposition is needed.	Must somewhat obey syntax rules.
Visual Program Design Language	Can be translated into program code. Details can be fleshed out. Quickly determines whether further task decomposition is needed. Generally easier to edit than text-based program design languages.	Difficult to modify if specification details changes. Difficult to modify if underlying code changes.
Formal Computer Language	Ready to compile.	Forces concentration on syntax and declarations rather than on specification. Difficult to modify and update as specification changes.
Decision Table	Handles complex sets of conditions and actions. Tabular (visual) representation. Easy to spot inconsistencies and gaps. Easy for end-users to understand.	No procedural capabilities.
Decision Tree	Handles complex sets of conditions and actions. Graphical (visual) representation.	No procedural capabilities.

Figure 5.13   Summary of Mini-Specification Techniques.

provide *state transition matrices* for real-time extensions to the normal data flow diagram paradigm. Figure 5.13 summarizes the Structured Analysis mini-specification techniques described in this chapter.

Mini-specifications serve as a bridge between the requirements-oriented data flow diagram and the design-oriented structure chart discussed in the next chapter. Once the mini-specifications are written for each process node in the leveled set and an appropriate specification review completed, the requirements specification is complete. The next step is building the design specification for the actual software implementation. CASE methodologies for building design specifications are detailed in the next two chapters, "Structure Charts" and "Data Modeling Methodologies."

Chapter 6

Structure Charts

This chapter describes how CASE technology can help with the transition from the requirements analysis stage to the design specification stage of the software life cycle. Just as computer-aided software engineering leveraged the requirements analysis stage, so can it simplify and expedite the design specification process. CASE technology provides assistance by offering mechanical aids to translate detailed requirements specifications into software architectures for implementation.

On a cautionary note, the bridge between these two critical phases is narrow and should not be crossed until the requirements analysis phase is fully complete, and the requirements specification has passed a thorough audit by both end-user community representatives and the development organization. Once the requirements specification is approved, however, CASE technology is waiting to smooth the transition into design and implementation.

The *structure chart*, which depicts a hierarchy of software modules, is the design specification's backbone. Structure charts graphically illustrate the interconnections between software modules and frequently show execution information, such as calling sequences and iteration. Sometimes, structure charts are used simply to portray subroutine groupings, as is shown in the Quick Schedule structure chart repeated here in Figure 6.1; the higher-level modules, constituting the user interface, call the lower-level modules to process information.

Other times, structure charts delineate specific calling hierarchies for individual subroutines as shown in Figure 6.2. No matter how detailed, the structure chart, coupled with data structure and file format definitions, comprises a software system's basic architectural design.

If you obey all the rules you miss all the fun.
— Katherine Hepburn

The structure chart, coupled with data structure definitions, comprises a software system's basic architectural design.

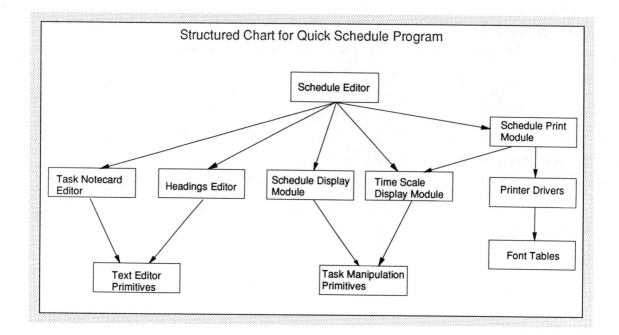

Figure 6.1 Each module is completely separable from the others with clearly defined data paths connecting the modules. Notice that modules tend to call vertically and not horizontally. This is a good organizational principle of structured design.

This chapter presents two structure chart development methodologies commonly implemented in CASE tools. The first is an extension to Structured Analysis that allows a structure chart to be automatically derived from a data flow diagram. The second is the Jackson Structured Programming methodology which gained popularity in the early 1970s in many data processing departments.

Basic Structure-Charting Principles

Good design principles dictate that each module in the structure chart should be independent from and viewable as a *black box* by the other modules. Structuring a large software system is difficult even for seasoned application developers. Creating and editing a structure chart with hundreds or thousands of individual modules becomes an enormous task, especially if the design must be updated at some point after implementation has begun.

In the past, large software applications exhibited a high degree of functional redundancy among code modules, and structure charts often grew to resemble bowls of spaghetti instead of neatly organized hierarchical structures.

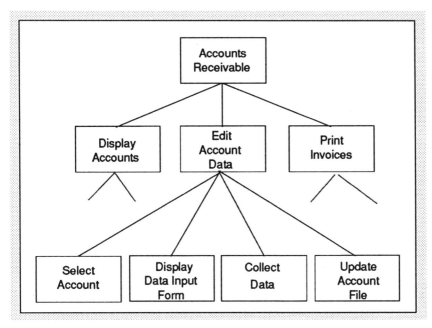

Figure 6.2 A Detailed Structure Chart. Structure charts frequently show detailed calling hierarchy and execution information.

Fortunately, CASE technology can assist the software developer in assembling structure charts for the software design specification. As is discussed later in this chapter, many CASE tools implementing the Structured Analysis methodology can automatically transform data flow diagrams and their process specifications into structure charts.

The principles of good software design are remarkably simple and concise. As Ken Orr, a pioneer in the structured systems and CASE fields, states, "Something is structured if and only if (1) it is hierarchically organized and (2) the pieces of each function are related to one another either by sequence, alternation, or repetition—the basic forms of logic." Modules that exhibit black-box characteristics have the following properties:

- **Simplicity.** The module's function should be simple and easy to understand.

- **Well-defined invocation.** Each module should have a well-defined set of input and output data elements. The invocation (execution) of any procedure in a module should be obvious.

- **Locality.** The module should contain all code and data necessary to perform its function except for data passed into the module as part of its invocation. The module should only call modules beneath it in the structure chart.

- **Free of side effects.** The module's invocation should not influence another module's operation, except by the direct return of data.

Many of these fundamental design principles were first quantified by Larry Constantine and Edward Yourdon in *Structured Design*, one of the classic references on structure charts. The ideal program module performs only one well-defined function and has no relationships with or dependencies on other modules, except through the data passed directly into the module and the data returned directly out of the module. The resulting modules are highly reliable and easy to verify and maintain.

Coupling and Cohesion

The structure chart is a tool for graphically depicting program structure. Structure charts aid the designer in minimizing the *coupling* and maximizing the *cohesion* among program modules. Coupling is an indication of how tightly the modules are interconnected. High coupling, that is, a large number of connections, is generally bad. Cohesion, on the other hand, is a measure of how well a particular module's components—its code and local data structures—belong together. High cohesion—that is, a strong measure of locality—is good. Figure 6.3 shows the effects of both high and low coupling.

Well-coupled programs pass discrete data structures between program modules. On a particular invocation, a module's operation should be completely determined by the data passed into the module; the operation should not depend on values in global data structures or inside other modules. Poorly coupled programs contain a large amount of global data, and its modules generate and rely on many "side effects." For example, one module may post a value (or record) to a global data structure for other program modules to

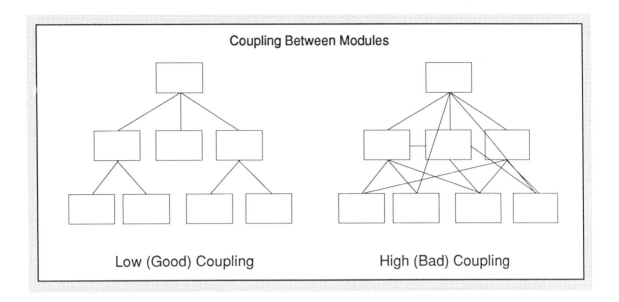

Figure 6.3 Coupling indicates the tightness of interconnection between modules. A high degree of coupling—a significant amount of interconnection—indicates a poorly structured program.

reference in determining their course of action. Although some amount of global data is required in all programs, well coupled programs restrict its use.

Another characteristic of a poorly coupled program is the existence of modules with enough knowledge of other modules' internal contents to use or even modify them. For example, a subroutine in module A may modify the local data in module B in order to achieve some desired effect when a routine in module B is executed. In this case, the modules should be redesigned so the required effect is achievable by some other means, such as adding an input field containing the needed data.

Programs exhibiting good module cohesion are organized into modules that perform only one or a small set functions. Modules do not rely on each other except through well-articulated interconnections (good coupling). Modules with poor cohesion contain functions grouped together only for spatial reasons (they fit on the disk) or some other arbitrary reason (functions whose names begin with A through F are in the first module). Figure 6.4 demonstrates both high and low module cohesion.

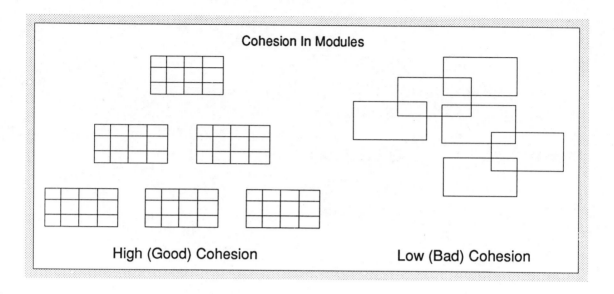

Figure 6.4 Cohesion in a program module measures the isolation between it and other modules. High cohesion—well-isolated modules—indicates a good, well-structured design.

Deriving Structure Charts from Data Flow Diagrams

How are good, well-designed program architectures synthesized from the underlying requirements specification? One way is to manually derive the structure chart from data flow diagrams using the following algorithm:

1. Select an external data source.

2. Trace the input data stream from the external source through the data flow diagram until it disappears.

3. Back through each output stream from its external data sink until it disappears.

4. Identify the "central transform" (the point of highest abstraction) which marks the split between input and output.

5. Build a multibox diagram which refines the system into smaller, more manageable pieces.

6. Continue to refine the boxes until you have "primitive" modules which are easy to code.

Using the data flow diagram in Figure 4.4 as an example, start with the *Phone Call* data flow input to the Enter Order process bubble as shown in Figure 6.5. Trace this path from the Enter

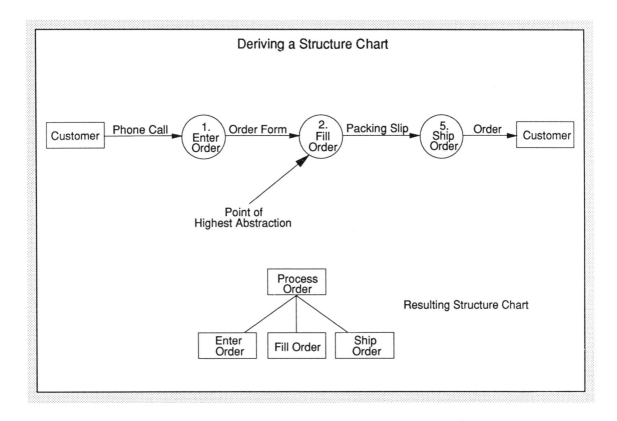

Order process to the Fill Order process, through the Ship Order process, and then out of the diagram to the Customer data sink. Now ask the question, "Where does the flow stop being an input stream and start being an output stream?" This is always a subjective decision since the point of highest abstraction must be selected. For this example, this point is probably the Fill Order process. Up to this point, every process on the path has been involved in data collection and refinement. But once past the Fill Order process, all process nodes along the data flow path are contributing to "sending something out the door."

Applying this algorithm to the context diagram (the top-level data flow diagram) produces the topmost portion of the structure chart hierarchy. Repeating the algorithm for the lower-level (subordinate) data flow diagrams generates the lower levels of the structure chart. Figure 6.6 shows the partial results of applying this algorithm to the subordinate data flow diagram in Figure 4.6 for the Fill Order process.

Figure 6.5 Structure charts can be derived directly from data flow diagrams by tracing single paths from input to output through the data flow diagram. The top structure chart module is the process bubble with the "highest point of abstraction."

Figure 6.6 After the topmost portion of the structure chart is generated from the context diagram, the remainder of the structure chart is produced by applying the refinement algorithm to the subordinate data flow diagrams. The primitive processes may have pseudocode mini-specifications that can be translated into compilable code.

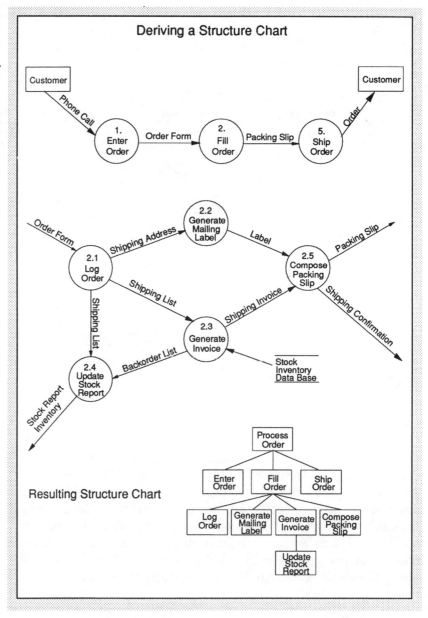

This manual "tracing" procedure is somewhat tedious, especially on large data flow diagrams with hundreds (or thousands) of process bubbles. Fortunately, integrated CASE tools help simplify this process by *automatically* deriving structure charts from data flow diagrams. Chapter 9

describes Structured Analysis tools supporting the design specification phase with structure chart creation and editing facilities. One of these tools, PowerTools from Iconix, will automatically transform a network of data flow diagrams into a hierarchical set of modules using its program design language as the guiding framework.

Jackson Structured Design

Jackson Structured Design, developed during the early 1970's by Michael Jackson, is a structure charting methodology for specifying program operations, such as sequencing and iteration among program modules. Jackson structure charts convey the program's dynamic execution structure in addition to the static calling hierarchy information found in traditional structure charts. Using Jackson Structured Design, the entire program is represented as a hierarchical tree of boxes. The lower-level boxes show fine-grained sequencing and iteration detail, and the higher-level boxes delineate program module organization. In fact, Jackson Structured Designs are typically more detailed than traditional structure charts because they are useful for diagraming small blocks of code as well as large program modules.

These structured programming techniques are best described by example. Figure 6.7 illustrates the basic operations of program sequence, selection, and iteration. A *calling sequence* is shown as a series of program modules or blocks of code which are assumed to be called, or executed, in a left-to-right order. A selection between code blocks is shown diagrammatically as a sequence of modules each with a zero ("0") in the upper right-hand corner. Iteration is depicted as a code block with an asterisk ("*") in the upper right-hand corner.

Figure 6.8 shows a code fragment designed using the Jackson Structured Design methodology. As you might expect, building one of these detailed designs involves a substantial amount of refining and editing. With pencil, paper, and flowcharting template, this is an onerous task, and the programmer is more likely to try writing the code first before building the design. But with a graphically oriented CASE tool implementing the Jackson Structured Design concepts, this tedious

Figure 6.7 Jackson Structured Programming merges the conventional structure chart with a notation to specify algorithmic execution. Program sequence, selection, and iteration are indicated on Jackson designs.

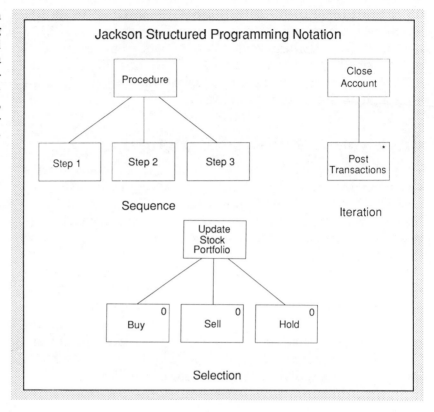

design editing is simplified. Just "button" the desired box with a mouse and drag it to the desired location, a process which is easier and perhaps more enjoyable than writing code.

Jackson Structured Programming has always been a favorite design technique in commercial data processing organizations, although few implementations exist in CASE tool form at this time. This situation is rapidly changing, however. An alternative is offered by many of the more sophisticated CASE tools, especially those organized around the Yourdon/De-Marco Structured Analysis methodology. These tools can be modified by the software designer to include custom symbols, allowing designers to install entirely new design methodologies on top of the existing data dictionary and project development framework.

This customization is not as difficult as it may seem. At the drafting level, most design methodologies are composed of

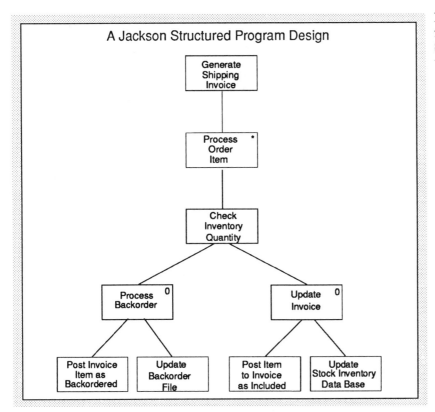

Figure 6.8 A program fragment using Jackson Structured Programming techniques.

circles, boxes, and ovals connected by lines or arrows. So the CASE tool has only to provide a general-purpose graphics editor with built-in rules for object connectivity; the underlying data dictionary framework remains intact for most of the design methodologies one could invent. After all, most of the meaning in a design diagram is conveyed by the semantics of the diagram, not the "visual syntax" of the bitmaps. Specific customization facilities are described in Chapter 9.

This chapter presented two similar structured design methodologies for developing design specification structure charts. The next chapter, "Data Modeling Methodologies," completes the design specification phase with methodologies for developing application program data structures, file formats, and data base schemas.

Chapter 7

Data Modeling Methodologies

*Beware of all
enterprises that
require new clothes.*
— Henry David
Thoreau

Data structure and file format definition are important parts of the Design Specification stage in the software development cycle. The major data structures should always be designed before mapping out a module's subroutines and algorithms. Good data structure design *suggests* appropriate design architectures and processing algorithms, while poor data structure design leads to redundant, clumsy, and excessive code. Data is all in how you represent it!

Data base programmers have been using schema layout mechanisms for years. They have discovered the secret of intelligent data design: simple queries and rapid execution. Poorly designed data bases lead to labyrinthine queries and poor access times. From the initial schema design methodologies came more elaborate data and information modeling concepts. Today's software engineer has CASE tools available for all three:

- **Schema design tools** for logical data base record layout.

- **Data modeling tools** for data structures and file formats.

- **Information modeling tools** for modeling the flow of information through an organization or a process.

The concept of information modeling, which grew out of data modeling, has gained wide recognition during the last few years because of its importance in business operations. More than just a requirements analysis and systems design technology, information modeling now reflects business' growing recognition of the importance of *information* and *information flow* throughout an organization. The importance of information is obvious in data-base-intensive businesses such as credit card transaction processing and airline reservations systems, and other types of businesses are now becoming aware that *management information systems* can be an excellent tool for extracting up-to-date information on a business's condition.

Indeed, current and reliable information is now regarded as the most important competitive edge in many rapidly changing businesses. An example of such an advanced management information system is the sales tracking system at Mrs. Fields Cookies. Each retail store is linked to a central computer in their Utah headquarters where store sales information is updated continuously throughout the day. This allows regional managers to review sales trends and suggest immediate corrective actions, such as distributing free cookie samples to generate walk-up retail traffic if a product's sales begin to wane.

Several different data and information modeling methodologies have evolved over the years, but two, *Warnier-Orr diagrams* and *entity-relationship diagrams,* are of particular interest because they are common components of analysis and design CASE tools. Warnier-Orr diagrams are useful for both data structure and program architecture design, and entity-relationship diagrams are well-suited for information modeling and describing relationships between data elements. Indeed, even data flow diagrams can be used to model the information flow throughout an organization, so it should come as no surprise that entity-relationship diagrams are a common facility in Structured Analysis CASE tools. In fact, these tools typically use entity-relationship diagrams to portray the relationships between elements in the data dictionary.

Warnier-Orr Diagrams

The Warnier-Orr diagram is an important data modeling technique. Warnier diagrams were invented by Jean-Dominique Warnier in France and later enhanced by Kenneth Orr in the United States. The Warnier-Orr diagram is a simple and straightforward technique for representing *system structure* and can be used either as a data modeling tool or as a software module structuring tool. Although originally developed for expressing program architecture, they are most often used to describe data structure composition.

Warnier-Orr diagrams are primarily a design specification methodology for data modeling.

The basic component of the Warnier-Orr diagram is the brace, or bracket, as shown in Figure 7.1. Warnier-Orr diagrams can be regarded simply as an organizational chart laid on its side. The leftmost bracket is the outermost, or highest level, view of the system or data structure. Moving to the right are successively more refined and detailed views, all organized in a hierarchy. That is, the sequence of refinement or activity is presumed to be left to right and top to bottom. Warnier-Orr diagrams show the composition of structures, be they subroutine calling hierarchies, data structure definitions, or file format specifications.

Conceptually, an interactive Warnier-Orr diagram layout editor might function like the ThinkTank outline processor (for the IBM PC, it allows users to expand and contract outline segments on-screen), allowing the designer to expand the Warnier-Orr diagram to reveal successive layers of detail or to collapse the diagram to hide detail. Like the Yourdon/DeMarco Structured Analysis methodology, Warnier-Orr diagrams are tedious when designing with pencil and paper, since the slightest change in architecture requires redrawing the entire diagram. Warnier-Orr diagrams are not amenable

Figure 7.1 Warnier-Orr diagrams depict data structure and program organization. CASE tools implementing the Warnier-Orr data modeling methodology allow designers to expand and collapse parts of the structures to reveal and hide levels of detail and refinement.

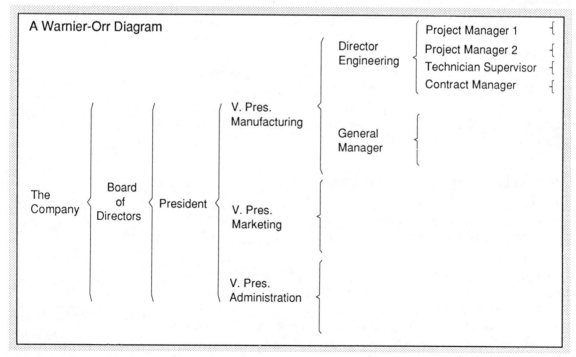

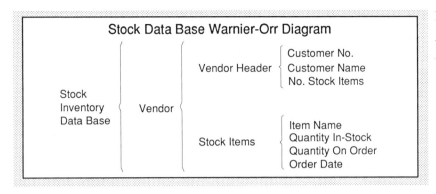

Figure 7.2 The Stock Inventory Data Base in Warnier-Orr diagram format.

to quick "patches" because designers frequently move entire substructures around the diagram, combine two substructures to form a single structure, or break out a structure into its components. In each of these cases, more than a few simple lines are needed to update the diagram.

With interactive, graphical Warnier-Orr CASE tools, redrawing is almost instantaneous once a change is made to the diagram. Entire substructures can be moved with a few keystrokes, and diagram segments can be expanded or collapsed on-screen to reveal an appropriate level of detail.

Data Structure Design. The principle use of Warnier-Orr diagrams is designing data structures and file formats. For example, Figure 7.2 illustrates the file format for the Stock Inventory Data Base used in Chapter 4 for the order entry and shipping system. In Figure 7.2, the Stock Inventory Data Base is composed entirely of Vendor records. Each record has a Vendor Header identifying the vendor, which is followed by a series of Stock Item records. Each vendor may have any number of stock items, the number of which is specified as part of the Vendor Header. Each substructure in the Warnier-Orr diagram can be further decomposed until the individual atomic data elements are revealed. Integer values, such as Customer Number, and character strings, such as Customer Name, typify these atomic data elements.

Warnier-Orr diagrams also express the *sorting order* of files, a property lacking in traditional data structure specification. The sorted sequence of structures runs from top to bottom, left to right. So if the Stock Inventory Data Base in Figure 7.2 has only one type of substructure, Vendor, these vendor records are assumed to be in sorted order based on some value in the Vendor Header. Furthermore, for each vendor, the Vendor Header record always precedes the Stock Items records for each vendor, so the actual physical file layout might appear as in Figure 7.3.

In Figure 7.4, the scope of the Stock Inventory Data Base is expanded to include individual company divisions, all of which purchase products. The data base is sorted by the purchasing division first and then on the vendor. Some detail has been omitted from the Purchasing Division portion of Figure 7.4, such as the purchasing division's name, which might appear in a Division Header record preceding the individual Vendor records. Such detail hiding demonstrates the Warnier-Orr diagram's ability to present only the important information while screening out the unimportant. In Figure 7.4 the important information is the file's sorting order.

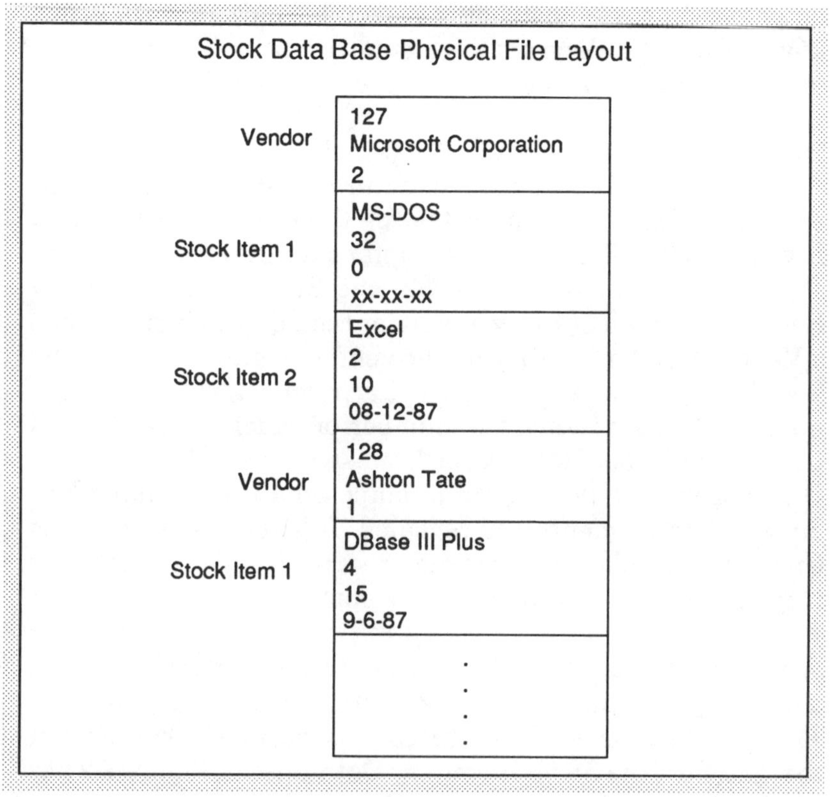

Figure 7.3 The War-nier-Orr diagram speci-fies the sequential sorted order of the individual records in a file. Here the file is sorted by vendors and then by stock items for each vendor.

Stock Data Base Physical File Layout

Vendor	127 Microsoft Corporation 2
Stock Item 1	MS-DOS 32 0 xx-xx-xx
Stock Item 2	Excel 2 10 08-12-87
Vendor	128 Ashton Tate 1
Stock Item 1	DBase III Plus 4 15 9-6-87
	. . . .

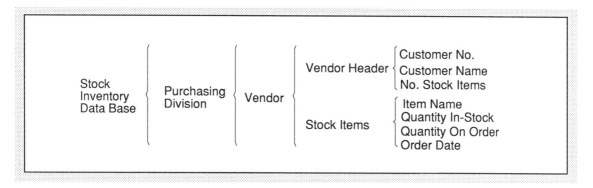

From one perspective, data structures and file organizations expressed in Warnier-Orr format are similar to the data dictionary format discussed in Chapter 4. Both partition complex structures into simpler components. The Warnier-Orr diagram uses a visual outline-style representation, in contrast to the BNF (Backus-Naur Form) production ruler representation used by the data dictionary. However, the Warnier-Orr diagram is a tool for designing data structures and file formats, while data dictionaries function as data element repositories in a data flow diagram. Data dictionaries can be used to design data structures in addition to cataloging and viewing them. But its primary access is through the data flow diagram while Warnier-Orr diagrams are meant to be directly edited.

The Warnier-Orr diagram does have limitations as a data modeling tool. Generic Warnier-Orr diagrams lack a formalized annotation capability for specifying details, such as legal value sets and range bounds for data elements. For example, the Order Date has a finite set of date values ranging from January 1 through December 31, and Customer Numbers are restricted to positive integer values. Most Warnier-Orr diagram editors allow the designer to enter arbitrary amounts of text at any position and level in the diagram, which provides a convenient means for recording such information, although the text cannot be extracted in any meaningful format except by printing the diagram. This means range and legal value set information cannot be extracted and input to a user interface development tool, for example. This capability would be beneficial when the data structures map on to a visual form where, for example, each form field has a range of acceptable values.

Figure 7.4 This Warnier-Orr diagram specifies a primary sort on the purchasing division and a secondary sort on the vendor.

Program Structure Design. Warnier-Orr diagrams can illustrate program structure as well. Instead of data structures, the outer (leftmost) levels of a Warnier-Orr diagram might be modules and files, and the inner (rightmost) levels are subroutines, DO loops, and IF-THEN statements. This is similar to a visual program design language such as the FLOWForms system by Intelligent Micro Systems, Inc. discussed in Chapter 5.

Figure 7.5 illustrates several program fragments designed in Warnier-Orr style. Figure 7.5 introduces several new symbols. The Greek theta character, θ, denotes a selection among alternatives. The notation (1, N) denotes iteration from 1 to N times where N may be replaced with a specific constant. For example, a task that is performed once or not at all would be annotated as (0, 1).

The astute reader will notice a high degree of similarity between program representation in Warnier-Orr diagrams and in Jackson Structured Programming (see Figures 6.7 and 6.8). Both Warnier-Orr diagrams and Jackson diagrams are hierarchical in structure; only their directions are different. Warnier-Orr diagrams show lower-level detail to the right, but Jackson diagrams and structure charts show increasing levels of detail at the bottom. Both Warnier-Orr diagrams and Jackson diagrams have a notation for selection, and both have a notation for iteration. Both show implicit sequence among operations on the same level.

Figure 7.5 Warnier-Orr diagrams are useful for designing program structure and module hierarchies as well as data structures.

The one crucial difference is that Warnier-Orr diagrams were designed with interactive editing in mind. It is intended that brackets be expandable and contractible on-screen, although there is no reason why boxes in a Jackson diagram couldn't be "buttoned" to expand and contract as well.

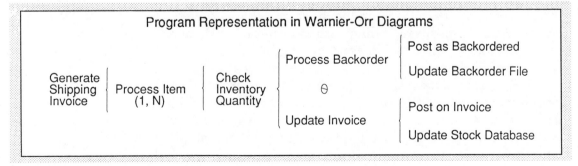

Entity-Relationship Diagrams

The previous section described how Warnier-Orr diagrams are used for data modeling, that is, designing and refining data structures. In fact, entire file structures can be designed using Warnier-Orr diagrams. This section discusses *information modeling*, a generalization of data modeling. Information modeling looks beyond the simple design of data structures, examining the relationships between information and data used throughout an organization or business enterprise.

Entity-relationship diagrams are used to describe the relationships between data in an organization or in a conceptual model of a system or process. These diagrams are useful for modeling information that is to be stored in a data base or information that is to be extracted and summarized in some new fashion. Entity-relationship diagrams are very straightforward and consist of only two components: *entities* and *relations*. Entities are the objects (data structures) being described—something about which data is, or can be, stored. Entities may be specific objects, such as people and invoices, or entities may be abstract concepts, such as positions and services.

Relationships are associations or links which show how one entity or a group of entities relates to another entity or group of entities. Figure 7.6 shows a simple list of entities and relationships.

A simple entity-relationship diagram is shown in Figure 7.7. It highlights several of the more common relationships likely to be present in an entity-relationship diagram. Obviously,

ENTITY	RELATIONSHIP	ENTITY
Order	Has	P.O. Number
Invoice	Contains	Customer Address
John	Is The Parent Of	Mary
Alan Fisher	Manages	Project
Project	Is Managed By	Alan Fisher
Project Manager	Is A Part Of	Development Organization
Schedule	Belongs To	Project
Customer	Pays	Accounts Receivable

Figure 7.6 Entities are objects or attributes of objects. Relationships link one entity or a group of entities to another entity or group of entities. Entity-relationship diagrams, which are composed of entities and their relationships, show how information and data fit together within an organization or enterprise.

Figure 7.7 This entity-relationship diagram shows the relations between an invoice, its component parts, and its originator and recipient.

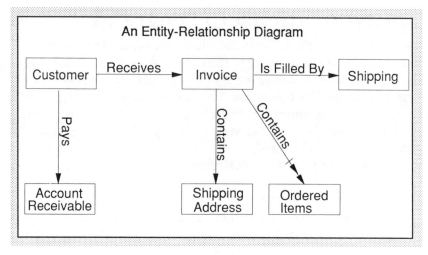

An Entity-Relationship Diagram

there is a tremendous amount of latitude in determining the exact entities and the appropriate relationships linking them.

Entity-relationship diagrams are almost the inverse of the data flow diagram. In data flow diagrams, the data items are thought of as being "fluid," flowing from process to process but in entity-relationship diagrams, the data (entities) are stationary relative to their linking relationships.

There are different types of relationships, or correspondences, between entities as shown in Figure 7.7. These "links" are necessarily one-way because they describe a single relationship between two entities (or groups of entities).

There are several competing diagrammatical notations for entity relationships used in commercial CASE tools. The notation used in Figures 7.7 and 7.8 was developed by Peter P. Chen, who is considered the original inventor of entity-relationship diagrams. This notation is used in Chen's CASE product, ER-Designer.

A competing notation has been developed by James Martin, a widely known and well-respected industry author and consultant. Martin refers directly to his notation as "information models." Martin's company, KnowledgeWare, markets Information Engineering Workbench, a CASE tool set using his information model notation. These tools perform Yourdon /De-Marco Structured Analysis (data flow diagrams) and struc-

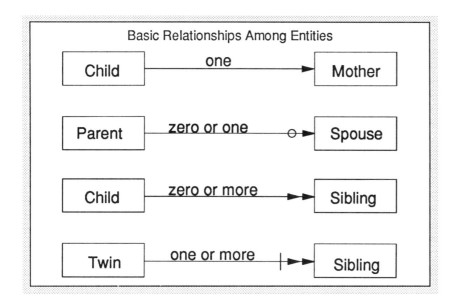

ture chart diagramming in addition to entity-relationship diagrams. Although there are differences between Chen's entity-relationship diagrams and Martin's information models, they are not important for the discussion in this book.

Entity-relationship diagrams are most often used to model the information relationships in an organization. Certain CASE tools generate entity-relationship diagrams for data dictionary entries to depict their relationships between entries. For example, Excelerator from Index Technologies, Inc., described in Chapter 9, builds entity-relationship diagrams (called data models) that graphically illustrate the composition of data dictionary entries. For example, one data element might contain a field which itself is comprised of several other data elements. This is a visually useful way of understanding the relationships between data elements in the central data dictionary.

The previous several chapters in Part 2 of this book have focused on modeling end-user requirements with CASE tools and organizing program structure for maximum flexibility and minimum complexity. We have discussed at great length the technology underpinning many CASE tools, and it is now time to turn our attention to the end-user's only view of the application program—the user interface. The next chapter,

"User Interface Design Methodologies," is the last in this section and describes the different types of command metaphors and information presentation styles available in specialized CASE tools for user interface design.

Chapter 8

User Interface Design Methodologies

The user interface is the most important and critical portion of an application program. The user interface is the only part end-users can see. Users cannot peer inside the software package to marvel at the elegance and efficiency of the internal design; all they can see is what is in front of them on the screen. If that on-screen view is clumsy, slow, unresponsive, or hard to learn, then by all rights the end-user will judge the application to be of low quality.

Yet the user interface is usually the last component to be specified and designed. Many development teams postpone its design to be completed as an exercise during the implementation phase. This is partly historical because until recently, display technology limitations restricted user interface design. The de facto user interface was a command line interpreter to which the user typed commands, and the application responded with output (or a syntax error message!) that scrolled by on the screen. This style of interaction was all the glass Teletype CRT terminals with display capabilities limited to scrolling text from the bottom of the screen to the top) display hardware would support.

Data base applications prompted developers to design form-based user interfaces which gathered input from visual screen forms and presented output in tabular format. Certain mainframe displays, such as the IBM 3270 terminal family, provided built-in support for form input to off-load much of the keystroke processing burden from the main CPU. For data base input, retrieval, and updating, this performed quite well, and IBM developed the screen-form-based query-by-example (QBE) technique to simplify end-user data base queries.

Still, on most minicomputers, user interfaces were simple, TTY affairs. With the advent of the personal computer, the user has a dedicated CPU capable of displaying

The user interface is the program.
— Dr. Alan Kay,
Apple Computer
Corporation

117

computationally expensive graphics, windows, forms, menus, icons, and tables. Initially, no interface design methodology for personal computers existed other than the traditional minicomputer and mainframe-style interfaces. These simplistic interfaces reflected in early personal computer software designs. But as legions of small-scale software developers embraced the personal computer, completely new interface paradigms were invented through countless iterations of trial-and-error design.

Many of these innovations are still effective interface techniques. Out of these efforts emerged several consistently good *display metaphors* and *command interaction metaphors*. Standard operating system interfaces emerged as well, such as Microsoft Windows for the IBM PC (and the Presentation Manager) and the Apple Macintosh Finder. These standardized interface environments make it easy to develop CASE tools for interface design. Such tools are usually design and code generation facilities for:

- **Window layout.** Windows are rectangular screen regions used for segmenting the user interface display. In many windowing environments, several application programs can run simultaneously, each in its own window.

- **Form and dialog-box generation.** Form-filling interfaces, among the most common interface paradigms, are very effective for data entry. Dialog boxes are used for command dialogues completion and for parameter selection.

- **Menu system composition.** Menu-based interfaces, usually in conjunction with dialog boxes, are rapidly becoming the de facto personal computer user interface.

Many user interface design tool vendors do not consider themselves to be CASE tool vendors. Nevertheless, they are considered CASE tools in this book since these tools aid in the requirements analysis and design specification phases of the software development cycle, and since many of these tools automatically generate code.

Basic User Interface Principles

User interfaces are almost without exception the most difficult and time-consuming part of a software application to design and implement. Getting a user interface design right means constant end-user involvement from the beginning of the requirements analysis phase. An interface developer can expect to go through countless iterations of an interface specification before end-users are happy, and once the specification is complete, there is no guarantee the *realization* of that interface will work in practice.

In fact, many user interfaces look good in paper screen drawings, only to collapse under regular daily use because the keystroke sequences are clumsy or because the implementation failed to achieve some unspecified goal, such as performance (speed of execution) or ease-of-learning by novices.

How do you specify a good user interface? There are several heuristics for greatly enhancing the chances of designing a successful user interface:

- **Identify the *real* end-user community.** Frequently, the contracting organization (the expected end-user customers for a commercial software package or for a custom-built application) is not the organization that will actually use the package. An operations manager may decide to automate a group in his organization and engage the MIS (Management Information Systems) department to build a system without consulting the individuals that will use the system on a daily basis. For an application to be workable, the end-users must be involved from the beginning and feel a sense of ownership and involvement in the system.

- **Carefully target the end-user community.** The end-users' needs must be carefully identified and articulated. End-users must be interviewed thoroughly to determine the best user interface presentation and layout from their perspective. For example, cash management traders in banks and brokerages are notorious for rejecting new software systems ostensibly designed to make their excruciatingly harried business life less stressful. The reasons for these rejections vary, but they frequently cite lack of speed and poor screen layout as common complaints.

■ **Show users the interface on-screen, not on paper.** End-users will, after all, use the interface on a terminal screen and not on paper, so common sense dictates that the designer should work as closely as possible with actual operating conditions. Because screen resolutions are usually lower than paper renditions, a paper-based design will portray a higher-quality layout than is actually achievable. Do not accidentally beguile users (or yourself) into an un-realizable look and feel.

■ **Mock up, or prototype, the interface to demonstrate the *feel* of operation.** Prototyping a system so that actual keystrokes lead the user from screen to screen and operation to operation is the next step beyond on-screen presentation. Prototyping a user interface gives the user the illusion of a functional software package, allowing a level of user feedback not attainable in a paper-based specification.

Prototyping, however, can be quite costly and time consuming. This is how CASE tools can provide leverage by allowing a designer to quickly mock up an interface.

■ **Use several groups of end-users as the specification progresses.** Having a large group of end-users available to test the user interface design is obviously better than having a limited group. It helps to try ideas and designs on small groups of users and switch end-user groups for each new design iteration to achieve a continually fresh perspective. End-users acquire particular biases and become attached to specific features they suggest during the design process. Also, as the design evolves, jettisoning a particular feature in favor of a better one may offend the suggesting party.

■   **Specify performance goals and metrics.** Even with a prototype, the user will not be able to operate the program with the actual processing occurring behind the interface. To prevent surprises once the software is delivered, the software designer should always specify the acceptable performance criteria and establish a set of metrics to measure the performance.

User Interaction Models

Application programs treat their end-users differently. Some applications assume a high level of end-user sophistication, but others are oriented toward relatively naive or unsophisticated end-users.

For example, many word processors and page composition programs assume a very high degree of user sophistication. Because these packages are designed to be used for several hours per day, users are expected to become very familiar with the software package. Therefore, most word processing programs are designed to give their users maximum control and flexibility and to operate as quickly as possible, with very short, but more difficult to learn, command sequences. Designers expect users to sacrifice some amount of ease-of-learning for performance, flexibility, and control because, after the learning period, the users become *power users* of the application.

On the other hand, videotex terminals, such as those found in airports, assume a very low level of user sophistication. These systems usually display locally pertinent topics, such as hotel locations and prices, weather, and shopping information. Because Videotex systems are used infrequently by any single user—typically only once—they are designed to lead the user by the hand. Because they are unfamiliar, users can *not* control the application; they must be presented with menus of choices from which to select. Each option or choice must be obvious.

These examples illustrate two common interaction models: the first where the user is in complete control and the second where the application program guides the user's choices.

Figure 8.1 Sophisticated or experienced users *issue* commands to the application program. The application responds with an output result. Sophisticated users *drive*, or control, the application rather than being prompted for input.

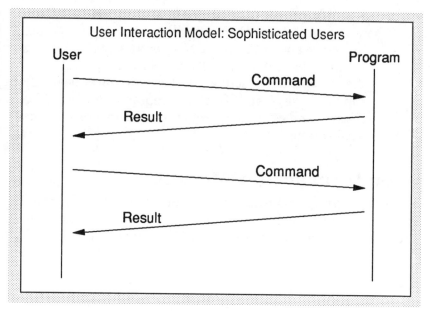

With the *sophisticated-user* model, the user is placed in the driver's seat (Figure 8.1). The user is responsible for selecting the next command and operation to perform. The application program is subservient and always waiting for the user's instruction. The user commands the software to perform some action and the software responds to the command. This sophisticated-user model is best suited for applications with one or more of the following characteristics:

- **High-volume use.** The application is used for large amounts of work, such as transaction processing and text editing.
- **Frequent use.** The application is used frequently by the same individual user or group of users.
- **Familiar users.** An individual user or group of users has invested a significant amount of learning or training in the application program.

In the *unsophisticated-user* model, the application program is in the driver's seat and the user is the passenger (Figure 8.2). The application program presents the user with a menu of options or a prompt indicating the user's choices. The user selects a choice and the result of the selection is displayed on-screen, followed by another menu of options.

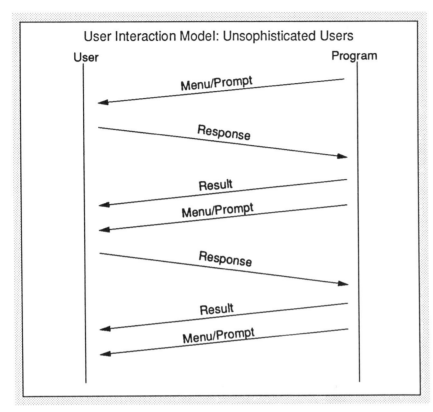

Figure 8.2 Unsophisticated or infrequent end-users are presented with a menu of possible selections from which to choose. They respond to the application program's menu with a selection and are then presented with the result and another menu of available selections.

The term "unsophisticated" is not meant in a derogatory sense. It simply implies the user is either computer naive or does not interact with the particular application often enough to warrant giving the user absolute control. The unsophisticated-user model is best suited for applications with one or more of the following characteristics:

- **Low-volume use.** The application program processes a small amount of work.

- **Infrequent use.** The application program is used infrequently by any single user.

- **Casual users.** The individual user has little or no training or learning investment in becoming familiar with the application's operation.

These two interaction styles represent extremes across a range of interaction models. A sophisticated word processing package may streamline the text editing keystroke sequences, but switch to a different interaction style, such as form-filling panels, in the less-often-used spelling checker module. Other applications have "novice" and "expert" modes. For example, the WordStar text editor for the IBM Personal Computer has three different help level settings. In the novice setting, on-screen command menus are always present to guide novice users through each command sequence. In the intermediate setting, menus only appear on-screen after a delay of two seconds while entering a command sequence. After two seconds, WordStar assumes the user needs help completing the sequence and displays a help screen. Finally, in the expert mode, the command menus never appear except by resetting the help level.

Now that we understand several of the man-machine interface approaches taken by applications, we turn our attention to the different output display and data presentation metaphors.

Information Display Metaphors

Most modern software applications emphasize the *direct manipulation* of data. Not only is data displayed in a convenient and logical format, but the user can "place the cursor" on the object and alter its value simply by entering a new one. This is certainly true in text-oriented programs, such as word processors and data bases, and direct manipulation is rapidly becoming de rigueur for graphics applications as diverse as CAD (computer-aided design) and project scheduling.

There are at least as many ways to display information visually as there are application programs. The personal computer software industry offers a gold mine of different visual display metaphors. Out of these seemingly unique metaphors, however, several common information presentation techniques emerge:

- Tables and Lists
- Forms
- Text Objects
- Graphical Objects and Pictures

Of these information display metaphors, tool vendors have concentrated on tables and forms because they are the best understood and easiest for which to implement general-purpose design tools. Developing general-purpose tools for the design and code generation of text and graphical objects is more difficult because of the wide diversity of semantic meanings associated with such objects.

Tables. People have been presenting data in tables for years, making columnar information display one of the most appealing presentation formats available to the interface designer. The classic example is the financial spreadsheet, churned out by countless MBAs with pencil and paper for years. Spreadsheets present financial information, such as balance sheets and income statements, in a tabular, line-by-line format.

The Apple II personal computer and VisiCalc brought an end to the drudgery of recalculating spreadsheets by hand whenever a parameter or value in the spreadsheet changed. Spreadsheet programs are successful because they present financial information in a format identical to that used on paper for years—a consistent and familiar display metaphor. Electronic spreadsheet users retain the direct access to the computer-based spreadsheet's "cells" they had with the pencil and paper version. This *direct manipulation* of the table entries makes the spreadsheet easy to use by giving the user direct control over the spreadsheet layout and contents.

Tables are also popular as a data base presentation metaphor, especially for relational data bases, which are usually presented to end-users and programmers alike as a set of columnar tables. New tables (views) are created by "joining" (a relational data base operation) other tables using query languages like SQL to select the desired rows and columns. In most personal computer applications, these tables are scrollable, allowing the end-user to move up and down and left and right through the table.

Forms. Another common display metaphor is the form, which is used for everything from order entry to loan applications. Filling out a form on a computer screen is a natural extension and an immediately familiar metaphor. Users are comfortable filling out forms, so there is little pondering over what to do. Their only concern may be what values to enter into the form fields.

Forms are inherently *transaction* oriented (Figure 8.3). People generally fill out forms when they are requesting something, such as registered mail service at the post office or money from a loan application. For this reason, form-based applications are usually high volume, performance-oriented applications like data base requests and order entry and fulfillment systems. Forms are used as output displays as often as they are used for data input. What better way to display a collection of related items?

Forms take many shapes, not just the traditional full screen "fill-in-the-fields" form seen in most data base and accounting applications. One type of form described in Chapter 11 is the dialog box. Dialog boxes are used in interfaces to gather more information from the user, generally in response to a user-selected command. Dialog boxes are used to enter file names, to select application program options, and to enter small

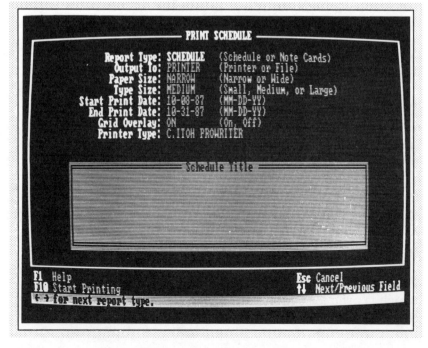

Figure 8.3 A Quick Schedule Form Screen Interface data entry form from the Quick Schedule project scheduling program. The user enters or selects the appropriate printing parameters and then presses "F10" to begin the schedule printing operation. Notice that the "Schedule Title" field allows scrollable, multiline input.

amounts of text. Dialog boxes may contain checklist menus (discussed in the next section) for selecting program and command options, or tables, such as a file directory.

Form interfaces have attracted the most attention from interface tool vendors because of their universal appeal and because forms are easier to generalize than other display metaphors. Although forms differ widely in appearance, ranging from simple text input fields to sophisticated dialog boxes, they possess the same internal architecture. The basic properties are as follows:

- **Data Input Fields.**   Input fields are the sole means of gathering information from the user. Fields range from simple one-line text input boxes to cursor-activated pop-up selection menus.

- **Text and Graphic Display.**   In addition to input fields, forms display static, or *protected* information, such as explanatory text and graphics. Such text and graphics material may be so extensive as to mask the fact that a screen is actually an input form.

- **Form Processing Control.**   Each form requires a certain amount of customization in its processing. Some forms require users to enter data values in a certain order. Others require only selected fields to be filled before the form is exited and processing begins. Still others calculate default field values based on the values entered in other fields.

Data input fields are the most important elements in a form. All forms have input fields, and most input fields automatically validate input data against illegal values. For example, users are not allowed to enter text strings into fields where numerical values are expected. In addition to input validation, form fields have the following general characteristics:

- **Data Types.** All form design packages support field input data validation to ensure the acceptable data values are entered into the field. The most common field data types are integer number, floating point number, single line text, currency (fixed point dollars and cents), dates, and Boolean (yes/no). The more sophisticated packages include general text entry (using the form package's text editor) and menu item selection.

- **Protected Fields.** Protected fields are display-only areas of the form where the user may not enter data. Protected field values may be automatically calculated from other input values on the form.

- **Must-Fill/Optional Fields.** Input fields can be designated as must-fill or optional. Must-fill fields require the user to enter an acceptable value before the form can be exited and processing can begin. An insurance policy number may be a required field but the insured's social security number may be an optional field.

- **Field Specific Help Messages.** Most form packages have the capability to display a help or prompt line message for each form field. As the user moves the cursor to a field, that field's help message automatically appears at the bottom of the screen. Such prompting messages are very beneficial for novices.

Chapter 11 highlights several form design and creation packages.

Text Objects.   Text objects, such as words and paragraphs, lend themselves to word processing applications, like text editors and page composition systems. Text objects are also frequently found in news and document retrieval systems, such as Dialog and the Dow Jones News Retrieval Service. User interfaces designed around text objects require capabilities for conveniently browsing, editing, and manipulating text objects in a useful fashion.

Graphical Objects and Pictures.   Most people are visually oriented and find it easy to understand information expressed in a graphical or iconic format. For example, tasks in a project plan are expressed visually as task boxes with arrows linking the boxes to graphically illustrate their temporal sequence; or schematic circuit diagrams are expressed as collections of individual icons representing the discrete circuit elements connected by lines representing wires.

DISPLAY METAPHOR	APPLICATIONS
Tables	Financial spreadsheets
	Relational data bases
	Reminder/appointment schedulers
	Disk directory listings
Forms	Data base records
	Individual account information
	Order entry systems
	Configuration/setup applications
Text Objects (words, paragraphs)	Word processors
	Page composition systems
	On-line news retrieval systems
	On-line help facilities
Graphical Objects (boxes, circles)	Computer-aided design (CAD)
	Graphics editing programs
	Page composition systems
	Project management/scheduling tools
	Process Control Graphics
	Business graphics display

Figure 8.4 User Interface Display Metaphors. Even though user interfaces vary greatly, they are composed of just a few basic information display metaphors.

Only now are graphical engineering workstations achieving widespread market penetration, displacing the traditional character text displays. The introduction of Microsoft Windows is, at this writing, just beginning to transform the IBM Personal Computer into a graphical workstation. The area of graphical interface layout tools is a challenging research topic and much remains to be done, but new tools, such as Apple's HyperCard, are appearing on the market.

Graphical pictures and diagrams are excellent for presenting information that is difficult to visualize from a text description. For example, financial data such as market share is frequently displayed in pie charts, and earnings growth often appears in bar graphs. This presentation metaphor is useful for constructing composites of information found in data bases.

Graphical displays communicate ideas and designs much more quickly than text descriptions.

Summary. The four different data display metaphors examined in this section are summarized in Figure 8.4. In the next section, we investigate the commonly used command interaction metaphors, the vehicles for program interaction.

Command Interaction Metaphors

Just as there are an infinite number of ways to display information on a computer screen, so are there an infinite number of ways to interact with, or command, the application program. These two concepts—display presentation and interaction control—are entwined, and altering one will assuredly affect the other. For many of today's applications, especially on the personal computer, the distinction between information display and command execution is blurred.

Several basic command interaction metaphors are available to an application designer. Few programs exhibit just one of these metaphors, and most use a mixture to satisfy conflicting goals, like ease-of-learning and efficient operation. These command interaction metaphors are:

- Command Line Interpreters
- Full screen Menus
- Pull-Down Menus
- Lotus-Style Menus
- Function/Control Keys

Individual user interface design CASE tools tend to emphasize only one or two of these command styles, although this is changing.

Command Line Interpreters. The command line interpreter is the oldest and still one of the most prevalent forms of command interaction. Basically, the user types instructions to the program, usually followed with one or more options (such as a file name) and a carriage return. Then the software parses and executes the command. Most operating systems, such as MS-DOS on the IBM PC, UNIX on most minicomputers, and VM and MVS on IBM mainframes, use command line interfaces, as do many utility programs. Command line interfaces are simple to understand, inexpensive to build, and effective in terms of performance.

The chief drawback to command line interfaces is that individual commands and options are difficult to remember. Only sophisticated end-users using an application on a frequent basis prefer the command line interface. To their credit, command line interfaces are very rich and expressive. Usually, command line options, parameters, and file specifications can be mixed to produce highly customized results with a minimum of steps. Several operating systems, most notably Unix, encourage chaining commands together, called "piping" in Unix parlance, as shown in Figure 8.5. Data base query languages, such as SQL, also exploit the flexibility afforded by the command line interface.

Although many developers craft command line interfaces by hand, there are software tools available, like the YACC (Yet Another Compiler Compiler) package on most Unix systems, for implementing command line interfaces. YACC, which is a *parser generator*, processes a BNF (Backus-Naur Form) file of grammar rules for a target language and produces a compilable C-code implementation of the language parser. The target language could be a command language for a software application or it could be a programming language such as C or COBOL. The BNF file itself is a simple ASCII file that can be created with almost any text editor. After running the BNF file through YACC, a parser for the language is produced in

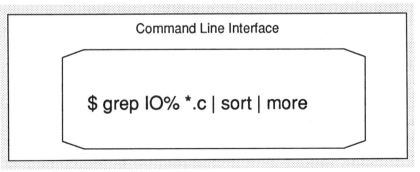

Figure 8.5 Command line interfaces are easy to develop. Parser generators are generally available for most computing environments, like YACC (Yet Another Compiler Compiler) on Unix, that will automatically create a command language parser for a given syntax.

the form of compilable C-language code. The generated parser code is itself a single callable subroutine, and the application programmer need only supply an input routine for reading characters (called the "scanner" by parser technologists). In fact, the generated parser code is machine independent because the application developer provides all the input and output routines. The generated code may be compiled on any machine with a C compiler, even non-Unix environments.

YACC is a very flexible tool. It allows the application developer to install calls to application-defined subroutines at any point in the BNF grammar productions. These calls are embedded in the generated parser code, and whenever the YACC-generated parser parses a sentence in the language (e.g. a command line), the appropriate subroutine calls are made. The subroutines themselves must, of course, be provided by the application programmer and linked (bound) to the generated parser code along with the rest of the application's code. Typically, calls to symbol table building routines or similar functions are placed at strategic points in the production grammar.

YACC is a form of CASE tool, although it and other parser generator programs have been used by software developers for so long that they lack the novelty of being called CASE. This is a pity, because parser generators provide great leverage by allowing the application architect to focus on the design of the language rather than on its implementation. The software developer literally inserts a BNF file and working code appears out the other end.

Full Screen Menus.   Full screen menus and command line interpreters are at opposite ends of the ease of learning spectrum. Command line interfaces assume the user is very conversant with program features and options, but the full screen menu makes no such assumptions. The full screen menu displays all available options, perhaps with one or two sentences describing each option. As one might guess, full screen menus are an excellent choice for unsophisticated and infrequent users. They are commonly found in applications such as automatic teller machines, many order entry applications, and frequently in accounting packages.

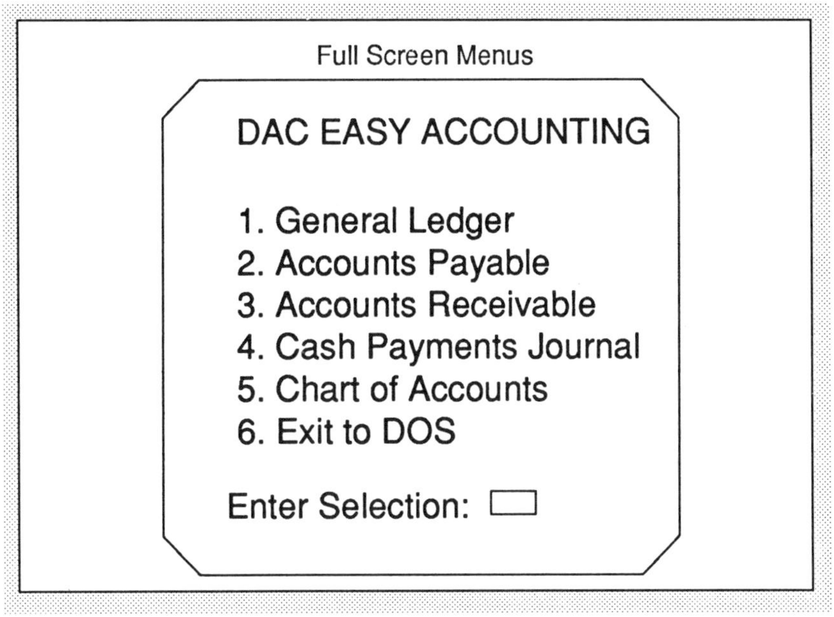

```
                    Full Screen Menus

              ╭────────────────────────────╮
              │                            │
                   DAC EASY ACCOUNTING

                 1. General Ledger
                 2. Accounts Payable
                 3. Accounts Receivable
                 4. Cash Payments Journal
                 5. Chart of Accounts
                 6. Exit to DOS

                 Enter Selection:  ☐
              ╰────────────────────────────╯
```

Figure 8.6 Full screen menus are commonly used in low-volume applications and applications with a low frequency of use. Full screen menus are good for novice or infrequent users.

Full screen menus are inappropriate for high-volume applications and applications where the user must conduct a rich or intricate interaction with the software; full screen menus simplify applications by removing (or reducing flexibility and functionality (Figure 8.6).

Pull-Down Menus. Pull-down menu systems, which are usually operated with a mouse, are the standard command interfaces on the Sun and Apollo minicomputer workstations and on the Apple Macintosh personal computer. In pull-down menu systems, a bar of menu titles resides at the top of the screen or within an individual application's window. The user positions the cursor over the desired menu, "buttons" the selection, and a pull-down menu appears, listing several commands. Again using the mouse, the user moves a highlighted scroll bar to the desired command and buttons the selection to activate the command.

Pull-down menus are becoming increasingly more prevalent on personal computer and minicomputer hardware platforms. Xerox initiated this style of user interface by building pull-down menus into the Xerox Altos, Dorado, and Star operating systems. Apple Computer popularized the interface on the Apple Lisa and Apple Macintosh personal computers, and Microsoft followed suit with Microsoft Windows and the Presentation Manager for the IBM PC.

In many systems, pull-down menus are implemented as part of the operating system software, establishing a consistent command metaphor across all applications running under that operating system (Figure 8.7). The foundation of a consistent command metaphor shortens the entire learning curve substantially. Operating systems providing pull-down menu facilities also typically offer a suite of *dialog box* capabilities for user input, such as prompting and option selection.

Pull-down menu systems segregate application commands into logical groups, quickly conveying the application's conceptual organization to the end-user. Because a set of pull-down menus can hold a large number of commands, single-screen applications are common. This is fortunate because single-screen applications are inherently easier to learn and understand. The users perceive the system to be "mode-less" because they are not required to navigate a maze of sub-screens.

Figure 8.7 A Pull-down Menu System. A bar of menu titles indicates the major command groupings. Individual commands are selected from the pull-down menus. Upon selecting a comand, the application may display a dialog box to collect additional user input necessary to execute the command.

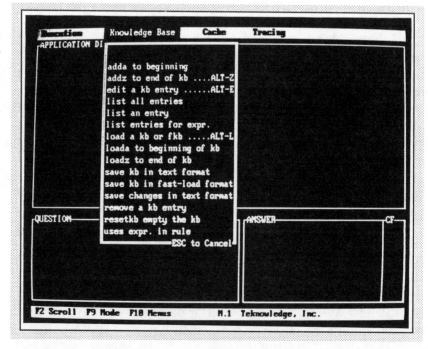

Lotus-style Menus.   Lotus-style menus are really a variant of pull-down menus. In Lotus-style menus, a horizontal one-line or two-line menu resides at the top of the screen, listing each menu entry. Directly underneath the menu line is a one-line sentence describing the command currently highlighted. A scrollable selection bar highlights each menu entry as the user uses cursor pad keys or a mouse to move left and right among the options. Pressing the *Enter* key or clicking a mouse button selects the highlighted command. Depending on the command, a submenu may replace the top-level menu, presenting the selected command's options. For example, selecting the "Files" command may produce a submenu with "Save" and "Retrieve" options.

Because of Lotus Development Corporation's dominance in the personal computer software market, other software packages have adopted the Lotus-style menu as their command structure. Several subroutine packages provide facilities for creating Lotus-style menus. For example, the Windows for Data package by Vermont Creative Software gives the application programmer both pull-down and Lotus-style menu capabilities. The programmer simply fills in a data structure defining each menu entry. The programmer also defines the application program routines that process each menu entry selection. To display the menu on-screen, the application program calls a single Windows for Data menu processing routine which, after the user has made a selection, calls the designated application program routine to process the command.

Windows for Data also has a Form Design Utility package which reads a design file prepared with any standard text editor, translates it into C code, and writes the code to a definition file. This definition file contains the definitions and function calls needed to define data entry forms and menus, fields, and text. The definition file is not a complete program in itself but rather a program fragment that can be used in a larger program.

This type of subroutine package is not considered to be a CASE tool since it lacks an interactive layout editor. Interface designers should, however, investigate these packages because they do provide significant leverage during the

COMMAND METAPHOR	PROS	CONS

Command Line Interpreters	Very efficient
	Rich and expressive
	   interactions
		Steep learning curves
		Easy to forget if not
		   continuously used

Full Screen Menus	Easy to use Easy to learn Options always visible	Slow, cumbersome interaction

Pull-Down Menus	Consistent command
	   metaphor
	Logical command groupings
	
	Facilitates single-screen
	   applications
		Must know what commands do
		
		Must shift attention to
		   command menu

Lotus-Style Menus	Used in many PC
	   applications
	Prompt/info line visible
		Slow for advanced users
		
		Must shift attention to
		   command menu

Function/Control Keys	Very fast operation	Options not visible on-screen Steep learning curve Keystrokes easy to forget

Figure 8.8   User Interface Command Interaction Metaphors.

application implementation phase. They can save a tremendous amount of development time and substantially reduce the debugging and testing efforts.

Function/Control Keys.   For large volume, high-speed interaction, function and control keys are commonly used for command execution. In this command style, keystrokes are bound to individual commands, and simply pressing those keystrokes invokes the commands. Function and control keys are pervasive in word processors and graphics editors and are often used with other command interaction styles, particularly pull-down and Lotus-style menus. In this case, the single keystroke commands are termed *accelerator keys* because they shorten the normal keystroke sequences used by novices.

Accelerator keys are provided for the more advanced users to expedite the commonly executed commands.

Figure 8.8 summarizes the basic command interaction metaphors described in this section. Clearly, many of the newer application software packages are incorporating pull-down menus and dialog boxes, especially in the personal computer environment. This convergence on a single command metaphor will encourage interface design tool vendors to build standardized CASE tools. Already such tools are appearing for a variety of hardware environments, several of which you may already be familiar with. Chapter 11 highlights these tools, many of which are quite new. Hopefully, you will find something applicable to your interface design work.

Part 3

Specific CASE Tools

Chapter 9

Analysis and Design Tools

The following three chapters focus on *commercially available* CASE tools—products available for building today's software applications. The tools included in this section were chosen to provide a balance of different technologies and certain commonalities between CASE tools. By comparatively evaluating both similar and dissimilar tools, you can develop a better understanding for their relative strengths and weaknesses. Focusing on commercially available tools reveals the underlying issues in assimilating computer-aided software engineering technology into your organization. The careful reader will not only evaluate the tools and their technologies but also the level of vendor-supplied product support and training.

Obviously the tool descriptions in the following chapters will become obsolete the day this book is printed. Several underwent major revisions just before going to press! New vendors are appearing almost daily with advertisements in the trade press. However, these profiles accurately portray the overall capabilities of each tool and the different classes of CASE tools as a whole. By no means is the list of tools selected for detailed examination fully inclusive. Many other tools and vendors are listed in Appendix A.

Although many advanced software engineering tools are under development in academic computer science departments and in corporate research laboratories, they are not discussed because they are not available for use in a commercial application development setting. For those interested in the forefront of CASE technology, Chapter 15, *"Technological Trends in CASE Tools,"* describes the new directions likely to develop during the next several years.

The author makes no implied endorsement of any of the tools discussed in the following chapters. For readers wishing to contact tool vendors, Appendix A lists the addresses and

Thunder is impressive, but it's lightning that does the work.
— Mark Twain

phone numbers of the companies discussed throughout this book.

This chapter describes six different commercially available *requirements analysis* and *design specification tools.* Most of these tools implement the popular data flow diagramming techniques emphasized by the Yourdon/DeMarco Structured Analysis Methodology. Although there are competing analysis and design methodologies, such as Gane and Sarson Structured Systems Analysis, IBM's JAD, and SofTech's SADT, the data flow diagram has gained the widest acceptance in the commercial marketplace. The tools described in this chapter differ greatly in their focus. Some are vertically integrated tools providing extensive mini-specification capabilities, structure chart editing, and code generation. Others are horizontally integrated, offering data modeling facilities, such as entity-relationship diagram editors, in addition to data flow diagram and structure chart editors.

Teamwork—Cadre Technologies

Cadre Technologies, Inc., of Providence, Rhode Island, is one of the larger CASE tool vendors. Teamwork, Cadre's flagship product, is a family of tools which collectively implements many elements of the Yourdon/DeMarco Structured Analysis methodology, including data flow diagrams, process specifications (mini-specifications), and data dictionaries. Teamwork is available on most of the popular minicomputer workstation environments.

The Teamwork tool set contains the following modules for specifying and designing software systems:

Teamwork/SA	This "Structured Analysis" module is an editor for creating and editing data flow diagrams and mini-specifications. Teamwork/SA will build input/output lists for each process node in the data flow diagram and allow the developer to attach code to the individual process node mini-specifications.
Teamwork/RT	This "Real-Time" Analysis module extends Teamwork/SA with several

extensions to the standard Yourdon/
DeMarco data flow diagrams for real-
time control.

Teamwork/IM   The "Information Modeling" module
provides entity-relationship modeling,
data dictionary building, and data base
schema generation.

Teamwork/SD   The "Structured Design" module provides for the definition of software
modules in a typical top-down structure
chart fashion.

One goal of the Teamwork products is to automatically build
DOD-STD-2167 requirements specification documents which
the Department of Defense requires for mission critical defense related software work. Teamwork provides document
output interfaces to a variety of text-formatting packages,
including Interleaf, Context, and Scribe. Teamwork also provides a tool for the back-end documentation preparation work
after the software system has been specified and designed.
Teamwork/DPI (Document Production Interface) allows system designers to press the "magic button" that automatically
generates analysis and design documents based on specifications in the other modules.

Teamwork/SA.   Teamwork/SA is an editor for creating
Yourdon/DeMarco Structured Analysis data flow diagrams.
Starting at the highest level in the data flow diagram, each
process (bubble) can be partitioned into its "child" diagram or
process (Figure 9.1). Progressing to the lowest level, beyond
which there are no further process decompositions (subordinate data flow diagrams), each process can be described by a
simple textual description called a *process specification* (P-
Specs in Teamwork). Throughout the model, the data
elements in the data flow diagram are described in *data
dictionary entries*. Process specifications and data dictionary
entries are attached to diagrams for retrieval and updating.
All elements, data flow diagrams, process specifications, and
data dictionary entries are stored in a central project data
base which serves as the basis for communication within the

Figure 9.1 Teamwork/ SA Data Flow Diagram. Teamwork/SA is a structured graphics editor for creating data flow diagrams. Each data flow is logged into a central, project-wide data dictionary. Data flow diagrams can be automatically checked for consistency and balancing, ensuring the data flows are consistent from one level to the next in a hierarchical data flow diagram.

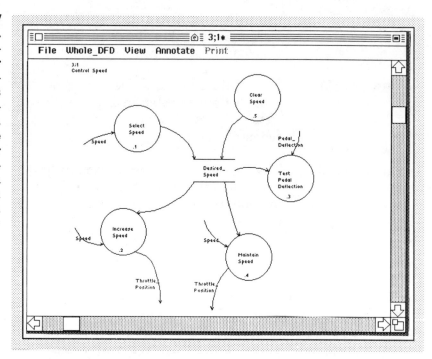

project team. The project data base can be printed to create specification documents.

The purpose of automating Structured Analysis in this manner is the ability to perform automated checking. Checking a design for completeness ensures that all processes have complete process specifications and all data flows have associated data dictionary entries. A second form of checking, called *balancing*, verifies that the various hierarchical data flow diagrams are consistent (balanced) from one level to the next. In its simplest form, balancing checks to ensure the input and output data flows match between levels. Balancing is crucial to a design's completeness but is seldom performed satisfactorily with manual techniques because of the tedium.

Teamwork/RT. This "Real-Time" Analysis module extends Teamwork/SA with several real-time control extensions. In particular, Teamwork/RT introduces two new symbols to indicate control flows (dashed lines) and control specifications (vertical bars), as shown in Figure 9.2. Control specifications are similar to process specifications in that both describe a set of actions to be performed upon activation.

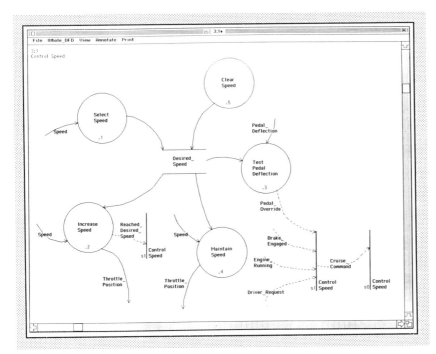

Figure 9.2 Teamwork/RT Real-Time Data Flow Diagram. Teamwork/RT extends the Structured Analysis methodology that is implemented in Teamwork/SA with real-time primitives.

However, control specifications in Teamwork/RT are indicated by *state transition diagrams, state event matrices, process activation tables, and decision tables.*

Teamwork/IM. Teamwork/IM is an "information modeling" system that allows system analysts and data base designers to construct data models using entity-relationship diagrams. Entity-Relationship diagrams visually describe a system's data elements by showing the relationships between individual data elements. Definitions and attributes of entities and relationships are stored in the data dictionary common to all Teamwork modules.

An interesting and important feature of the Teamwork family of tools is a concept called Teamwork/ACCESS, which opens the Teamwork project data base to allow integration with the Teamwork tools. This allows sophisticated user organizations to connect the Teamwork tools with back-end documentation, project management, and software development packages. For example, the Teamwork tools could be connected to a documentation system in order to build the DOD-STD-2167 specifications required for military contracts. Access to the

Teamwork project data base is provided via a C programming language interface.

Teamwork/SD.   The Teamwork/SA, Teamwork/RT, and Teamwork/IM modules all implement the Structured Analysis methodology for building structured requirements specification. Teamwork/SD, an editor for creating structured designs, focuses on the next development phase, design specification. Structured designs articulate a software system's *internal* architecture, while Structured Analysis methodologies, such as data flow diagrams, articulate a software system's *external* or user view. The elements used in Teamwork/SD are structure charts, a data dictionary, and module specifications. Structure charts consist of three elements: boxes representing modules, arrows (called invocations) connecting the modules, and short arrows with circular tails (called couples) representing data passed from one module to another.

As shown in Figure 9.3, inside each box on the structure chart is a module specification. Module specifications contain the "code," usually pseudocode, that specifies the module's function in an algorithmic manner. Notice that module invocations are separated from the actual data passed between the modules. This is because the data may come from a different source than the module's invocation. Frequently, however, one module will invoke another module in order to retrieve data.

DesignAid/CASE 2000—Nastec Corporation

Nastec Corporation's CASE 2000 product line is a set of integrated CASE tools with DesignAid being the cornerstone component. Like many other CASE tools, DesignAid is workstation oriented, running on the IBM PC and minicomputer workstations, such as the DEC VAX.

One of DesignAid's unique characteristics is its open architecture, allowing the integration of traditional written specifications with the graphically based data flow diagrams and mini-

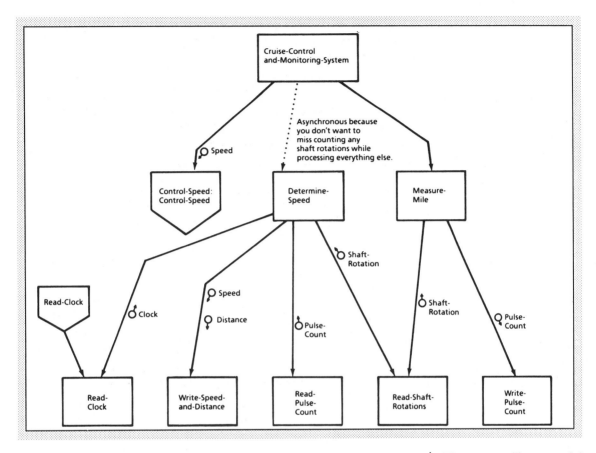

Figure within the chart contains the following labels:

Cruise-Control and-Monitoring-System

Asynchronous because you don't want to miss counting any shaft rotations while processing everything else.

Speed

Control-Speed: Control-Speed

Determine-Speed

Measure-Mile

Shaft-Rotation

Read-Clock

Clock

Speed

Distance

Pulse-Count

Shaft-Rotation

Pulse-Count

Read-Clock

Write-Speed-and-Distance

Read-Pulse-Count

Read-Shaft-Rotations

Write-Pulse-Count

specifications generated using the Yourdon/DeMarco Structured Analysis methodology. For Nastec, this is a major feature because it integrates the end-user documentation with the program's requirements and design specification.

A major reason for combining the system specification with the graphic diagrams, like data flow diagrams and structure charts, is the production of DOD-STD-2167 requirements documents, required in all mission critical military software systems (see Chapter 14). To support DOD-STD2167, DesignAid has facilities to search, identify, and catalog requirements from specification documents. DesignAid will also generate trace reports and compliance reports to ensure the design meets the specified requirements.

File Management.   Like other requirements analysis and design specification tools, DesignAid has built-in capabilities

Figure 9.3 Teamwork/ SD Structured Design Chart. Structure charts consist of boxes, connecting arrows and couples representing data passed between modules.

for creating Structured Analysis data flow diagrams and structure charts. Unlike other tools, however, DesignAid is a file-based system with sophisticated hierarchical file management capabilities. It combines file-handling techniques, an interactive design dictionary, and design validation capabilities. DesignAid uses a word processing metaphor throughout the tool by allowing designers to construct arbitrarily large documents from nested groups of files and can embed file references within diagrams or documents to read the contents of the files. For example, there might be one hundred individual data flow diagrams, each in its own file. Inside each of these data flow diagram documents might be references to the underlying process specifications, each again in its own file. Figure 9.4 illustrates a hypothetical document hierarchy for a set of data flow diagrams and mini-specifications (process descriptions).

Separating the design into a large number of files makes it easy to rearrange individual design components as the design evolves during development. Figure 9.5 illustrates this file management perspective for a retail inventory system. The file shown in Figure 9.5 is called "menu." It lists the files related to the retail inventory system. These files contain data flow diagrams, process specifications (called *process narratives* in DesignAid), structure definitions, and other

Figure 9.4 DesignAid is a hierarchical file manager that supports the compartmentalization of individual design components, like data flow diagrams and mini-specifications, into separate files. The .DFD files contain data flow diagrams; the .PN files contain mini-specifications. Throughout DesignAid is a strong word processing metaphor that encourages designers to mix text with graphical designs.

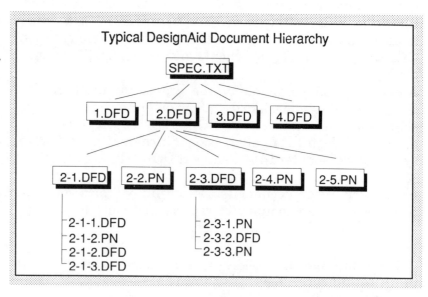

```
****** Start of file:        (menu)*************************************************
Project Deliverables for:
                          RETAIL INVENTORY SYSTEM
(CD.DFD)        Context Level Data Flow Diagram
  (CD.STR)          Context Level Structure Input File
(0.DFD)         Zero Level Data Flow Diagram
  (0.STR)           Zero Level Structure Input File
  (DB.STR)          Data Store Structure Input File
    (2.PN)          Update Inventory Process Narrative
    (3.PN)          Produce Price List Process Narrative
      (3.STC)           Price List Structure Chart
    (4.PN)          Inventory Master Process Narrative
    (5.PN)          Inquire Vendor Master Process Narrative
(1.DFD)         Collect Inventory Transactions Data Flow Diagram
  (1-1.PN)          Process Receipts Process Narrative
  (1-2.PN)          Process Adjustments Process Narrative
  (1-3.PN)          Process Sales Process Narrative
  (1-4.PN)          Create Inventory Transaction Process Narrative


                          PRACTICE FILES
```

Figure 9.5 A Nastec DesignAid file structure for a retail inventory system. The top-level file—shown here—contains references to lower-level files. These lower-level files may, in turn, contain references to still lower-level files.

deliverables created during the systems development process. File references are enclosed in braces, and each file's type can be indicated by the file extension (file suffix). For instance, files containing data flow diagrams might end with the .DFD suffix. Files containing process narratives might end with the .PN suffix.

Each file, as illustrated by "menu," can contain text in addition to other file references. DesignAid uses the braces to distinguish file references from other text contained in the file. Files can contain text, as well as graphics, or a combination of the two. The DesignAid user can view more than one file at a time, which is accomplished by "nesting" one file into another for viewing. With this background in place, we can examine DesignAid's analysis and specification technologies.

Structured Analysis. DesignAid implements the traditional Yourdon/DeMarco Structured Analysis methodology consisting of data flow diagrams, data dictionaries, and minispecifications (process specifications). DesignAid's underlying data dictionary provides consistency checking to verify that each data dictionary entry is unique; balancing the parent and child process node diagrams verifies that all lower-level data flows and process nodes are appropriately connected and that there are no orphaned data flows. Figure 9.6 shows the context data flow diagram for the retail inventory system. DesignAid calls these context diagrams *zero level diagrams*, following Yourdon's conventions.

Figure 9.6 DesignAid Context Data Flow Diagram. Data flow names are enclosed in angle brackets to separate them from the rest of the text in the diagram.

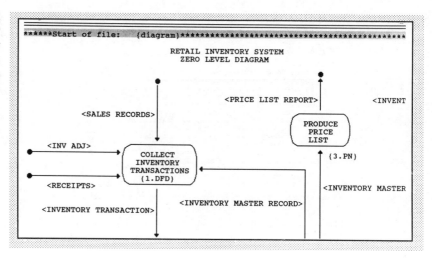

Notice that these data flow diagrams are created within a file. In addition to the word processing functionality, DesignAid's *Data Flow Diagram Menu* contains commands for creating process bubbles, data flow vectors, and external file structure symbols (called *data stores* in DesignAid). The designer encloses data flow labels in angle brackets to separate them from the rest of the text in the file. The only other requirement is that data flow labels be placed one line above or below horizontal data flow lines or within two columns of vertical data flow lines. DesignAid recognizes these data flow name delimiters as containing data flow names during consistency-checking operations. Text not within process bubbles or angle brackets is ignored during the consistency checking operation.

DesignAid is really a smart *structured document editor* in its treatment of data flow diagram files. Symbol sizes can be expanded or contracted so that longer or shorter labels can be entered. Single data flow symbols or entire blocks of symbols and text can be copied and pasted within a file. Symbols with lines—data flow vectors—can be moved, and the attached lines (vectors) will be stretched to meet the moved symbol. Whenever a symbol is moved, it can overlay whatever is present on the screen if it is in the destination area chosen. However, the symbol can be moved wherever desired to uncover anything that may have been covered.

Each diagram type on the DesignAid *Diagramming Menu,* such as the data flow diagram, has its own menu listing the valid symbols for that diagram and all the operations needed to complete it. The designer also has the option of creating customized menus which list user-defined symbols. This is an interesting capability that, within limitations, allows the more sophisticated tool user to implement software engineering methodologies other than the traditional Structured Analysis and structured design techniques.

Data Dictionaries. DesignAid includes a project dictionary where all information about a design is stored. One type of information is *object definitions* describing the function of each object in a system. An object might represent a specific symbol on a data flow diagram, like a process node or data flow, or perhaps an entire data flow diagram. Figure 9.7 illustrates a dictionary entry for the Update Inventory data flow from the retail inventory system.

Before adding an object definition to the dictionary, Design-Aid performs an interactive inquiry which checks to see if the definition automatically exists. For instance, placing the cursor inside the Vendor Masters data store and activating the Object Definition command will automatically fill in the Object Name and Object Type. Only the Object Name and Object Type fields are required to define an object to the

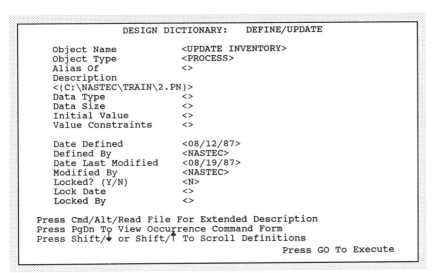

```
               DESIGN DICTIONARY:    DEFINE/UPDATE

     Object Name              <UPDATE INVENTORY>
     Object Type              <PROCESS>
     Alias Of                 <>
     Description
     <{C:\NASTEC\TRAIN\2.PN}>
     Data Type                <>
     Data Size                <>
     Initial Value            <>
     Value Constraints        <>

     Date Defined             <08/12/87>
     Defined By               <NASTEC>
     Date Last Modified       <08/19/87>
     Modified By              <NASTEC>
     Locked? (Y/N)            <N>
     Lock Date                <>
     Locked By                <>

   Press Cmd/Alt/Read File For Extended Description
   Press PgDn To View Occurrence Command Form
   Press Shift/↓ or Shift/↑ To Scroll Definitions
                               Press GO To Execute
```

Figure 9.7 DesignAid Data Dictionary Entry. Notice the file reference in the *description* field. This field can either display a description of the object or, in this case, a reference to a file containing a longer description. This extended description file can be formatted in any way the designer chooses, which includes containing text, another diagram, or even compilable source code.

dictionary, but the other information provides a useful tracking mechanism on larger design projects. In addition, designers can define their own object types as well as use the DesignAid provided types. This allows the designer to enter definitions for objects contained in any one of the system development files.

At any point in the design process, the designer can *validate* the data flow diagram. Validation records the location of each object represented in the data flow diagram by entering this information into an occurrence file of the data dictionary. Validation also identifies any errors in the data flow diagram, such as a process node (bubble) with several input data flows but no output data flows.

Structures are used to represent a hierarchical arrangement of data in the data dictionary. These structures are used to define the components of individual data flows and data stores in data flow diagrams. Structures are entered into the dictionary through a structure input file that describes how the structures are to be defined in the dictionary. An example structure is shown in Figure 9.8.

An important DesignAid capability is the ability to relate objects through the data dictionary. This allows analysts, for example, to query the data dictionary and locate all uses of a particular data element, be they in data flow diagrams or process narratives.

Process Narratives.   Process narratives, or mini-specifications, describe how a process node transforms the input data flows into output data flows. DesignAid treats process narratives as simple text files which can contain anything from structured English to a program design language (see Chapter 5).

Figure 9.8 DesignAid Data Structure Definition. DesignAid data structures are created in the familiar BNF (Backus-Naur Form). Parenthesis surrounding an entry signify it as optional. Braces indicate an item may be repeated any number of times.

```
INVENTORY TRANSACTION = RECORD TYPE
                      + VENDOR NUMBER
                      + ITEM TRANSACTION
                      + ITEM DESCRIPTION
                      + CATEGORY CODE
                      + CATEGORY DESCRIPTION
                      + UNIT COST          ⬅
                      + (ADJ CODE)         ⬅
```

Structure Charts.   Creating structure charts (see Chapter 6) is much like creating a data flow diagram. DesignAid contains a number of built-in symbols for constructing structure charts, including boxes and data couples, as shown in Figure 9.9. Structure charts may contain module descriptions in external files, as indicated by the suffix ".MD".

Screen Prototyping.   One of DesignAid's more interesting features is a screen prototyping facility. Since DesignAid is built around a word processor metaphor with built-in capabilities for creating diagrams, it is easy to lay out screen mockups. The designer simply opens a file, draws rectangular boxes, adds in data fields, and so forth. This process can be repeated for any number of screens. Once a screen layout has been created, DesignAid allows the user to simulate the *presentation* of the screen. One feature supporting this capability is the ability to change screens with a single keystroke.

DesignAid's "learn mode" is used to record the entry of data into a screen. Then once the keystrokes necessary to enter the data have been recorded, they can be assigned to a function key. This sequence of keystrokes—a keystroke macro—can be replayed each time the data needs to be entered to give the impression of a user entering actual data on a screen. The designer can scroll through the screens, giving the impression that the data is changing, not the actual screen. Although this is an extremely simplistic mock-up facility in light of the user

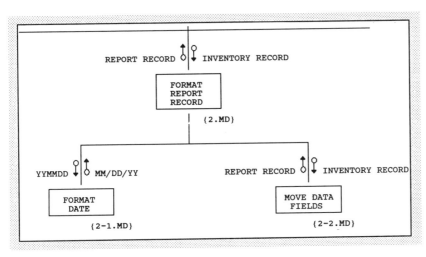

Figure 9.9 A Design-Aid Structure Chart. DesignAid provides facilities for creating structure charts with module boxes and data couples (called flow symbols). Structure charts may contain module descriptions in external files.

interface design tools described in Chapter 11, this "slide show animation" is effective for straightforward types of interaction such as form input.

Copies of portions of mini-specifications can be merged into the specification text document, and files can be attached to individual process nodes in the data flow diagram as part of the process' mini-specification. These attached files typically contain source code. Facilities are provided for building the attached files, usually ASCII text, into a form presentable to a traditional language compiler.

DesignAid provides no automatic code generation features and no mechanism for cataloging and indexing the code written in the individual files other than by their binding to mini-specification nodes. However, because of the open integration strategy underlying the tool, it is possible for analysts to make these connections themselves in order to construct a customized software development environment. This integration requires additional work, but it does allow the development organization to streamline its design and implementation process.

Development organizations can use their existing software tools, such as application code generator packages, by integrating them to DesignAid, which provides analysis and design specification capabilities. Several other software vendors have already interfaced their packages with DesignAid. For example, both Pansophic Systems and Sage Software provide interfaces for their respective code generator products, Telon and APS Development Center.

Excelerator—Index Technology Corporation

Index Technology Corporation of Cambridge, Massachusetts markets the Excelerator and Excelerator/RTS products for the IBM Personal Computer and compatibles. Excelerator is targeted for the commercial data processing (MIS/DP) organization, and Excelerator/RTS has additional capabilities for real-time application developers such as the aerospace industry. Like other analysis and design tools, the Excelerator products are built around a data dictionary which supports a number of modules providing different views on the design (Figure 9.10).

Excelerator supports six different diagrams:

1. Data Flow Diagrams
2. Structure Charts
3. Data Model Diagrams
4. Entity-Relationship Diagrams
5. Structure Diagrams
6. Presentation Graphs

Excelerator/RTS supports these diagrams and adds state transition diagrams, transformation graphs, and block diagrams, which are useful for developing timing and action sequences for real-time systems. The Excelerator product is one of the few CASE tools integrating the Yourdon/DeMarco Structured Analysis methodology with data modeling and structured design methodologies—a combination that makes very good sense. Excelerator also contains facilities to support multiple designers/developers.

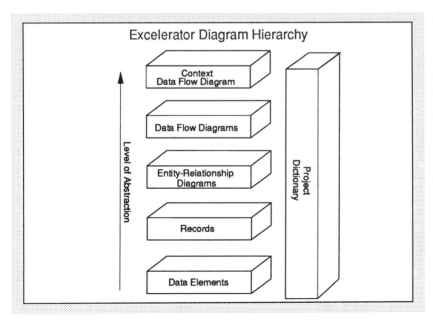

Figure 9.10 Excelerator from Index Technology Corporation, supports various levels of design abstraction. At the highest level are data flow diagrams which can be "exploded" into lower-level data flow diagrams, structure charts, structure diagrams, or entity-relationship diagrams. Individual data records (data flows) are composed of atomic data elements.

Excelerator and Excelerator/RTS can be configured to use either the Yourdon/DeMarco or the Gane and Sarson™ notation for data flow diagrams. In the Gane and Sarson representation, square bubbles are used to represent processes instead of circular bubbles. Data flows are viewed as "pipes" through which data travels. As illustrated in Figure 9.11, the data flow diagramming capability follows the conventions very closely. Data flow diagrams can have up to nine levels underneath each process node. Excelerator terms this level traversal as *exploding* the diagram.

Individual data stores (external data files and data bases) can be exploded to reveal *data model diagrams* as shown in Figure 9.12. Arrows can have several styles of arrowhead indicating the type of relationship between the data elements. For example, a single-to-double arrow indicates a one-to-many

Figure 9.11 An Excelerator Data Flow Diagram. Index Technology Corporation's *Excelerator* product implements the Yourdon/DeMarco Structured Analysis methodology data flow diagrams.

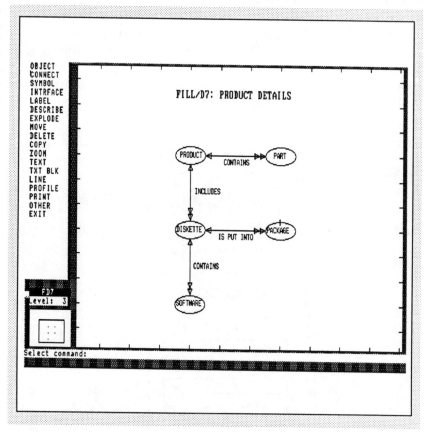

relationship. In Figure 9.12, a single product can have many parts. Individual data model diagram entities can be further exploded to reveal *records,* as shown in Figures 9.13 and 9.14.

Associated with each entity within Excelerator is a description screen that defines the entity within the project dictionary. A graph's data dictionary description screen lists all the entities that exist in the graph. Figure 9.15 illustrates two different data dictionary entries. Notice that their formats are slightly different, depending on the type of entity being cataloged.

The Excelerator XLDictionary facility lets the designer probe the data dictionary in a variety of different ways to examine different data elements and graph objects. In addition to providing access to the project dictionary, the XLDictionary

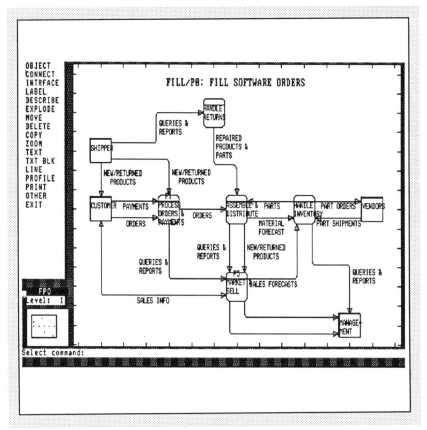

Figure 9.12 An Excelerator Data Model Diagram. Excelerator implements data modeling methodologies in addition to the Structured Analysis methodology. In this diagram, an external data store called "Product File" has been exploded to reveal a *data model diagram.*

Figure 9.13 An Excelerator Data Model Diagram Record. Exploding a data entity reveals a *record*.

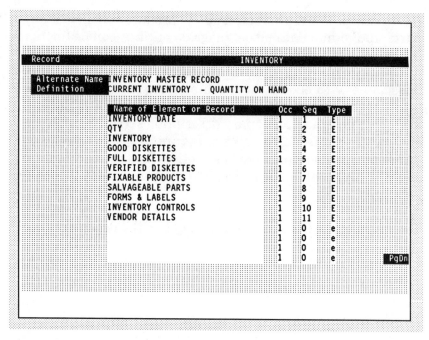

Figure 9.14 An Excelerator Record Element Definition. Individual data model record elements are "exploded" to show detailed information about that data element. This information includes display characteristics such as the element's data type and picture display string.

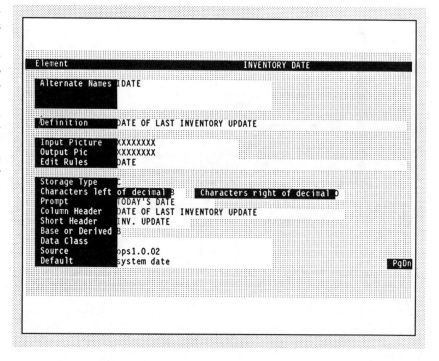

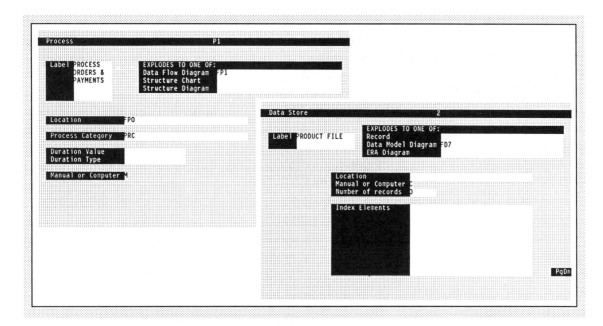

Figure 9.15 The Excelerator Data Dictionary. Excelerator's data dictionary centralizes the recording of data flow elements as well as processes and mini- specifications.

facility is the only way to define elements to the dictionary and look at relationships among the entities. For example, once several data elements have entered into the project dictionary, a record can be created that contains them. A record called "Item" might be composed of the elements "Item Number," "Item Name," "Unit Cost," and "Price." From record entities, Excelerator will generate data structure definition code in the BASIC, C, COBOL, and PL/1 languages.

Excelerator has a "Screens and Reports" facility that allows designers to create mock-ups of system inputs and outputs— screens and reports. This facility enhances the designer's prototyping capability. In the Screen Design module, screens are created by adding fields and text to a blank drawing area on the screen. If an element has been described to the data dictionary, it can be automatically referenced as a field on the screen. Figure 9.16 shows two screens. The first is a completed screen layout; the second is the screen with a "field definition screen" overlaying the finished screen. The field definition screen overlay is used to enter display characteristics of the field being defined for inclusion on the screen.

In addition to field definition screens for defining form fields, there are also "scroll region definition screens" and "text block

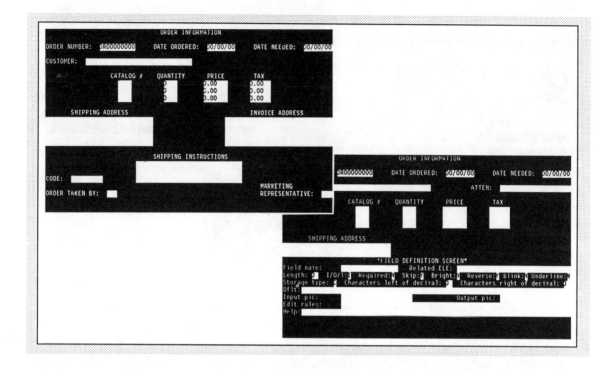

Figure 9.16 User Interface Screen Mockup in Excelerator. User interface screens can be designed with Excelerator. The left display shows the completed screen design. The right display shows a field definition screen overlaying the screen. Field definition screens allow designers to specify the properties of individual form fields.

definition screens." Scroll regions are vertically contiguous fields that appear as a column and can be scrolled. The fields comprising a scroll region are treated as a group of related fields. Data is entered one field (row) at a time, but the region may scroll vertically when the user accesses a field not currently in view on the screen. Text blocks are text input areas that resemble scroll regions on the screen but allow the user to input a stream of text, like a paragraph.

Once the screen has been defined, it can be tested. In this mode, users can input data into the fields. Data entered is validated against the specified data type for the field in the data dictionary. The data entered into a screen can be saved in a text file for analysis.

A separate product, XL/Interface Micro Focus, allows Excelerator users to automatically create structured "skeletal" COBOL source code from Excelerator designs. The COBOL used is Micro Focus's VS COBOL Workbench. This product does not yet generate fully functional code, but it does provide an outline from which programmers can work.

PowerTools—Iconix Software Engineering

PowerTools from Iconix Software Engineering, Inc. is an integrated set of CASE tools for the Macintosh environment. The tools support the popular methodologies, such as Structured Analysis and structure charts. Like many CASE tools implementing the Yourdon/DeMarco Structured Analysis methodology, the PowerTools CASE products are integrated and contribute to the analysis and design phases of the software life cycle as well as to the implementation and maintenance phases. The PowerTools programs are:

FreeFlow   FreeFlow is a data flow diagram editor and consistency checker with extensions for real-time software development. FreeFlow includes a mini-specification editor for writing pseudocode for the primitive-level data flow diagram processes (bubbles). As data flow diagrams are built, FreeFlow automatically collects the data from each process into a mini-specification file (process specification) which the analyst can edit with pseudocode. FreeFlow collects these pseudocode designs into a skeletal pseudocode design language file for use with other PowerTools modules during the design phase.

FastTask   FastTask is a tool for the development of real-time software using the Hatley real-time design techniques. The analyst uses FastTask to model state transition diagrams as control specifications for the control flow diagrams created with FreeFlow. Where the control flow diagram maps the flow of control signals through a system, the state transition diagram illustrates the various states a system can be in and what events and actions trigger movement between states. The software also automatically transforms the state transition diagram into corresponding tables and matrices. This gives the analyst alternate views of the system to better identify potential errors. FastTask shares Free Flow's dictionary to permit automatic checking between control flow diagram control signals and trigger events.

ASCII Bridge   This is an import/export function that translates FreeFlow and FastTask files into ASCII text format for export into an external environment. This allows textual descriptions of diagrams and data dictionaries to be imported into the PowerTools Environment.

PowerPDL (Program Design Language Processor)

The PowerTools Program Design Language Processor is a pseudocode processor that takes the output of the FreeFlow module and generates formatted documentation. In conjunction with SmartChart, PowerPDL initiates the "iterative loop" between preliminary and detailed design. The processor creates formatted documentation, including design body, data item, and subprogram cross-reference lists, a nesting tree, and a table of contents.

SmartChart   SmartChart is a structure chart generator and language-sensitive editor. With PowerPDL, the software designer uses SmartChart to transform the nesting tree files created by PowerPDL into structure charts (Figure 9.17). SmartChart contains an editor with keyword templates for several languages including Ada, Pascal, C, and Modula-2. Using the PDL (program design language), the designer fleshes out a skeleton program design language file of FreeFlow mini-specifications. The designer then reviews the program graphically with the structure charts and refines the design in the PDL file.

FreeFlow.   With FreeFlow, analysts decompose a system, moving level by level into finer detail. Beginning with a context diagram (see Chapter 4) that portrays system

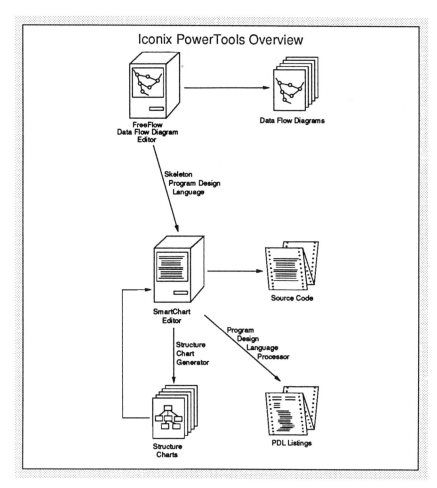

Figure 9.17 The Iconix PowerTools tool set emphasizes program design language (PDL) generation during system design. The SmartChart editor uses the PDL code to automatically generate source code in several languages, including Ada and C.

boundaries, the analyst creates a network, called a data flow diagram, of related functions showing all interfaces between components. By exploding each process in the data flow diagram, the engineer moves down into the system until reaching a level that cannot be further decomposed. This is called a *functional primitive* and the set of primitives is called the *leveled set*. Identifying a system's functional primitives and their interrelations is the goal of the data flow diagram.

For real-time software needs, the engineer creates leveled sets of control flow diagrams in the same manner as data flow diagrams. Where data flow diagrams model the flow of information through a system, the control flow diagram denotes movement of control signals. Control flow diagram elements are also housed in the same data dictionary as data items from the data flow diagram. Just as primitives in data flow diagrams have corresponding process specifications, all control flow diagrams have a control specification. The control specification can take several forms, including state transition diagrams, matrices, and tables.

The PowerTools tool set as a whole places more emphasis on mini-specifications than do other Structured Analysis tools. The data flow diagram editor has graphics editing facilities and commands similar to the MacDraw program provided as part of the Macintosh system software. Data dictionary elements are logged into the data dictionary as data flows are created on the data flow diagram; the designer can invoke the data dictionary module to provide the data element definitions.

FreeFlow is built around a central data dictionary and includes a consistency checker that verifies the completeness of the data flow diagram (Figure 9.18). The consistency checker identifies over twenty different errors, including unnamed or unconnected data flows, processes, and data files, and undefined entries or circular definitions in the data dictionary.

Figure 9.18 Iconix PowerTools FreeFlow Data Flow Editor. FreeFlow is the data flow diagram editing module of the PowerTools tool set. The data flow diagram editing and layout is similar to the MacDraw graphics editing program.

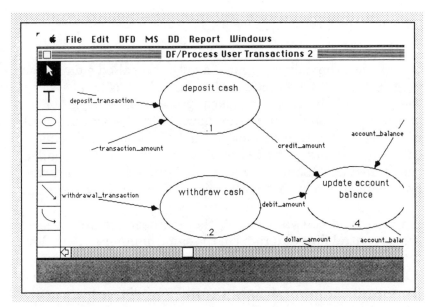

FreeFlow's data dictionary editor defines data element entries in terms of "formulas" (Backus-Naur Form productions) as shown in Figure 9.19. The data dictionary contents (entries) may be output as an ASCII file using the "ASCII Bridge" facility in order to interface with external programs and data bases. All FreeFlow and FastTask files are exportable via the ASCII Bridge.

Once the data flow diagrams have been constructed and the primitive process nodes identified (the leveled set) the FreeFlow mini-specification editor is used for building process specifications. This editor is a text editor with the capability to import and export text from external sources such as MacWrite documents using the Macintosh Scrapbook, or by writing and posting text from a clipboard with Switcher (a program that allows users to rapidly switch between different application programs). The designer designates a process as being a "primitive" process and FreeFlow generates a mini-specification file for the process. The inputs, outputs, and name of the primitive process are automatically inserted into a header template in this file. The designer then writes the pseudocode and comments which form the process's functional description.

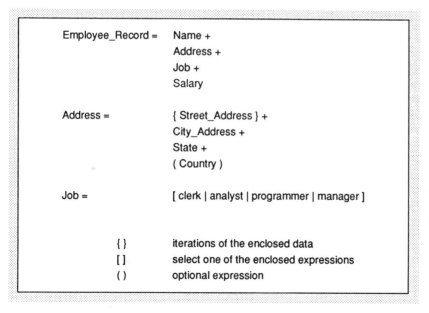

```
Employee_Record =    Name +
                     Address +
                     Job +
                     Salary

Address =            { Street_Address } +
                     City_Address +
                     State +
                     ( Country )

Job =                [ clerk | analyst | programmer | manager ]

            { }      iterations of the enclosed data
            [ ]      select one of the enclosed expressions
            ( )      optional expression
```

Figure 9.19 Power-Tools Data Dictionary Editor. PowerTools uses a data dictionary syntax similar to BNF (Backus-Naur Form) production rules. Data items are automatically logged into the project data dictionary as they are created on the data flow diagram. Software designers can use the data dictionary to add lower-level detail as needed.

FastTask. With the FastTask module, the engineer builds a state transition diagram articulating control specification information associated with the control flow diagrams created in FreeFlow. The state transition diagram models the system's movement from state to state using finite state machine techniques. As a state transition diagram is built, the software automatically regenerates the data into corresponding matrices and charts. With this approach, the engineer has a variety of review mechanisms, thereby enhancing the ability to detect logic errors before system construction begins.

SmartChart. FreeFlow extends the Structured Analysis conventions by allowing the mini-specification files to be grouped together to form a single output file which can be processed by the PowerTools Program Design Language (PowerPDL) processor. This serves as input to the SmartChart program where the PDL can be refined and compilable code subsequently generated. Although anything can be entered into a mini-specification file, the PDL source file requirements must be followed when editing mini-specification files if the mini-specification files are to be used as input to the PDL processor. In particular, the structure of the mini-specification header template must not be altered. The following control structures supported by the PDL processor can be used when writing the pseudocode in mini-specification files:

    begin-end
    if-then-end if
    if-then-else-end if
    loop-end loop
    select-end select

Control information is added to the PDL file by using PDL templates provided in the SmartChart structure chart editor. The resulting PDL file (mini-specification plus control information) is compiled by the PowerPDL Program Design Language processor and can be used by SmartChart to automatically generate a structure chart for the design (Figure 9.20). The application designer can edit and refine the PDL source file using SmartChart, recompiling with the PDL processor until the design is complete.

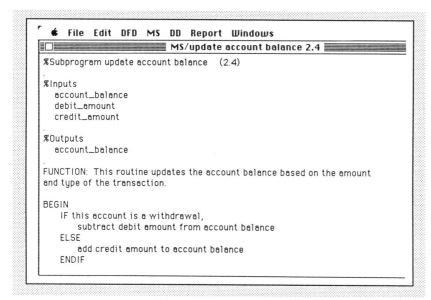

Figure 9.20 Iconix PowerTools Mini-specification Pseudocode. The PowerTools Design Language for writing mini-specifications is a procedural, block structured program design language.

Once the new structure charts are complete, source code is added to the PDL file using the SmartChart "language-sensitive" editor. The language-sensitive editor is a facility for building both pseudocode and program code text files. Keyword and control structure templates are provided for the PDL language, Pascal, Ada, C, and Modula-2. The original pseudocode is embedded within the application's source code as comments, allowing the structure chart to be used as a code browser. As the software evolves through the project's implementation and maintenance phases, the pseudocode comments can be edited and extracted to produce a current PDL file and structure chart listing. This keeps the design synchronized with the code.

ProMod—Promod, Inc.

Promod, Inc. of Lake Forest, California is a medium-sized CASE tool company. Their analysis and design tool, ProMod, runs on the IBM PC and VAX series computers. ProMod stresses Structured Analysis and structured design and provides capabilities for back-end code generation in Ada, C, and Pascal. This code generation capability is one of ProMod's differentiating features. Like other analysis/design CASE tools, it is highly graphical in nature, mandating a graphics display and plotter or a laser printer.

ProMod is composed of six modules:

1. SA (Structured Analysis)
2. SA-RT (Real-Time Analysis)
3. MD (Modular Design)
4. Pro/Source Code Generator
5. ProCap Code and Design Maintenance Facility
6. Re/Source Reverse Engineering Facility

SA (Structured Analysis).   ProMod's Structured Analysis module implements the widely accepted Yourdon/DeMarco Structured Analysis methodology. As in other design-oriented CASE tools, the principal graphic tool in ProMod's SA module is the data flow diagram. Corresponding to each data flow is a data dictionary entry describing the data form and content. Similarly, while each process node is described by a mini-specification. A typical data flow diagram is shown in Figure 9.21.

During the creation of a Structured Analysis model, ProMod checks for consistency and completeness. ProMod performs global or local leveling and balancing checks to insure full consistency between the data flow diagrams, mini-specifications, and the data dictionary.

ProMod's Real Time Analysis module, SA-RT, extends the Structured Analysis module by adding control flow diagrams, control specifications, and state transition diagrams. As with other Structured Analysis tools, ProMod relies on a central data dictionary, the output of which is shown in Figure 9.22.

MD (Modular Design).   The Modular Design component of ProMod transforms a model created in the Structured Analysis module into a hierarchical structure of subsystems, modules, functions, and data elements. This structure diagram is used as the basis for further stepwise refinement of the design into a more detailed system structure. Figure 9.23 illustrates a typical structure chart designed using ProMod.

Part of the Modular Design module is a pseudocode editor that allows program-code-like structures to define details of functions embedded in modules and functions. This permits the

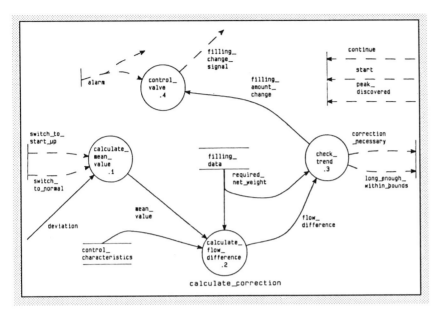

Figure 9.21 ProMod Data Flow Diagram.

Figure 9.22 The Pro-Mod Data Dictionary.

```
****************************************************************
* ProMod V1.4c    09-APR-1987  14:21          PAGE   21     *
*(714) 855-3046                                              *
* ProMod, Inc.       PROJECT:paint     Analysis Report (RA&D) *
****************************************************************


     DATA_DESCRIPTION

     commands
       =  [ "read"
              * read planned filling data  *
          | "print"
              * print statistical report  *
          | "start"
              * activate the filling process  *
          | "continue"
              * after an abnormal situation  * ]

     continue

          *
          operator command
          *

     filling_data
       =   date
         + production_number
         + filling_number
         + "number_of_cans_to_fill"
         + required_amount
         + required_net_weight
         + order_number
         + can_number
         + lid_type

     last_can_filled

          *
          signal to indicate that enough cans have been
          filled to the required weight;
          the end of this filling process
          *

     planned_filling_data
       =   date
         + production_number
         + filling_number
         + "number_of_cans_to_fill"
         + required_amount
         + required_net_weight
         + order_number
         + can_number
         + lid_type

     start

          *
```

Figure 9.23   ProMod Structure Chart.

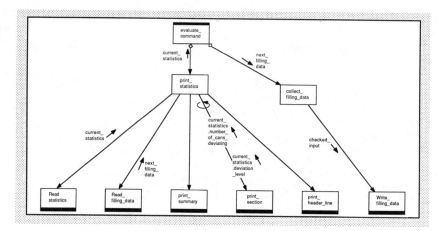

integration of key logic algorithms into a structure that is consistent with the preceding analysis and design. Examples of the pseudocode statements are constructs such as If-Then-Else and Do-End.

Pro/Source Code Generator. ProMod's Ada, C, and Pascal language code generator translates the architectural design written using the Module Design component of the ProMod package into compilable code constructs and statements. This is one of ProMod's most unique features. For example, ProMod's Modular Design structures, such as subsystems, modules, and functions, are directly transformed into Ada packages and procedures. The subordinate detail within ProMod structures, such as purpose statements, function calls, export/import relationships, and pseudocode statements, are transformed into their Ada equivalents.

The ProMod data type dictionary is transformed into a global *Type Declaration Package. Record Type* structures consistent with ProMod's data structures are automatically created, as summarized in Figure 9.24.

ProCap. ProCap maintains Ada, C, and Pascal source code and design abstractions in a multilevel file structure. Report generators automatically produce program-level documentation. ProCap accepts source code and design information generated from Pro/Source. ProCap also accepts source code developed elsewhere and serves as a stand-alone

Figure 9.24 ProMod
Data Type Dictionary
Correspondence.

Data Type Dictionary Correspondence

ProMod	Code Generator
Single Name Definition	Derived Type declarations

Sequence Definitions of:
  Simple Names
  Nested Structures
	
	Simp[le Record Types
	Nested Record Types

Selection Definition
  Alternates Defined
  Alternates Undefined
	
	Discriminant Record Type
	Enumeration Type

Option Definitions	Flagged for analyst conversion
Iteration Definition	Array Type

Pseudocode Correspondence

Function Call If-Then-Else-End If Do-End Do	Procedure Call If-Then-Else-End If Loop-End Loop
Case	Case
Purpose-End Purpose Text Comments	Text Comment Text Comments with flag

Architecture Correspondence

Function	Procedure
Module	Package Declaration including: • Context Specification • Procedure Interface Specification • Package Body Declaration
Subsystem	Package Declaration including: • Context Specification • Data Declaration Package Specifications

development tool for the creation of detailed designs and source code using stepwise refinement.

Re/Source.   Re/Source accepts Ada, C, and Pascal source code and generates design constructs for ProMod/MD (Modular Design). This effectively "reverse engineers" existing source code so that the full power of ProMod/MD can be applied at the design level. Used in conjunction with ProCap, Re/Source ensures overall design consistency when changes are made at the source code level.

Summary

This chapter presented only a few of the commercially available Structured Analysis and design specification tools. The reader should only consider the selected tools as representative of the offerings in the marketplace. However, they were selected to highlight their differences in capabilities and features. Different vendors stress different methodologies or combinations of features. Where one tool may embrace program design languages, such as Iconix's PowerTools, another may emphasize data modeling, such as Index Technology's Excelerator. You must select the feature set that provides the most benefit for your organization.

Many of the tools described in this chapter provide a variety of specification techniques in addition to data flow diagrams. Data and information modeling is as common as structure charting. The general industry trend is for vendors to offer more capabilities, both for design and for implementation. Increasingly common are code generation facilities. While still embryonic at this time, expect these facilities to become much more robust during the next five years. This trend and others are discussed in Chapter 15.

The chart in Figure 9.25 summarizes the capabilities of each tool presented in this chapter. This chart is *not* meant to compare, weigh, or rank one tool against another. Its goal is to merely itemize the methodologies emphasized by each tool. Unfortunately, as any software technology evolves, wholesale ranking and rating checklists will be devised that supposedly calculate the relative value of each tool. Numerous magazine

Tool/Vendor	Capabilities
Teamwork Cadre Technologies, Inc.	Data flow diagrams Real-time extensions to data flow diagrams Structure charts Data dictionaries Entity-relationship diagrams
Execelerator Index Technology Corporation	Data flow diagrams Data dictionaries Entity-relationship diagrams Data structure code generation (COBOL, C, BASIC) Screen prototyping
DesignAid Nastec Corporation	Design document building Data flow diagrams Data dictionaries Structure charts Screen prototyping
ProMod Promod, Inc.	Data flow diagrams Real-time extensions to data flow diagrams Program design language Structure charts Code generation (ADA, C, Pascal)
PowerTools Iconix Software Engineering	Data flow diagrams Data dictionaries Program design language Structure charts Code generation (ADA, C, Pascal)

Figure 9.25 Summary of Design Specification Tools.

articles and research reports will appear containing large checklists of all the computer-aided software engineering features known to mankind. The tool with the most check marks wins, and for this reason, Figure 9.25 is not constructed in a feature checklist format. Needless to say, these ranking schemes ignore ease-of-use, learning curves, vendor support, training, price, and most importantly, the benefit to *your* organization. This unfortunate rating practice occurs with data base and with expert systems tools; it will happen with computer-aided software engineering tools. Beware!

Chapter 10

Specialized Design Tools

'Necessity is the mother of invention' is a silly proverb. 'Necessity is the mother of futile dodges' is much nearer the truth.
— Alfred North Whitehead

There are many CASE tools and technologies that resist being pigeonholed into categories. Unlike the previous chapter, in which each tool implemented the Yourdon/DeMarco Structured Analysis methodology, the tools in this chapter emphasize two different, specialized methodologies for data modeling and real-time control design. Unfortunately, the length of this book limits the diversity of different tools that can be included. Nevertheless, this chapter should convey the notion that there are alternatives to Structured Analysis and that CASE vendors are indeed supporting these alternative methodologies.

Two individual tools are highlighted in this chapter. The first, Brackets from Optima, Inc., implements the Warnier-Orr methodology on the IBM PC. The second, TAGS from Teledyne Brown Engineering, is a tool for designing real-time systems using a methodology that focuses on input and output data requirements.

Brackets—Optima, Inc.

Brackets is an interactive Warnier-Orr diagraming tool for the IBM PC and compatible machines marketed by Optima, Inc. (formerly Ken Orr and Associates, Inc.) of Schaumburg, Illinois. Brackets uses an outline processor format for creating and editing Warnier-Orr diagrams, allowing the designer to expand or collapse any part of a Warnier/Orr diagram with a single keystroke.

Warnier-Orr diagrams and Brackets are designed to support the program design code generation phases of software development. With Brackets, code can be maintained through the Warnier-Off design documentation in a more structured fashion (Figure 10.1).

Brackets has many of the properties of a conventional outline processor, and in fact, Brackets can be used as an outline processor. Brackets also incorporates the spreadsheet metaphor. For instance, the Lotus-style command menu structure is used, as is the notion of a worksheet "cell." The cursor pad keys (arrow keys) are used to move a "highlight bar" from one cell to the next, either vertically or horizontally. The entire worksheet scrolls as necessary. At the top left of the screen is the "cell display" showing the value of the currently highlighted cell (area) on the worksheet. This area is used for subsequent editing.

Substructures (called brackets) can be closed by moving the highlight bar anywhere to the left of the bracket and pressing the "Grey +" key. The "Grey +" key is used as a toggle to expand and contract substructures. To create a new element in a blank cell to the right of and adjacent to an existing bracket, the user simply places the highlight bar on the blank cell, types in the text for the new element, and presses the "Enter" key. To insert a new element between two existing ones, the user places the bar on the element above the insertion point, presses the "Insert" key, types in the text, and presses "Enter." The delete operation works similarly. Brackets draws

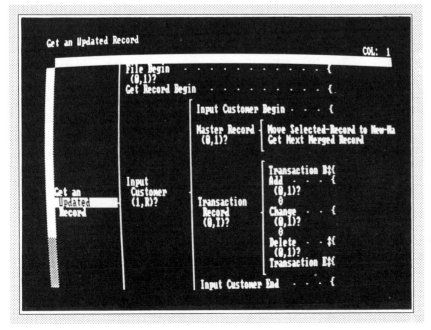

Figure 10.1 Brackets Warnier-Orr Diagram Editor. Brackets is a Warnier-Orr diagram editor that operates much like an outline processor and has many of the characteristics of a spreadsheet program.

new brackets automatically as they are needed. The user simply places the highlight bar to the right of an existing cell and enters in new text, followed by "Enter." To edit text in an existing cell, the user places the highlight bar over the cell and presses the "Enter" key. The line of text is then edited in the cell display window in the upper left corner of the screen, again like many spreadsheets.

Brackets utilizes the important Warnier-Orr diagram properties of hierarchy, sequencing, repetition, alternation, concurrency, and recursion. Warnier-Orr diagram *hierarchy* is used to establish the relationship between a *set* and its subset elements. To establish a hierarchy (a Warnier-Orr bracket) the designer positions the cursor at an appropriate position and enters the name of the hierarchy. Moving the cursor one column to the right and entering data causes a bracket to appear, designating the next lower level in the Warnier-Orr diagram hierarchy. Inside the bracket, each new entry will cause the bracket to automatically expand vertically.

Inside each bracket, the entries establish a *sequence*, or ordering, of a set of data or actions. New sequential entries can be added or deleted using the "Insert" and "Delete" keys. To define a sequence, the designer just keeps creating entries inside a set and the bracket expands to accommodate each new entry.

Repetition in Warnier-Orr diagrams indicates that the enclosed data elements or actions are to be repeated up to some maximum limit. In Brackets, the number of iterations, (1, N), is specified by typing the "#" sign preceded by at least one space. The text that follows will be shown inside the iteration parenthesis "( )" on the line below the entry. For example, payments can be excepted or refunds issued once or not at all:

Accept Payment
(0,1)
 θ
Issue Refund
(0, 1)

Two or more sets can be shown as mutually exclusive (*alternatives*) using the exclusive-or symbol. The designer indicates alternation by typing an "o" on a line by itself, which Brackets translates into the Greek letter theta (θ). *Concurrency*, a property indicating two or more actions can be performed simultaneously (an "and" condition), is indicated in Brackets with the "+" symbol. The "+" is entered on a line by itself between the two concurrent elements. (Concurrency is rarely used for data structure definitions.) Finally, Brackets can indicate *recursion*. Recursion occurs when a set contains a "duplicate" of itself, a concept that is useful both in data structures and in program design, as shown in Figure 10.2.

The top-level command menu at the top of the screen employs a very simple set of commands: Block (block marking), Move, Copy, Duplicate, Wedge, Yank, Search, Print, File, Options, and Quit. Wedge and Yank are functions that permit inserting or removing levels of the diagram. Using the Block Mark command, portions of the hierarchy can be marked and then moved or copied from one part of the diagram to another. When blocks are moved or copied, they can ascend or descend levels in the hierarchy as needed.

Brackets has a "duplicate" feature, called "cloning" in outline processors, that allows the designer to create several copies of

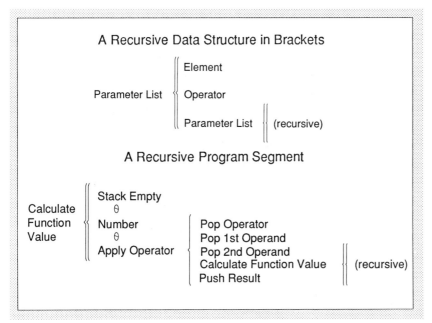

Figure 10.2 Recursive structures and procedures are represented with double-lined brackets in Brackets. The Greek theta (θ) symbol indicates alternate, or mutually exclusive, operations or structures.

an individual structure (elements to the right of a bracket). These copies are linked, and changing any copy will likewise change the others. The duplicate feature is useful because the designer only has to change one copy of the structure, regardless of level or position in the diagram, to modify all copies of the structure. "Duplicate" brackets are distinguished visually as a double-line bracket rather than the single-line bracket used for regular structures. In program design, the duplicate feature is used to define subroutines that are called from more than one place in the design, or subroutines that are recursive. Brackets also supports "linking" diagrams together, which allows designers to traverse from one diagram to another via a link between diagrams.

Brackets can automatically generate complete COBOL code from detailed program designs. Brackets files can be imported from or exported to the STRUCTURE(S) COBOL Code generation program, also from Optima, Inc. Likewise, STRUCTURE(S) source code can be imported and displayed as a Brackets diagram (Figure 10.3).

TAGS/CASE—Teledyne Brown Engineering

Teledyne Brown Engineering is one of the largest companies in the computer-aided software engineering market. Their product, TAGS (Technology for the Automated Generation of Systems), is a computer-aided software and systems engineering environment that provides for automated definition, design, documentation, simulation, testing, and maintenance of complex integrated hardware/software systems. TAGS supports the full implementation of Teledyne Brown's Input/Output Requirements Language (IORL) and consists of several interactive software packages in a workstation environment that build IORL documents. TAGS provides components to graphically build and edit Schematic Block Diagrams, Timing Diagrams, Process Diagrams, and Data Structure Diagrams. This is accomplished by a series of software packages which function in a distributed workstation environment.

```
              IDENTIFICATION DIVISION.
              PROGRAM-ID.   EMP-LIST.

         *      THIS PROGRAM PRINTS AN EMPLOYEE ADDRESS LIST
         ..................................
         * GENERATED FROM FILE   COBOLPGM  *
         ..................................

              INPUT-OUTPUT SECTION.
              FILE-CONTROL.
                 SELECT NAME-ADDRESS-FILE-IN
                    ASSIGN TO "DISK-TITUS.DAT".
                 SELECT EMPLOYEE-LIST-OUT
                    ASSIGN TO "PRINTER-TITUS.PRN".

              DATA DIVISION.
              FILE SECTION.
              FD  NAME-ADDRESS-FILE-IN
                    RECORD CONTAINS 80 CHARACTERS
                    LABEL RECORDS ARE STANDARD
                    DATA RECORD IS NAME-ADDRESS-RECORD-IN.

              01  NAME-ADDRESS-RECORD-IN.
                    02  EMPLOYEE-NAME-IN             PIC X(21).
                    02  EMPLOYEE-ADDRESS-IN          PIC X(24).
                    02  EMPLOYEE-CITY-STATE-ZIP-IN   PIC X(25).
                    02  EMPLOYEE-HIRE-DATE-IN.
                      03  EMPLOYEE-HIRE-MONTH-IN      PIC 9(2).
                      03  EMPLOYEE-HIRE-DAY-IN        PIC 9(2).
                      03  EMPLOYEE-HIRE-YEAR-IN       PIC 9(2).
                    02  FILLER              PIC X(4).

              FD  EMPLOYEE-LIST-OUT
                    RECORD CONTAINS 132 CHARACTERS
                    LABEL RECORDS ARE OMITTED
                    DATA RECORD IS EMPLOYEE-LINE-OUT.

              01  EMPLOYEE-LINE-OUT.
                    02  FILLER              PIC X(1).
                    02  EMPLOYEE-NAME-OUT            PIC X(21).
                    02  FILLER              PIC X(1).
                    02  EMPLOYEE-ADDRESS-OUT         PIC X(24).
                    02  FILLER              PIC X(1).
                    02  EMPLOYEE-CITY-STATE-ZIP-OUT  PIC X(25).
                    02  FILLER              PIC X(59).

              WORKING-STORAGE SECTION.

                77  END-OF-NAME-ADDRESS-FILE        PIC X(3).

              PROCEDURE DIVISION.
              MAINLINE-PRINT-EMPLOYEE-LIST.
                 OPEN INPUT NAME-ADDRESS-FILE-IN
                    OUTPUT EMPLOYEE-LIST-OUT.
                 PERFORM INITIALIZE-VARIABLE-FIELDS.
                 READ NAME-ADDRESS-FILE-IN
                    AT END
                      MOVE YES-VALUE TO END-OF-NAME-ADDRESS-FILE.
                 PERFORM PROCESS-NAME-ADDRESS-RECORD
                    UNTIL END-OF-NAME-ADDRESS-FILE IS EQUAL TO "YES".
                 CLOSE NAME-ADDRESS-FILE-IN
                    EMPLOYEE-LIST-OUT.
                 STOP RUN.

              INITIALIZE-VARIABLE-FIELDS.
                 MOVE NO-VALUE TO END-OF-NAME-ADDRESS-FILE.

              PROCESS-NAME-ADDRESS-RECORD.
                 MOVE SPACES TO EMPLOYEE-LINE-OUT.
                 MOVE EMPLOYEE-NAME-IN TO EMPLOYEE-NAME-OUT.
                 MOVE EMPLOYEE-ADDRESS-IN TO EMPLOYEE-ADDRESS-OUT.
                 MOVE EMPLOYEE-CITY-STATE-ZIP-IN
                    TO EMPLOYEE-CITY-STATE-ZIP-OUT.
                 WRITE EMPLOYEE-LINE-OUT
                    AFTER ADVANCING 2 LINES.
                 READ NAME-ADDRESS-FILE-IN
                    AT END
                      MOVE YES-VALUE TO END-OF-NAME-ADDRESS-FILE.
```

Figure 10.3 Brackets-Generated COBOL Program. Brackets will automatically generate complete COBOL programs from detailed program designs.

The Main Menu shown in Figure 10.4 provides an overview of TAGS. The first option enables the user to log into TAGS and to either access an existing system or create a new one. The next four options have their indicated support functions. The Edit Mode (shown in reverse field) enables the creation and/ or modification of IORL *sections* through a software package called Storage and Retrieval (SR). Note that IORL is maintained at the graphical level and not at the code level. Storage and Retrieval is also used in the Display Mode to enable the easy elaboration of lower-level IORL sections by selecting their corresponding abstraction symbols within higher-level sections (using a mouse.)

The next four options of the TAGS Main Menu are application packages which operate on IORL systems established by Storage and Retrieval. The first is the Analysis Library, a series of ten diverse tools to aid the user in manipulating and gaining insight into an IORL system. The Configuration Management package protects a system's documentation during maintenance by maintaining a baseline and closely managing changes at the page level. The Diagnostic Analysis package is used to ensure that a system design is a complete, consistent, and syntactically correct IORL. Finally, the

Figure 10.4 TAGS. Teledyne Brown Engineering's TAGS (Technology for the Automated Generation of Systems) system focuses on real-time software specification. TAGS uses the Input/Output Requirements Language (IORL) and provides graphical editing facilities to build schematic block diagrams, timing diagrams, process diagrams, and data structure diagrams.

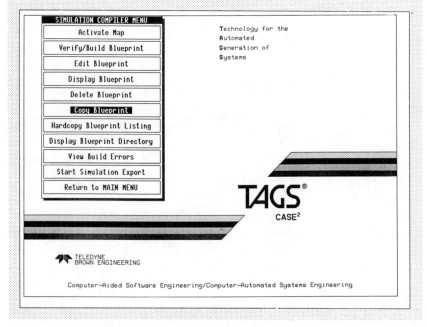

Simulation Compiler executes the design to provide dynamic error analysis and system performance evaluation of real-time systems, including the identification of race conditions and timing faults.

The following discussion presents IORL sections in terms of a variety of Storage and Retrieval displays. Some of the IORL constructs are exemplified to show the power of this graphics-based language. After this, the various functions of the TAGS environment will be reviewed briefly.

Example IORL Sections. Figure 10.5 presents an example of the highest-level Schematic Block Diagram (SBD) section of IORL. This particular system (called TS, an acronym for Tracker System) has been successfully compiled and simulated. The schematic block diagram is the highest level of both data and procedural abstraction. Rectangles on the schematic block diagram, called *components*, represent independently functioning processes. The only way that one component can affect any other component is by sending data over the connectors, called *interfaces*. An interface is the highest level of data abstraction, merely indicating

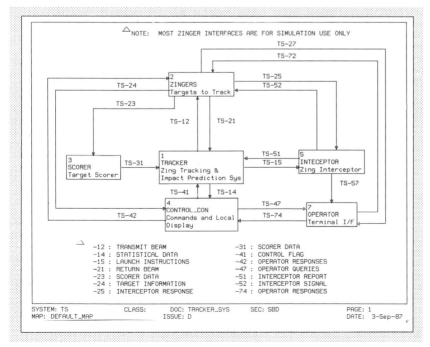

Figure 10.5 An Example Schematic Block Diagram Section in TAGS/IORL.

that data are allowed to flow between the two components in the direction indicated. While the degree of information-hiding is extremely high within the schematic block diagram, it results in a structural understanding that otherwise would be obscured if IORL mixed control and data flow, or if separate interfaces were required for each message type. Note that the schematic block diagram shows only the interaction between components; no temporal or control relationship is inferred.

Other IORL sections support stepwise refinement. Further analysis might be required if a component consisted of independently functioning processes within it. Each of these processes are components in their own right, and thus their interactions could be modeled by a lower-level schematic block diagram. Figure 10.6 gives an example of this for the CONTROL_CON component of the Tracking System (TS) example. The identification fields at the bottom of the page show that the SYSTEM is still the Tracking System, but now the DOC, or *documents*, is CONTROL_CON (i.e., the name of the component which it elaborates). An IORL document consists of all of the sections needed to elaborate a component as though it were itself a system. This recursive

Figure 10.6 A Lower Level Schematic Block Diagram. This diagram was created by stepwise refinement of the diagram in Figure 10.5.

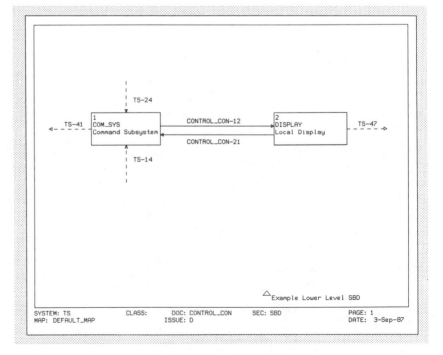

GRP	PARAMETER DESCRIPTION (DIM)	NAME	VALUE RANGE	UNITS/VALUE MEANING
1	<Control Group>			
		&XOFF	<True, False>	
2	<Target Generation Times>			
	Average Time of Arrival	AveTA	<1,2,...>	
3	<Sim Limit>			
	Maximum Run Time	MaxTimeLimit	[0,∞)	
4				
	Control Flag	ControlFlag	<0,	Stop Tracker
			1,	Search Only
			2,	Search/Track Only
			3,	Search/Track/Intercept
				All
			4>	Launch Only to Defend
				Scorer
5	<Time Delay Between Queries>			
	Time Delay	TDBQ	R	Time Delay Between
				Queries to/from Operator
6	<Illumination Debug>			
		IRDEB	<0,	DEBUG OFF
			1,	DEBUG ON DETECTIONS ONLY
			2>	DEBUG ON ALL XMIT BEAMS
7	<TARGET OBSERVATION DEBUG>			
		TODEB	<0,	DEBUG OFF
			1>	DEBUG ON
8	<STATISTICS DEBUG>			
		STATDEB	<0,	DEBUG OFF
			1>	DEBUG ON

SYSTEM: TS	CLASS:	DOC: TS	SEC: IOPT-74	PAGE: 10
MAP: DEFAULT_MAP		ISSUE: 1		DATE: 9-Jun-87

Figure 10.7 A TAGS Input/Output Parameter Table. I/O Parameter Tables enumerate the data moving between components. These tables are similar to the data dictionary for data flow diagrams.

generation of sections gives IORL rich cross-reference and traceability characteristics for any number of levels of analysis. Figure 10.6 also introduces another symbol, the dotted connectors, called *external interfaces*, which represent data flow at the higher level. Also, free-form comments may appear anywhere outside of the symbols.

Parameter tables are used to elaborate the data represented by each interface. Figure 10.7, shows the *Input Output Parameter Table* (IOPT) for the interface between component 7 and component 4. Since the interface has been numbered -74, the corresponding parameter table section reference is IOPT-74. IOPTs contain *groups*, each indicating a temporally contiguous transmission of data. Looking ahead, Input/Output symbols within the procedure diagrams will reference the interface and the group number, thus providing a definitive specification of the sender/receiver as well as the quality and quantity of data. This not only makes the data visible upon request to the user (via Display Mode), but it also forces the establishment of timing requirements for the I/O.

The structural and data flow modeling of a system with components, interfaces, and I/O Parameter Tables facilitates the procedural analysis of the components. The section used to elaborate the timed sequence of activities within a given component is its Input/Output Relationships and Timing Diagram (IORTD). Figure 10.8, presents the logical flow for Component 1 (IORTD-1) in the Tracking System document.

To understand the sequence of activities within Figure 10.8, note that the major loop begins with a process block, the symbol which generally contains assignment statements. In this case a single assignment increments the Time variable. Control then drops to a decision node where a test is performed on Time. This is followed by five Predefined Process Reference (PPR) symbols. The predefined process reference is the major symbol for procedural abstraction. As shown with PPR-20000, multiple entries and exits are allowed. Each predefined process reference references its corresponding Predefined Process Diagram (PPD), which is a grouping of I/O relationships and timing diagram symbols, including predefined process references. The merge symbol in Figure 10.8, the Fan-in OR, allows control flows to merge.

Figure 10.8 Timing Sequence in TAGS. These frames show the timing sequence of activities for a system software component designed using the Teledyne Brown TAGS system.

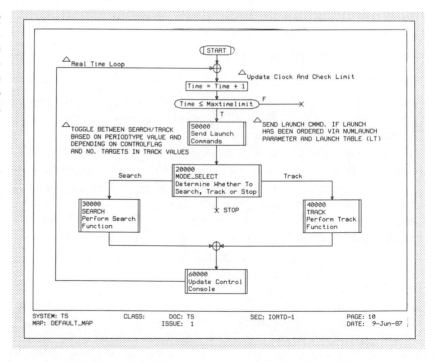

Designers using IORL can package the details of the procedure at an optimal level of abstraction. "Optimal" means the design that leads to maximum communication (understandability). Usually a grouping of seven to twelve symbols satisfies this objective and fits conveniently on one page. (The use of page connectors are allowed but not encouraged.) Too much detail obscures the intent of a section, and too much hiding requires unnecessary references to lower-level sections.

Moving to a lower level, (Figure 10.9) gives an example of PPD-46000, which is called within PPD-40000. In addition to having two decision primitives, this predefined process diagram also references three other predefined process diagrams. The process of stepwise refinement and procedural analysis shown in this example continues to the "atomic" level, as seen in PPD-46100 (Figure 10.10). The absence of any abstraction symbols indicates that the design on this branch of the I/O relationships and timing diagram tree is completed.

The details of a component can be analyzed in two possible directions: lower-level schematic block diagrams or I/O

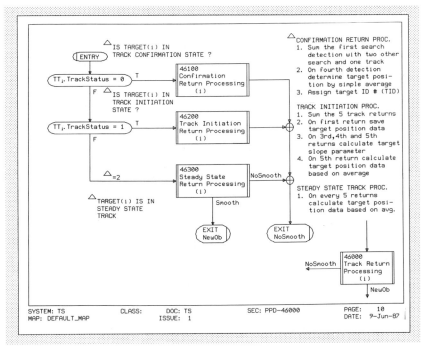

Figure 10.9 This predefined process is called within PPD-40000 in Figure 10.8.

relationships and timing diagrams. A thorough analysis proceeds in both directions. The I/O relationships and timing diagram is used for a high-level view of the component; and the lower-level sections in the document, resulting from the new schematic block diagram, are used for more detailed specification and ultimately for implementation. Generally, the structural decomposition which creates an entire document should be performed only if the presence of concurrency within an I/O relationships and timing diagram can best be modeled by the creation of a lower-level schematic block diagram.

Several other sections further support those presented. The first is the *I/O Macro*, which is a grouping of I/O symbols. Macros are much like predefined process diagrams, but they elaborate I/O procedures, usually from the initial handshaking through the final data transmission. For this reason they are parameterized with interfaces, groups, and other I/O primitive syntactical elements rather than variable values. The presence of the I/O macro reference symbol in I/O relationships and timing diagrams or predefined process diagrams makes I/O visible in these higher-level diagrams. A

Figure 10.10 "Atomic". This process diagram contains no abstraction symbols indicating there is no further process decomposition.

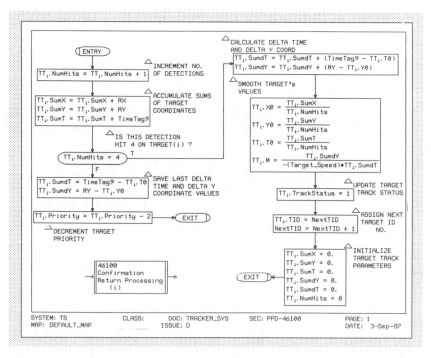

second section, the Data Structure Diagram (DSD), can accompany any parameter table. The data structure diagram is quite flexible, ranging in use from the rapid prototyping of input requirements and output reports to mapping data elements into specific memory locations. Finally, two parameter tables are used for variables that do not flow over the interfaces of the schematic block diagram. These are the Internal Parameter Tables (IPT) for each I/O relationship and timing diagram and the Predefined Process Parameter Tables (PPPT) for each predefined process diagram.

TAGS Environment. The TAGS Storage and Retrieval tool enables the IORL sections to be easily created and modified. All maintenance is done directly on the graphical representation without concern for the underlying representation. Icons, as shown in Figure 10.10, are used in conjunction with the workstation mouse to place and move symbols on the page. The normal text character set is augmented by a Greek/mathematics keyboard mode to enable great flexibility in variable naming and manipulation. Many mathematical and set symbols are directly supported (such as the summation and iterated product). These, coupled with

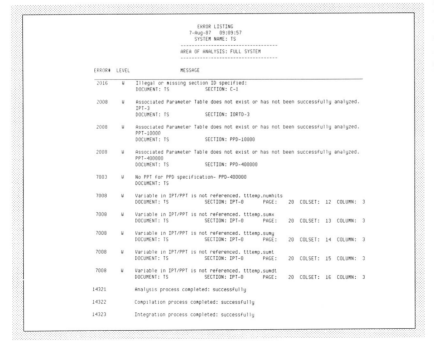

Figure 10.11 The Diagnostic Analyzer performs consistently, checks for completeness, invalid parameter names and syntax errors.

true subscripting, lead to a natural form of mathematical abstraction consistent with the engineering disciplines. Finally, TAGS assures traceability by furnishing or requiring proper identification field completion.

In addition to the creation and manipulation of IORL sections, TAGS creates an underlying representation which can be parsed and compiled into Ada language source code. The first step in this direction is the Diagnostic Analyzer package, which can be invoked at the completion of each section. An example Diagnostic Analyzer error listing is given in Figure 10.11. The Diagnostic Analyzer checks for completeness by assuring that there are no missing sections, symbols, symbol text, or parameters. It also checks semantic errors, such as invalid or illegal parameter names, characters, symbol numbers, and/or data values. Syntax errors, such as improper symbols, and a large variety of errors in cross-referencing, consistency, and control flow are also detected. The Diagnostic Analyzer assures that the underlying representation can be compiled into Ada and builds the necessary tables to support the Simulation Compiler and several other tools discussed below.

Figure 10.12 highlights three of the ten Analysis Library Tools. These three provide insight into the design database for a given system. The *Data Dictionary* provides an alphabetical list of the variables declared or used in the IORL system model, as well as a complete cross-reference of their

Figure 10.12 Additional TAGS Facilities. The TAGS environment includes Data Dictionary, Flow Analysis, and Cross-Reference tools.

```
                            DATA DICTIONARY LISTING
                            Date: 11-Aug-87

                    DICTIONARY TYPE    : ALL VARS/ ALL DEFS
                    DA INTEGRATION TYPE: FULL SYSTEM
                    SYSTEM             : TS
                    MAP                : DEFAULT_MAP


    VARIABLE NAME              DEFINED              DATA TYPE          REFERENCED BY
    ------------------------------------------------------------------------------------------
    J                    (TS) PPT-45000        INTEGER VARIABLE    (TS) PPD-45000
                         (TS) PPT-47100        INTEGER VARIABLE    (TS) PPD-47100
                         (TS) PPT-50000        INTEGER VARIABLE    (TS) PPD-50000
                         (TS) PPT-242000       INTEGER VARIABLE    (TS) PPD-242000
                         (TS) PPT-250000       INTEGER VARIABLE    (TS) PPD-250000
                         (TS) PPT-270000       INTEGER VARIABLE    (TS) PPD-270000

    k                    (TS) PPT-47100        INTEGER VARIABLE    (TS) PPD-47100
                         (TS) PPT-250000       INTEGER VARIABLE    (TS) PPD-250000

    l                    (TS) PPT-250000       INTEGER VARIABLE    (TS) PPD-250000

    lastvalue            (TS) PPT-3            INTEGER VARIABLE    (TS) PPD-3

    launchtablereo       (TS) IPT-0            STRUCTURE
        -lid                                   INTEGER VARIABLE
        -tl                                    REAL VARIABLE
```

use. The *Flow Analysis* tool shows where each interface and group of data are referenced throughout the system. These two tools require successful completion of the Diagnostic Analyzer. The third tool, the *SPPD Cross-Reference*, shows the inter-referencing between all control sections (I/O relationships and timing diagrams and predefined process diagrams). In addition to these three Analysis Library tools, there are seven others:

1. *Audit*, which lists all pages within a TAGS system for progress assessment and traceability.

2. *Document Processor Interface*, that merges the TAGS graphics into a document processor on the host workstation.

3. *Merge Library*, that enables TAGS systems to be moved between hardware installations.

4. *Page Copy*, which copies pages from one TAGS system to another.

5. *Page Rename*, that performs updates throughout a TAGS system as a result of renaming a page.

ENGINEERING CHANGE PROPOSAL (ECP)

| SYSTEM: TS | MAP: | DATE: | CLASS: |

| ECP NUMBER: | TYPE: | PRIORITY: | REVISION: | CORRECTION: |

RELATED TR NUMBERS: , , , ☐ READY FOR SCN DISTRIBUTION

DOCUMENT	RELATED SCN	☐ ICCB STATUS REQUIRED	☐ ECCB STATUS REQUIRED
		☐ APPROVED ☐ PENDING ☐ REWORK ☐ REJECTED DATE RECEIVED: DATE OF ACTION: SIGNED: _____ COMMENTS:	☐ APPROVED ☐ PENDING ☐ REWORK ☐ REJECTED DATE RECEIVED: DATE OF ACTION: SIGNED: _____ COMMENTS:

| DESCRIPTION OF CHANGE: | NEED FOR CHANGE: |

Figure 10.13 TAGS also includes an Engineering Change Proposal facility for the logging of design requests.

6. *Page Resequence*, that renumbers pages to facilitate the insertion of a page between two others.

7. *SPPD Resequence*, that renumbers predefined process diagrams to enable insertion while modifying the other IORL sections to accommodate these changes.

Configuration Management.   Once a system design has reached an advanced level of maturity through the use of the Storage and Retrieval Program, the Diagnostic Analyzer, and the Analysis Library tools, it can be taken out of *draft issue* (in the ident field: ISSUE:D) and put under Configuration Management. Once this occurs, problems such as design changes and oversights must be reported using a *Trouble Report*. Upon approval, the Trouble Report becomes the basis for an *Engineering Change Proposal*. This in turn motivates the dispatching of a similar form called the *Specification Change Notice Request*. All of these forms, along with the management structure for controlling maintenance, are available within the Configuration Management package (see Figure 10.12 for the Engineering Change Proposal frame). Once under Configuration Management, maintenance to the

Figure 10.14   A Simulation Compiler is used to "execute" the design on a trial basis.

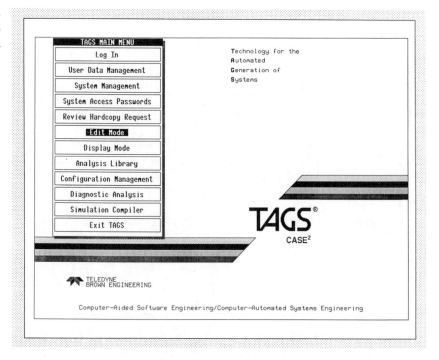

design documentation is very closely controlled through an automated management system such that arbitrary or disruptive changes are prohibited.

System Simulation. Although the Diagnostic Analyzer provides for static checks, the detection of certain errors, such as timing faults and race conditions, require the design to be executed. This is performed through the TAGS Simulation Compiler, in which realistic data values can be input or generated for an accurate simulation of system processing to uncover dynamic error types. Figure 10.14 shows the Simulation Compiler Menu, a large portion of which is devoted to building/manipulating *blueprints*, which describe subsets of the system for the Simulation Compiler to execute. These blueprints must first run successfully through the Diagnostic Analyzer.

The Simulation Compiler provides a system performance analysis in the form of a detailed execution trace. This execution is redundant to the target system code, providing the means for verifying the test-case output once the target code is written. Prior to this, the Simulation Compiler trace aids

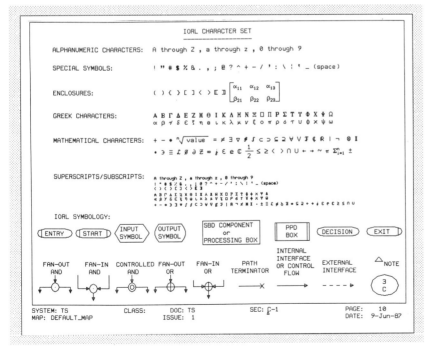

Figure 10.15 TAGS/ IORL Character Set and Symbols.

the designers by providing I/O event information, interface variable values, processing values, and control flow information. The Simulation Compiler interface also enables the building and exporting of the simulation model, which is built in Ada. Smaller systems may be compiled on a minicomputer workstation, and large complex designs may be exported to a larger target machine (e.g., DEC VAX) for compilation.

Summary.   Figure 10.15 summarizes the IORL character set and symbology. Although rich in abstraction capabilities, the IORL language does not have an overabundance of symbology. The Fan-in/out AND and OR and the Controlled AND symbols support a full range of parallel and concurrent processing specification. Experience has shown that two days of intensive training can enable mature designers to begin using TAGS/IORL, and one week of training with laboratory sessions provides a comprehensive knowledge of TAGS/IORL capabilities, even for the novice designer.

The dynamic nature of TAGS/IORL is clearly seen by the innovations that have been made over the past two years, culminating with the recent release of the Sim-Compiler. The continued development of the Sim-Compiler will ultimately result in the automatic generation of production-quality code. At the same time, however, the IORL language itself is evolving to a higher level, taking advantage of reusable macros and predefined process diagrams.

Summary

As summarized in Figure 10.16 this chapter has presented two well-focused, specialized CASE tools, one for constructing Warnier-Orr diagrams and the other for designing real-time systems. Brackets is an excellent tool that provides a low-cost ($695 at this writing) entry point into computer-aided software engineering. Although it may not be appropriate for designing large software systems, it certainly allows the designer to flesh out the initial ideas and concepts for an application. If your organization's budget is limited or you still have doubts about the practicality of CASE tools and methodologies, then PC-based tools like Brackets provide an excellent vehicle for technology exploration.

TAGS, on the other hand, is definitely a tool for building complex, sophisticated real-time systems and is robust enough to take the designer from project conception all the way through implementation. While several of the design specification tools highlighted in the previous chapter incorporate Ward and Mellor data flow diagram extensions for real-time systems, TAGS' simulation facility is particularly unique among the present state-of-the-art CASE tools. TAGS is one of the few tools focusing exclusively on real-time system development.

BRACKETS Optima, Inc.	Warnier-Orr diagrams Data structure diagrams Program organization diagrams COBOL data structure generation COBOL procedure generation
TAGS/IORL Teledyne Brown Engineering	Schematic block diagrams Real-time timing diagrams Data structure diagrams Code generation (ADA) System simulation Configuration management

Figure 10.16 Summary of Specialized Design Tools.

Both Brackets and TAGS generate code, an increasingly popular trend in CASE tools. In particular, Brackets treats designs, whether for data structures or programs, as a Warnier-Orr diagram hierarchy. This makes it very easy to generate code because the program structure and subroutine calls are already in place. Brackets also incorporates useful programming constructs such as iteration, selection, and recursion, which are similarly easy to generate.

The previous two chapters have concentrated on requirements analysis and design specification tools for specifying data flow, algorithmic, and control information. These tools all focused on the internal aspects of the application's operation. The next chapter turns away from the algorithmic and the procedural and toward the declarative and interactive part of application programming—the aesthetics of user interface design.

Chapter 11

User Interface Design Tools

*Pay no attention to
the man behind
the curtain!*
— The Wizard in *The
Wizard of Oz*

The previous two chapters dealt with general purpose analysis and design-oriented CASE tools. These tools work well for specifying a software application's function, and they are especially well suited for designing its internal architecture. This chapter deals with user interface design tools, a much more focused class of tools.

The nature of user interface tools is changing. In the past, they were used to mock up interfaces late in the requirements analysis state or early in the design specification stage. Now, because of the popularity of the personal computer and the new interface developments stemming from this platform, interface tools are leading the requirements analysis efforts. The user interface is becoming the *key* design component for most applications. Users now demand high quality interfaces, elevating the importance and necessity of interface design tools.

Graphically oriented by nature, user interface design tools allow analysts and software engineers to interactively *lay out* and edit user interfaces. Several provide *simulation* facilities for emulating the user-machine interaction, which gives end-users quick turnaround designs they can critique without the necessity of implementing the underlying code. Once the layout is finished, many user interface tools are capable of *generating* compilable code implementing the interface. These automatically generated interfaces are generally of two types. The first, which is common in form layout tools, is a series of user interface definition files accessed at run-time by a module that executes or interprets the interface definitions. The run-time module is linked with the application program code as part of the final executable program.

The second type of interface generator, common among tools producing window-based and graphical interfaces, generates application callable subroutines and data structures. In this metaphor, there is usually one or a small number of subroutines the application programmer must interface with. Much like the YACC parser generator described in Chapter 8, the design tool generates compilable code. The application program calls the entry point subroutine which passes control to the interface processing code. The generated interface code handles the screen display and user input, and when finished, control returns back to the calling application program routine.

Dan Bricklin's Demo Program

Dan Bricklin, the author of the original VisiCalc spreadsheet program, has created Dan Bricklin's Demo Program (Bricklin), a package which allows software designers to mock up IBM Personal Computer user interface screens. These mocked-up screens provide a very efficient means for specifying a user interface. A Bricklin mock-up is a set of screens, called "slides" in Bricklin's terminology, which can be linked together by a set of "keyboard handlers," allowing certain keystrokes to move from one screen to another in a slide-show fashion. This interactive slide show gives the impression of an implemented, working interface, even though it is only a mock-up.

The IBM PC has two modes, text and graphics. Bricklin allows interface designers to mock up *text-mode* interfaces only, although graphics screens can be included but not directly edited. In text mode, a set of 256 ASCII characters are is available, including 128 extended ASCII characters containing line and corner characters that are used for drawing window borders.

Bricklin has two modes, "edit" and "run." When in edit mode, the software designer can draw lines and boxes (with the extended character set), write text, and color regions to mock up user interface screens. The interface designer has the full IBM PC screen as his easel. The cursor pad keys are used to move around the screen, and text or other characters can be placed anywhere on the screen simply by typing the text. There are special function key commands for placing

Figure 11.1 Overlays Using Dan Bricklin's Demo Program. Dan Bricklin's Demo Program is an interactive screen layout design program for IBM PC applications. Individual screens are composed of overlays of other screen components. These screens can be "linked" together using "keyboard handlers" in a slide-show fashion to simulate the actual working application.

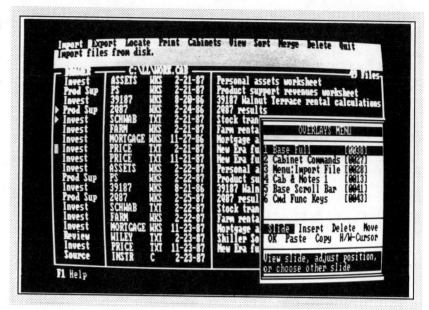

rectangular windows onscreen and for changing the screen attribute color of any individual character of group of characters. Bricklin commands themselves are accessed through pop-up menus which temporarily overlay part of the screen.

Screens can be composed of overlays that are other screens containing atomic user interface components. For example, an application program's screen may be the union of several overlay slides representing different windows and their contents. This gives the interface designer flexibility in composing sequences of screens. Figure 11.1 shows an example of overlaying technique.

The software designer can also specify certain keystrokes ("handlers") to move from one slide screen to the next when Bricklin is in run mode. In run mode, the user presses these predefined keystrokes to move from one interface screen to the next, giving the feeling of actually running the program. This rapid prototyping feature allows the software designer to go through many design iterations—and user feedback—before actually committing the user interface to code. Bricklin even has the capability to beep in several different tones and to make the disk drive spin in order to simulate a disk access from the mocked-up program!

Dan Bricklin's Demo Program does not generate software directly from this "slide-show" specification. However, there is an auxiliary product called C-scape (see Appendix A, *"User Interface Design Tools"*) that will generate software based on the screens built using Dan Bricklin's Demo Program. The C-scape system consists of two components that can be used individually or together. Look and Feel is a WYSIWYG (what-you-see-is-what-you-get) screen designer and code generator that allows the interface designer to interactively build data entry, menu, text, and other screens without writing any code. When the design is complete, Look and Feel automatically generates C code and the accompanying data structure declarations. Look and Feel will import screens created with Bricklin.

The second component of the C-scape system is a subroutine library of functions for data entry and field validation, windows, menus, text, and help screens. This subroutine library is not a CASE tool per se, but it does illustrate the common practice among user interface development tools of providing both a WYSIWYG design facility as well as a traditional subroutine package.

Microsoft Windows Dialog Box Editor

Microsoft Windows is a user interface environment for the IBM PC and PS/2 systems. The new IBM Presentation Manager, not yet released at the time of this writing, is visually compatible with Microsoft Windows. The Windows package itself is a subroutine library with over 400 individual subroutines. By using Microsoft Windows, application programs can achieve a standard look and feel that is the same among all Windows-based applications. This substantially reduces the learning curve for users of Windows applications.

Application program interfaces under Windows contain several components, such as windows, pull-down menus, and dialog boxes (Figure 11.2). Windows are rectangular display areas where text and graphics are displayed. The contents of a particular window is highly dependent on the nature of the application. A spreadsheet program would display a row and column spreadsheet in a window, while a CAD (computer-aided design) program might display a schematic. Pull-down menus contain all of the application program's commands, a command metaphor consistent from application to application. Other user input is entered via dialog boxes. Dialog boxes are used to enter file names, select application program options, and enter small amounts of text through a Windows-provided text editor. For example, selecting a command from a pull-down menu might cause a dialog box to pop up to gather further user input.

Each of these interface components—windows, menus, and dialog boxes—are called *resources* in Windows terminology. Resources for each application program are defined in an ASCII text file called a resource file. The resource file is a separate part of the application program, and the resources are made available to the application program by running the resource file through the Resource Compiler. Windows then knows how to access and use the program's resource declarations. In fact, application programmers can decide when a resource is to be loaded into memory during program execution.

Figure 11.2 Microsoft Windows Dialog Box Editor. The Dialog Box Editor is an interactive graphical layout editor for designing and generating "pop-up" dialog boxes. The Dialog Box Editor automatically produces executable code for these interface components that can be directly linked into and called from the application program.

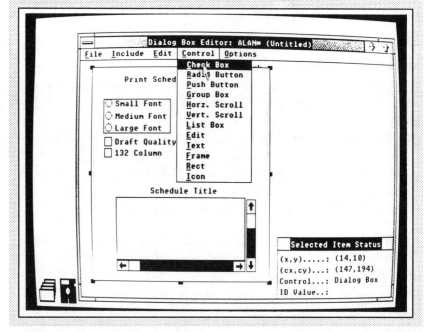

The advantage of a separate resource file is that resources become more manageable. Resource declarations are much simpler in form and syntax than application program code. Modifying a resource is a simple matter of editing the resource file with a text editor and recompiling with the Resource Compiler. No actual program source code has to be modified. There is nothing magical about resources—they are simply data objects. Windows applications can also create each type of resource at run-time via subroutine calls rather than through resource file descriptions.

However, writing a text description of a graphical resource object leaves something to be desired. The application programmer would rather interactively lay out the resource on-screen using a graphical editing program and then automatically generate the resource file when the editing is complete. For this reason, Windows includes the Dialog Box Editor as part of the Windows Developer's Tool Kit. This Dialog Box Editor allows application programmers to graphically lay out dialog boxes, the most complex type of display resource in the Windows environment.

The Dialog Box Editor can help the interface designer develop many dialog box components, including borders, text, check boxes, radio buttons, and scroll bars and size boxes for enabling the application programmer's user to adjust the size and shape of the dialog box once it appears during the course of program execution.

The Dialog Box Editor is the first step in having an interactive interface design and layout facility for Windows. Unfortunately, at this writing, the Dialog Box Editor does *not* allow for the creation of window and menu resources. This must be done outside of the Dialog Box Editor by editing the resource file containing the dialog box definitions generated by the Dialog Box Editor. Fortunately, Windows application programs can have multiple resource files, enabling the programmer to separate the interactively designed and automatically generated dialog boxes created using the Dialog Box Editor from the manually created windows and menus.

In Microsoft Windows there are two types of resource files: *.RC* Resource Script files for windows and menus, and *.DLG*

Dialog Box Resource files (Figure 11.3). Both are ASCII text files that when compiled, produce *.RES* Binary Resource Files which are linked into the application program. In operation, the Dialog Box Editor directly edits a *.RES* binary resource file, or creates one if a new set of resources is being created. When the programmer completes the dialog box editing, the .RES binary resource file is saved and a new *.DLG* dialog box resource file is created. The .DLG dialog box resource file is a text file containing the dialog box resource definitions just like the *.RC* file contains text descriptions of the other objects in the interface: windows, menus, and so on. The programmer can, of course, create and edit a .DLG dialog box resource using a text editor instead of the Dialog Box Editor.

JYACC FORMAKER

JYACC, Inc. is a New York City based computer consulting firm established in 1978 that markets two products for

Figure 11.3 Microsoft Windows provides two methods for developing dialog boxes: manually editing a dialog box resource file, which is then compiled; and using an interactive graphical layout editor, which automatically generates executable code.

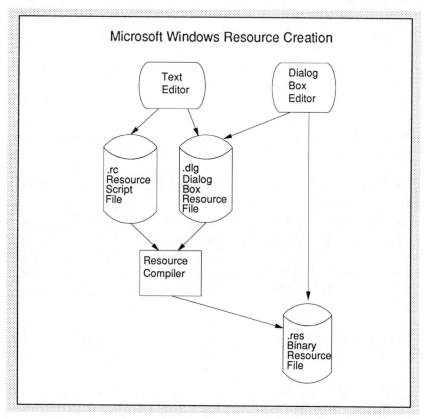

creating end-user interfaces. The first is JYACC FOR-
MAKER, a screen and window manager for interactively
creating and editing screens for application programs. FOR-
MAKER comes with subroutine library that allows the application program to "call up" screens and handle data entry. The
second product is the JYACC Application Manager (JAM), an
enhanced version of FORMAKER, which allows the application designer to specify the control logic that links screens and
windows to form an application interface. Both products run
on a variety of platforms, including the IBM PC, the Sun,
Apollo, and DEC VAX mini-computer workstations.

FORMAKER. FORMAKER is interactive, allowing the
screen designer to view the form or window as it evolves.
Configuration information, such as field display attributes, is
entered through pop-up windows. The FORMAKER library
subroutines handle all the keyboard and screen interactions,
relieving the application program from this burden. Application programs treat screen data like file data (i.e. like data
structures) and need not concern themselves with cursor
movement or field validation. Because JAM and FORMAKER
are designed to operation on a diverse set of hardware platforms and operating environments, the input operations have
been generalized so that individual keystrokes can be bound
to each operation separately in each unique environment.

For instance, the following is a subset of these generalized
operations:

<TRANSMIT>	Submit the form for processing.
<EXIT>	Abort the current form without processing.
<HELP>	Display a help screen or message
<TAB>	Move the cursor to the next form field.
<BACKTAB>	Move the cursor to the previous unprotected field.
<PFn>	Alters an application's control flow by signaling an event.

The ModKey utility is used to map the physical keys, which
vary from machine to machine, to the logical values that JAM
and FORMAKER understand.

FORMAKER itself has two modes, *draw* and *test*, much like
Dan Bricklin's Demo Program, discussed earlier in this chapter. The interface designer can toggle between the two modes

using a function key. In draw mode, the designer has full-screen editing capability and uses special pop-up field creation menus, invoked from a function key, to define field properties. The designer enters test mode by pressing the "test/draw" function key, allowing the designer to move from field to field, entering data just as an end-user would. The input fields behave exactly as specified with the configuration information. Figure 11.4 shows a mailing list form being interactively designed. The pop-up menus illustrate the types of properties assignable to individual fields.

The fields themselves can assume a wide range of properties ranging from simple display attribute information (foreground and background color) to word wrap in text fields. Fields can be designated as "protected" or "must fill." Protected fields are for display only and cannot be altered by user input. Must-fill fields must be filled by the user before the form can be processed. Fields can also be "arrays": consisting of multiple input lines, they are ideal for tables and lists. Two other interesting field properties are:

Shiftable   Input data, usually character strings such as names, can be longer than the field width

Figure 11.4 JYACC FORMAKER is an interactive form layout and editing tool. Individual field characteristics are defined via a series of pop-up menus. The function keys shown at the bottom of the screen toggle between *draw* and *test* modes and invoke the various field definition menus.

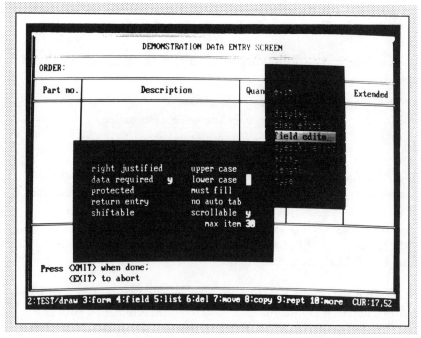

actually displayed on the form. When user input starts to exceed the field width, the field entry scrolls left.

Scrollable   Input data, such as lists, can have more lines than are actually displayed on the form. When the user is ready to input a line not visible on the form, the lines scroll up or down to reveal the next input line.

Fields can also have "attachments," such as an indicator of the next field to move the cursor to once the current field has been input. The "help screen" is also a useful field attachment and can be automatically displayed upon entry to a field or called only on demand when the user presses the help key. Help screens are usually pop-up paragraphs of text that overlay some portion of the form. Forms can, of course, be designed so they always reserve a portion of the screen for an automatically overlaid help screen. Another type of attachment is the application-defined field validation subroutine. This allows application programmers to construct fields of their own type. FORMAKER will automatically call the supplied validation routine to verify the entered data.

FORMAKER can automatically calculate field values based on the values input in other fields. This is much like defining a cell's formula in a spreadsheet program that automatically calculates the cell value based on a formula which references other cell values. For example, a telemarketing group might use a data entry form for logging information requests where a follow-up call date is automatically calculated based on the current date. Fields can be assigned symbolic names, like "current_date" and "follow_up_date," so the calculation might look like the following:

```
follow_up = @Date current_date + 30
```

The *@Date current_date* means interpret the value of the "current_date" field as a date; "+ *30*" means add 30 days to the current date to generate the follow-up date.

Once a form's design is complete, FORMAKER automatically creates C language data structures for each form in the application. These data structures are passed back and forth between the application program and the FORMAKER run-time library routines that handle the keyboard input and output display mechanics. The FORMAKER run-time library fills in the form's data structure with the values entered by the end-user and returns the structure back to the application program. Figure 11.5 shows the C language data structure for the mailing list form in Figure 11.4.

Notice that the designer specified several symbolic names, such as "follow_up" for use in the follow-up date calculation. FORMAKER automatically generated the other field names. Forms can also be "listed" in a human-readable ASCII text file format. List files contain renditions of the forms plus the configuration information for each form field: the display attribute, size, and other properties.

JYACC Application Manager (JAM). JAM, an enhanced version of FORMAKER, is a user interface editor with authoring tools for creating windows and screens. As a prototyping environment, JAM allows nonprogrammers to easily create screens, windows, and menus, and the control logic linking them together. Interface designers can build several prototypes and make modifications on the spot, making it easy to work with end-user groups. When the interface "shell" is complete, an application programmer must, of course, supply the routines that process the information entered onto the

Figure 11.5 JYACC FORMAKER Data Structure. FORMAKER will automatically generate C language data structures (in header file format) for inclusion into application programs. This structure is for the data entry form in Figure 11.4. Field 4 is a shiftable field of 51 characters; fields 6, 7, and 8 are scrollable fields of 10 lines each.

```
struct maillist
{
        char                    name[26];
        char                    date[17];
        unsigned int            _fld3;
        char                    _fld4[51];
        char                    address[3][30];
        char                    hardware[10][19];
        char                    operating_system[10][19];
        char                    languages[10][19];
        char                    follow_up[13];
};
```

forms and menus. Nevertheless, a large amount of the design and implementation work can be accomplished by nonprogrammers or those with human factors training.

JAM and FORMAKER run in a variety of different computing environments. Applications run and look the same on microcomputer and minicomputer systems, meaning that prototypes or entire applications can be developed on one system and then transferred to others.

JAM incorporates an integrated Data Dictionary and Data Dictionary Editor. The Data Dictionary includes the named data elements used in an application's interface and maintains the length, data type, and current value of each element. Data elements can be accessed at run-time using JAM library functions. A JAM run-time module is linked into the application program that performs the form and screen management during program execution. The JAM package also contains application-callable interface library functions.

Part 4

Managing CASE Technology

Chapter 12

A View From On Top

This chapter describes the computer-aided software engineering market. It examines the different categories of tool consumers, the different tool, training, and services vendors, and the marketing strategies and directions these vendors are likely to follow.

The characteristics exhibited by the CASE market as a whole are reminiscent of the markets created by similar software innovations such as data bases and expert systems. First, the market is pioneered by a few full-service companies which establish themselves by performing substantial amounts of "missionary selling," the process of forming and educating a market that must occur before any sales can be made into the new market. These companies emphasize training and support in addition to their software technology. As the market expands, a group of second-tier companies selling only software products appears on the scene. Finally, a market shake-out eliminates the less hardy firms, leaving the emerging market leaders in a stable market. At this writing, the full-service companies have established themselves, and the second-tier companies are starting to emerge. These trends and others are described in the following sections which explore the vendors and the consumers of CASE technology.

No attempt is made to determine which strategies are best and will prevail in the marketplace. Readers wishing more detailed market information may wish to consult one of the research reports assembled by the various market research firms (see Appendix C) specializing in computer software markets.

Character Traits of CASE Tool Users

On the whole, there is no single type of CASE tool user. They vary widely by type of organization, application development

People who like this sort of thing will find this the sort of thing they like.
— Abraham Lincoln

speciality, and computing equipment base. No matter what type, though, the highest leverage consumers of CASE tool technology are those organizations that perceive information as an asset. Such organizations employ staffs of software professionals to develop systems to collect, store, process, and analyze that information. We might expect these characteristics to be inherent in smaller, more agile organizations, but they are evident in larger data processing departments as well. Regardless of size, these are companies that see themselves as technological leaders and are willing to be the early adopters of important new technologies in order to retain their technological (and often financial) lead over their competitors.

The strategic objective for organizations is to build applications more quickly with less staff and with lower risk.

In particular, these organizations have already adopted structured methodologies, such as Structured Analysis (data flow diagrams), structure charts, and data modeling (entity-relationship diagrams), in order to standardize their software development practices. They are now ideally positioned to take advantage of design-oriented CASE tools, since after all, they are simply moving from a paper-based representation to an on-line, interactively edited representation.

A second common theme is the adoption of personal computers and engineering workstations within the software development groups. The graphics-intensive, highly interactive, tools demand more "individualized" hardware platforms. Organizations with large installed bases of personal computers and engineering workstations are well positioned to install CASE tools; the hardware base is already present and the organization has a *cultural bias* toward working in an individualized, interactive environment.

In summary, those organizations ideally positioned to introduce CASE technology exhibit the following character traits:

1. Institutional commitment to structured design methodologies.

2. Installed base of personal computers and engineering workstations.

3. Cultural bias toward working in an individualized, interactive environment.

You should scrutinize your organization in light of these characteristics when attempting to introduce CASE technology. Although none of these characteristics are mandatory requirements, their absence may be indicative of change that must take place before CASE technology can be successfully introduced. Chapter 13, "Introducing CASE into Your Organization," describes in more detail how to achieve organizational acceptance of CASE.

Major Consumers of CASE Technology

There are many different ways to dissect the computer-aided software engineering market. One simple cut is to examine the major categories of tool consumers and assess their progress in assimilating this new technology. At this writing, there are three major markets for CASE tools:

- Military contractors
- Corporate data processing department information centers
- Commercial software houses

Fundamentally, there is no real differentiation between these groups and how they use CASE technology. There is, however, a difference in how fast they have integrated this technology into their software development practices.

Military Contractors. Of these three markets, the military contractors have been the most willing to embrace CASE technology. In particular, the Department of Defense has identified the key issue of improving the quality and reliability of *mission critical software*, software required for proper equipment operation and the successful completion of missions. Military contractors have been very receptive to design-oriented CASE tools, due largely to the Department of Defense's adoption of DOD-STD-2167 as the standard guideline for mission critical software specification. By mandating all system requirements be traceable to the software and from the software modules back to the requirements specification, DOD-STD-2167's traceability requirements force most military contractors to utilize structured techniques. In large software systems, this chore is a very tedious, time-consuming task, forcing contractors to adopt computer-aided techniques. These tools generally implement structured methodologies capable of aggregating successive levels of design, such as data flow diagrams and structure charts.

Military contracting organizations are well positioned to adopt CASE technology. Because of the large engineering design activities inherent in military contracting companies, engineering workstations were quick to appear, putting in place the infrastructure needed to support the graphically oriented CASE tools. Military contractors never centralized around large mainframe computers for their engineering work in the same way that commercial software establishments have. Engineering design work is not transaction-oriented like commercial applications, so large, high-throughput machines were never required. The acceptance of CASE tools was almost a foregone conclusion because of their appeal to software engineering teams.

Corporate Information Centers.   Early in their development, commercial data processing shops and information centers centralized both their software development and production operations around large mainframe computers supporting many terminal connections. Because of the vast amount of input/output communication required to support a large number of users, the software applications running on these hardware platforms were structured to work in a *transaction*-oriented environment in order to off-load the central processing unit. These operating environment constraints make it difficult to field highly interactive graphical applications like CASE tools without seriously degrading the entire machine's performance.

Transaction applications programs typically send a screen form to the receiving terminal where the requested information is filled in and edited locally by the end-user before being transmitted back to the mainframe computer. While termed "interactive," these applications lack the same degree of interaction that is typical on personal computers and minicomputer workstations where the operating environments can support character-at-a-time I/O and frequent hardware interrupts from pointing devices such as mice. Most mainframe I/O equipment does not support character-at-a-time (asynchronous) I/O.

These interactive I/O and graphical display constraints have hindered CASE technology in gaining acceptance in the corporate data processing world. However, the popularity of personal computers has greatly diminished this problem, and CASE tool usage is on the rise. Several vendors are offering tools supporting micro-to-mainframe links so that central project data bases, such as a data dictionary, can be stored on a mainframe accessible by all, while the actual graphics editing is performed on a personal computer. The mainframe computer becomes the central project repository.

Commercial Software Houses. A high-leverage CASE technology consumer group is commercial software developers whose very existence depends on its ability to design, develop, and maintain software products for end-users. These software development houses are attracted to CASE technology because of its inherent ability to help them build high-quality, relatively problem-free software products. To date, few commercial software houses have adopted CASE technology in any meaningful way, a case of the cobbler's children going without shoes. Most software houses are small organizations of under 200 people. They typically fall under great pressure to continually revise and adapt their products to an ever-changing marketplace, leaving little time to plan and adopt a CASE technology assimilation program.

This, of course, will change over time, especially as the demand escalates for increasingly complex and feature-robust applications software. Commercial software houses are likely to adopt focused CASE tools such as user interface generators. For example, the Microsoft Windows/Presentation Manager environments and the Apple Macintosh windowing system have placed a substantial user interface burden on the software developer. No longer is a lean user interface acceptable. It must be thoughtfully conceived and well designed, feature rich, and so friendly that it has become *de rigueur* for end-users to expect to learn a program's operation without reading any documentation. The application can no longer display a simple screen, read the input data values, and move on to the next screen; end-users now expect to control the human-computer interaction by selecting which screen to view.

Increasingly, application developers are being required to interface with other software applications using a growing number of standards. On IBM personal computers, it is common to support the Lotus 1-2-3 and Ashton-Tate dBASE III file formats, the PostScript printing language, and the clipboard and Rich Text Interfaces under Microsoft Windows. An entire niche of CASE companies may spring up offering packages that help developers glue their applications to these interfaces. Already several vendors are offering subroutine library packages that access dBASE and Lotus files. The next step is the development of interactive CASE facilities.

Major Vendors in the CASE Market

Evaluating the different types of vendors is another way to examine the computer-aided software engineering market. How vendors orient themselves, their products, and their services has a tremendous bearing on the market, which strongly influences the types of products offered and the market segments encouraged to use CASE. Today the CASE market is composed of four major vendor groups offering products and services:

- Analysis and design tool vendors
- Focused tool vendors
- Software training companies
- Consulting practice companies

There is characteristic overlap between these vendor groups, especially among the mainstream tool vendors and the training companies, and among the training companies and the consulting practice companies. Many tool vendors offer introductory and advanced computer-aided software engineering courses as do the consulting practice companies, for example.

Analysis and Design Tool Vendors. It is difficult to characterize software tool vendors because of the diversity of their products and marketing positions. Each company positions itself differently with respect to its competitors, differentiations which are frequently subtle. For example, several vendors, such as Nastec Corporation, emphasize the ability to integrate their tools with other software, enabling their customers to extend the tool or even add in or develop new methodologies. Other vendors, such as ProMod and Iconix, emphasize automatic code generation from the data flow diagram and structure chart designs built using their tools. However, with these differences in mind, there appears to be three tiers of tool vendors:

- Full-service, market leader companies
- Major, well-known companies with CASE products
- Small, software-only companies

The first group of tool vendors are the full-service, CASE-only companies such as CADRE Technologies, Index Technology Corporation, and Nastec Corporation. Their only business is building, marketing, and supporting CASE tools. These companies tend to offer fairly good training for their tools and provide better product support than do the large companies with many diverse software products. The support services, however, vary from vendor to vendor and can range from product support through extensive application consulting. To date, these companies have focused almost entirely on Structured Analysis, structured design, and data modeling tools.

Several CASE tool vendors provide a mix of tools and application consulting. Optima, Inc. (formerly Ken Orr & Associates) is a good example of a tool vendor that provides extensive application consulting services along with hosting CASE seminars and user-group meetings throughout the year at locations across the United States. In many respects, Optima can be viewed as a training company that offers software tools.

Major, well-known companies such as Tektronix, Texas Instruments, and Teledyne constitute a second group of CASE tool vendors which have developed and are marketing computer-aided software engineering products in addition to their many other products. CASE tools, however, are not the major thrust of these companies' businesses. These large companies appear to be seeding the ground for future major markets. They fully expect many of these "seed" products in various industries to wither on the vine and not develop into profitable businesses. However, the ones that do grow and mature will offer major opportunities to these companies looking to expand beyond their traditional "cash cow" businesses.

The third group is the smaller, software-tool-only companies. These companies generally entered the market after the full-service companies and are not as well financed. Typically, they compete on price and do not offer training or support services as companion products. However, for organizations well along on the structured methodology learning curve, these tools may be very appropriate and save considerable amounts of money for organizations making multiple copy purchases.

Focused Tool Vendors. "Focused" tools are strongly oriented toward particular tasks, such as user interface design and source code organization and control. These tools are not oriented toward more *general* requirements analysis and design specification tasks, and although they play a very important part in the requirements analysis and design specification phases of the software life cycle, many such vendors do not perceive themselves as being CASE tool vendors. Rather, they see themselves as user interface tool vendors or simply as "software tool" vendors, a perception which will change (in fact, it is already changing) as these vendors realize there is marketing leverage in positioning themselves as CASE tool vendors. Look for this trend to cause considerable confusion until the markets and technologies stabilize and a well-accepted definition of computer-aided software engineering is adopted.

Software Training Companies. Companies specializing in professional development and training for software professionals are, at this writing, starting to field seminars and courses emphasizing CASE tools. Structured methodology courses have been a staple offering available for years from these companies, but most of the newer CASE courses teach the attendee the popular structured methodologies in addition to providing hands-on exposure to several different CASE tools. Courses of this nature, which range from three to five days in length, provide an excellent introduction to the fundamentals of computer-aided software engineering as well as impart a practical understanding of what can be accomplished with today's software tools.

Consulting Practice Companies. Consulting practice companies, such as Arthur Andersen, Arthur Young, and American Management Systems, develop or assist in developing applications on a custom basis for their clients. The services provided by these consulting companies usually include requirements analysis and design specification as well as implementation services, depending on the client's needs. Several of these companies have developed proprietary methodologies and companion CASE tools to speed application development. These tools and methodologies are not available to the general public.

Marketing Strategies and Directions

Major Vendors are Evident. Certain software tool vendors are readily identified as "CASE tool vendors," such as Cadre Technologies, Index Technology Corporation, KnowledgeWare Inc., and Nastec Corporation, although many others are becoming identified with the market. Interestingly enough, the tools developed by these market leaders all implement the Structured Analysis methodology and share many other characteristics. These market leaders promote their products in approximately the same manner through direct sales forces and encourage site license purchases by providing substantial quantity discounts for volume purchases. They emphasize the "full-service" strategy, stressing tool training and product support as key components of their product offerings.

Popular Methodologies Emphasized. Because computer-aided software engineering is, for the most part, an *evolutionary* technology rather than a revolutionary technology, vendor marketing strategies and directions have been fairly predictable. Since many of these tools are based on pencil and paper methodologies, there is a ready-made market in upgrading organizations already using these methodologies to computerized versions. This partially explains why vendors have implemented methodologies developed in the 1960s and 1970s. These methodologies have withstood the test of time on major projects in many development organizations.

Most of the commercially popular tools from companies commonly identified with the CASE industry implement the Yourdon/DeMarco Structured Analysis methodology, which uses multileveled data flow diagrams as the central design technique.

Many of the popular structured design methodologies, such as Structured Analysis (data flow diagrams), various mini-specification techniques, and structure charts, have been implemented in CASE tool form. These tools are, without exception, graphically oriented and typically run on IBM PCs, Apple Macintoshes, and minicomputer workstations like the Sun, Apollo, and VAX systems. These methodologies have proven successful in large software projects and will provide even more leverage now that they are software-based.

In addition to Structured Analysis, these tools frequently provide other methodologies, such as entity-relationship diagrams and Warnier-Orr diagrams.

Success Stories are Evident. The wide availability of personal computers and engineering workstations has enabled this technology to spread quickly. Many of the "major" tool vendors have large client lists and a variety of client software projects that have used their tools successfully. For example, Nastec Corporation boasts 8000 licenses of its DesignAid tool. Vendors are able to develop and sell their tools at prices attractive enough for most software development organizations to "buy in" to the technology.

Focused Tools are Appearing. Many software tool vendors are now jumping on the CASE bandwagon as a convenient marketing mechanism to give their products the cachet of being on the cutting edge of technology. Vendors of focused tools, user interface design tools for example, are slowly realizing that they are players in the CASE market and are moving to take advantage. These companies are well positioned in the short term because of their products' readily identifiable benefits. For example, most software developers realize that the user interface, if present, is a major component of any software application. The benefits of using a user interface generation tool are clear after even a brief demonstration, since working code can be automatically generated directly from the screen designs in many of these tools.

Automatic Code Generation is Coming.   Many Structured Analysis tools provide program design language facilities (for building mini-specifications) that assist in producing compilable code. ADA language templates for these program design languages are common, and other tools, such as data modeling tools, generate COBOL data structures.

Automatic code generation, discussed in greater detail in Chapter 15, is the crux of computer-aided software engineering technology. Without code generation, CASE will never reach its full potential. After all, the goal is to reduce the inherent risk in coding (and the drudgery) by focusing on the neglected development cycle phases of requirements analysis and design specification.

Chapter 13

Introducing CASE into Your Organization

He who hesitates is sometimes saved.
— James Thurber

Introducing a new technology into an organization is a very difficult process, regardless of the payoff in improved efficiency and increased earnings or reduced costs. Computer-aided software engineering is no different. Organizations are fundamentally resistant to change, especially with technologies like CASE that mandate a new way of performing an existing task (software development). *"If it ain't broke, don't fix it!"* is a frequently invoked saw when dealing with an evolutionary technology that improves a process rather than introduces something completely new.

This chapter presents an overview of the technology assimilation process and discusses criteria for selecting a tool vendor and for choosing a first project on which to apply CASE technology. This chapter also introduces the "construction crew approach" for organizing and managing development projects using CASE technology. CASE emphasizes requirements analysis and design specification while deemphasizing traditional coding and implementation, and with the pressure to "cut code" as soon as possible, organizations must recalibrate their expectations because of the changes CASE makes to the traditional development process.

The key to any organization's assimilation of new technology is the presence of a vocal *champion* for the technology. Organizations by themselves often suffer from inertia, and they need a motivating force to redirect their focus. The road for the technology champion can be long and arduous, depending on the support of the champion's management and the organization's willingness to understand and acquire CASE technology. As later sections in this chapter point out, the assimilation process is frequently political, adding an increased burden to our champion beyond merely proving that CASE technology is superior to the organization's current development methods. Hopefully, this chapter will serve as a navigational beacon for budding CASE technology champions.

The CASE Technology Assimilation Process

The political environment of many technological organizations sometimes resembles the perils of a Dungeons and Dragons™ adventure game. People in technological organizations tend to harbor technological prejudices, usually based on sound past experience. In addition, if the current procedures and policies are working, management is bound to respond in the negative. You, as a technology champion, must convince your management that by using CASE technology, you can increase the organization's productivity beyond its present level.

Positioning CASE technology for widespread use and selecting particular tools and methodologies requires a lengthy and potentially risky process of assimilation (Figure 13.1). The first three of the following steps, which are relatively straightforward and politically safe, are described in the following paragraphs. The remaining steps are treated in greater depth in the following sections because they represent a more difficult challenge to the technology champion.

1. A champion is born.
2. Education and understanding.
3. In-house tool evaluation.
4. Selection of a first project.
5. Use of tool on first project.
6. Evaluation of first project.
7. Preparation for larger projects.

A Champion is Born.   It is hard to pinpoint exactly when an individual becomes a supporter of a new technology. The seed may be planted after reading a few articles in the trade press. Maybe even reading this book has prompted you to

Figure 13.1 The Technology Assimilation Game. Championing a new software development technology like Computer-Aided Software Engineering can be fraught with risks.

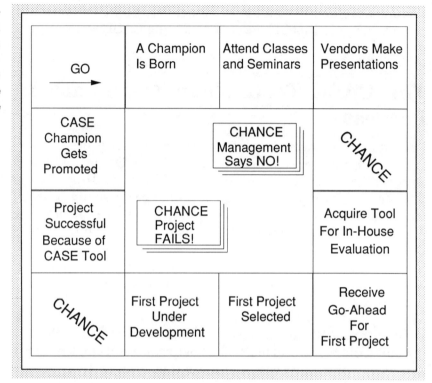

decide to champion the CASE technology cause! More likely, an individual slowly becomes an advocate as he or she becomes more educated about the technology and through countless hallway discussions (and a few debates) with colleagues (Figure 13.2).

Championing any new technology is a difficult task, even for a skilled organizational maneuverer. Management will always request hard, proven data to support your claims for this new technology's promise; and this is only rational. The first task is to gather information about successful projects using CASE tools in other companies or other development organizations within your own company. Most CASE tool vendors will be happy to furnish success stories of projects using their respective tools. The trade press is another source of success stories. Trade journals seldom enjoy printing failure stories; most articles emphasize the positive, successful elements of a new technology.

A second option is to persuade management to invest some time, money, and effort to investigate the technology. After

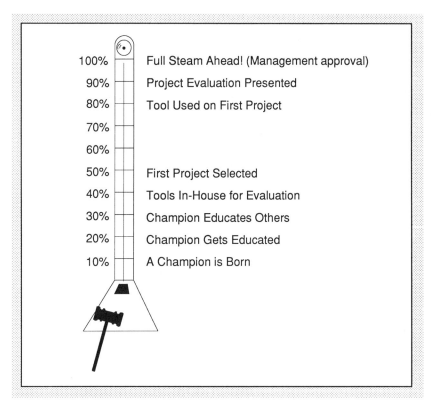

100%	Full Steam Ahead! (Management approval)
90%	Project Evaluation Presented
80%	Tool Used on First Project
70%	
60%	
50%	First Project Selected
40%	Tools In-House for Evaluation
30%	Champion Educates Others
20%	Champion Gets Educated
10%	A Champion is Born

Figure 13.2 Technology assimilation takes time and substantial effort. Rarely is it easy to introduce a new technology into an organization without careful planning and lots of education and training.

all, no software management group wants to be perceived as being a technology laggard. Most large organizations can spare one or two individuals on a study team investigation for several months. The larger the organization, the easier this option becomes and the more this exploratory time is perceived as an "investment." Individuals in smaller organizations must, of course, be prepared to invest some of their own personal time if a formal "investigative" assignment is not possible.

Education and Understanding. The education and understanding process occurs gradually over time. Champions start gradually, first reading about the technology and then taking a more active role in educating themselves. The first step is probably contacting a few vendors and requesting their product literature. The second step most likely is attending a local software engineering conference where CASE technology is being discussed. Finally, the champion may register for a specific, focused training course taught by a tool vendor or by a commercial training company. By this time, the champion has management's attention because training courses cost both time and money.

Suggest to your management that you take one or two training courses offered by the tool vendors or independent training companies. Also suggest you bring one or two tools in-house for evaluation by either yourself or someone politically neutral to CASE technology. Be careful, though, to select an opinion leader that your management will respect—an individual with a proven record and who has the requisite experience to carry out such an evaluation, and whose opinions and personality are not abrasive.

Another option is to hire an outside software consulting group with experience in CASE technology. These groups bring with them the collective experience of many different companies, software projects, and software project management styles. Sometimes managers are more apt to believe third party recommendations than their own personnel, and it is always sound counsel to seek an outside, nonpartisan opinion. Organizational outsiders do not bring with them the prejudices and conventional "wisdom" that may derail a sound technology assimilation program.

At this point, it is common for a technology champion to take a more assertive role in advocating CASE. The champion may give presentations to interested groups within the software development organization and to management. The champion may also invite CASE tool vendors to give presentations on their tools and the technology in general. This is part of the necessary internal selling process needed to convince others of the opportunity.

In-House Tool Evaluation.   Bringing a tool in-house for evaluation is the first step in the assimilation process that presents any real risk to both the champion and the development organization. The champion should be careful to select several tools for evaluation, not just one. A common mistake at this stage is to favor one vendor over the rest, and it is unlikely that the champion will understand the practical limitations of CASE technology well enough to recommend the "best" vendor. Remember, the goal of an in-house evaluation is to *educate* the organization, in addition to making a purchasing decision. That way, if one tool is not acceptable for some reason, the organization will not dismiss CASE as a fad. Rather, the organization will view the rejected tool as a package that did not meet the organization's needs because it lacked some capability. There are still other tools being evaluated that will fare better and may possess the requisite capabilities.

Plan to spend a month or so evaluating each tool. Spending this time in a detailed evaluation will make you much better prepared to make an informed purchasing decision. Once a likely candidate has been selected, prepare a detailed evaluation report for management. Remember to consider the business case behind the purchase. Most likely, you will be recommending a multicopy purchase, so the vendor's product training and support should be considered in addition to the strength of their tool's implementation. The next section examines the tool selection process in more detail.

Selecting the Right CASE Tools

Selecting a software tool is as much a process of establishing a vendor relationship as it is selecting a methodology or a tool. Unless your organization is very sophisticated, you will probably require help with training before the tool is installed and product support once the tool is in use. A little "hand holding" by knowledgeable trainers can substantially reduce the risk on your first project using CASE technology. Perhaps there is even the possibility you will require specialized consulting services to aid in your application's development (Figure 13.3).

There is probably no ideal CASE tool nor does one size fit all. Some CASE tools are general-purpose requirements analysis and design specification tools emphasizing data flow diagrams and structure charts. Others provide leverage in well-defined areas such as user interface design and data base report generation. The following questions are important issues to consider when analyzing CASE tools relative to your specific needs and requirements.

Figure 13.3 Selecting the Right CASE Tool. More than just the software products and technology must be considered when selecting a CASE tool. Organizations should also consider the vendor's product training and support services.

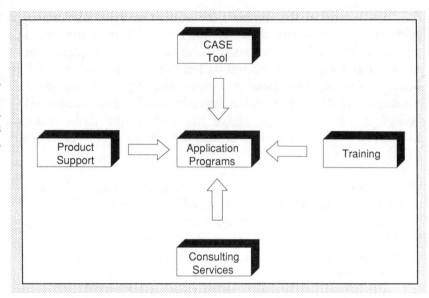

One size doesn't fit all. Acquire a tool box of well focused CASE tools.

Does the tool have a well-defined scope?

After assessing your needs, select a tool that best meets those needs. This sounds obvious, but many organizations are sold by the sizzle and not by the substance. For instance, if you need a requirements analysis tool, consider tools implementing the Structured Analysis methodology (data flow diagrams) with facilities for building detailed mini-specifications. However, Structured Analysis would be worthless for organizations needing a design specification tool that implements the Jackson Structured Design methodology, no matter how exciting the data flow diagram editor.

Can the tool be "customized" if necessary?

Many organizations use variants of the standard requirements analysis and design specification methodologies. For example, organizations performing large amounts of real-time system design probably have extended standard methodologies or have created novel methodologies for representing timing and control information. Several of the CASE tools provide facilities for installing custom methodologies by allowing developers to add their own symbols and connection rules on top of the built-in graphical editing and data dictionary facilities. Certainly most organizations will not need this capability, but it will be mandatory for some.

Is the interaction sufficient to leverage design and development efforts?

The CASE tool should provide a sufficiently greater benefit than your current practices (or lack of) are delivering. For example, if you already use a graphics editing program to create user interface designs, then selecting a user interface layout tool that does not generate code probably will not improve your productivity. However, if you are using a graphics editor to draw data flow diagrams, then a tool implementing Structured Analysis will provide much greater editing flexibility with features such as leveling, consistency checking, and data dictionary maintenance.

Does the tool automatically generate software from the specification?

If the tool generates code from a design specification, it should generate the "right" code. This is a relatively difficult capability to assess since the automatic code generation process is not yet well understood. Many tools generate data structure definitions from their data dictionaries. Others produce compilable code from mini-specifications written with program design languages. If code generation is an absolute requirement, then insist on a field test evaluation using a real example in your organization. A tool that generates only part of the code is hampered if it must be manually modified or expanded. This eliminates the benefit of automatic code generation because the flexibility of altering the design and regenerating the code is lost.

Selecting the Right First Project

Selecting the right project for introducing CASE technology to your organization is as important as selecting the right tools. There are many pitfalls to avoid when selecting the "shakedown" project. Obviously, your goal is to make the project succeed in less time and with lower cost than without CASE, so you must locate a project that will allow CASE technology to prove itself. The following issues should be considered when scouting for a "good" first project. Not all of these issues will be pertinent to you and your organization, but you should consider them when making your project selection decision.

Select a new project about to start, not one already in progress.

As discussed later in this chapter, computer-aided software engineering is not a technology easily retrofitted to a project failing due to poor requirements analysis, bad design, or bungled management. It is not a white knight rallying to the rescue. Rather, CASE technology demands a different project structure for optimum results than is typically followed in most development organizations. CASE places an increased emphasis on the software development cycle. Give CASE a chance to prove itself on a fresh project not clouded by elements of failure or other attributes that would jeopardize the project's chances for success.

The project team leader must champion CASE.

Obviously, the individual leading the project must want success. In fact, a good candidate champion is the project leader of the development team—someone who commands the authority and *respect* to demand that the selected tools be used in the proper manner. The best champion is someone who has a reputation and ego on the line and is "betting" on a successful project, not a project engineer who cannot control other project team members. Furthermore, the project champion should not be removed from the project team's day-to-day activities, such as a member of upper management. Often it is difficult to communicate goals "down the line" to those responsible for implementing them, and a new technology only exacerbates the problem. Even if the project succeeds, a nay-sayer may speak up and identify reasons, other than CASE technology, why the project succeeded.

Management must participate.

The presence of an organizational CASE champion, a manager higher up in the development organization, will greatly enhance the chances of the project's success. That individual should serve as the mentor for the first CASE-tool-based project and assume responsibility for selling the concepts of computer-aided software engineering to other peers in management. The organizational champion can also ensure that proper resources, budgetary and personnel, are allocated to the project.

Select a small to moderately sized project.

Select a project unencumbered with obstacles of size and complexity. Your goal is to prove that CASE technology has a place in your organization's software development arsenal, so choosing a project that will clearly establish the new technology's feasibility is a must.

Select a normal, straightforward project.

Do not accept a risky or complex project until your organization has gained experience with CASE technology and understands its strengths and weaknesses. Make sure there are no extreme or abnormal system requirements, such as ambitious real-time constraints, or an area where there is no development expertise (don't let an accounting-oriented data processing shop attempt to develop an expert system shell, for example).

Select a meaningful, high-payoff project.

Establishing CASE in your organization means selecting an application with visibility that will be enhanced by the new technology. Choose a project with measurable results that will "prove your case."

Ensure cooperative end-users.

A cooperative end-user community is essential to the project's success, regardless of whether CASE technology is employed. The Structured Analysis and information modeling methodologies are ideally suited for interacting with end-users, so take advantage of opportunities to engage in feedback sessions during the requirements analysis stage. Managing the developer/end-user relationship is critical. Ignoring this oppor-tunity for interaction can torpedo your chances for success.

Train the project team in the appropriate tools and methodologies.

Project team members should be as well versed as possible in the CASE methodologies and tools used on the project. Project members should attend training courses prior to the project's start, and they should be given an opportunity to learn and practice with the CASE tools before the project begins. Avoid on-the-job training during the project as this will only impede progress.

The project should be continuously monitored as to the effectiveness of the CASE technology and team members' reactions to working with the new software tools. Plan to conduct a postmortem on the project once it is complete. Prepare a full report for your management and, if nothing else, to satisfy yourself that you made the right choice of methodologies and tools.

Using a Tool on Your First Project

Computer-aided software engineering emphasizes requirements analysis and design specification while deemphasizing coding and implementation. The goal of this new technology is to let the computer do the tedious and time-consuming work, freeing you to concentrate on the more important requirements gathering and design tasks. With this in mind, plan to expect:

- Up-front focus on requirements and design details.

- More interviewing time with end-users.

- Lengthened design period.

- Many iterations during the design process.

These expectations may make sense conceptually, but they can cause an inexperienced project leader to fret as valuable development time slips away and no "progress" is being made (that is, no code is being written). This can be especially difficult for management to understand. They are more comfortable when the developers are working on "productive" tasks. It is best to prepare them with the facts before the project begins, and they should understand the requirements analysis and design specification periods will be lengthened in exchange for shortened coding and implementation periods. The next section, "The Construction Crew Approach," presents a project management philosophy that greatly ameliorates this risk. Even so, be prepared to stress the following *benefits* to recalcitrant management:

■ Shorter implementation period.

■ Vastly fewer surprises during implementation.

■ More maintainable code.

■ Better module organization and functional separation.

■ A code design that "writes itself."

During the first project using CASE tools, it is vital that success be quantified and measured in some fashion. If yours is a large development shop, then there are probably metrics already in place to gauge each project undertaken. If not, then several meaningful metrics should be designed and benchmarked against several previously completed projects so that success can be measured quantitatively as well as qualitatively. Several examples of project benchmarks are:

■ Duration of implementation and system integration periods.

■ Total person-months of development effort required for acceptable release.

■ Number of design change requests from users during beta test.

■ Number of design change requests from users after fielding.

■ Number of bugs per line of code (after release).

Even without measurable productivity benefits, using CASE tools will help instill better analysis and design practices within your development group. CASE technology emphasizes the philosophy of separating the software development process into clearly defined, manageable segments with well-documented deliverables at each stage.

Successfully completing your first "CASE-based" development project will win converts to your cause throughout the development organization. The next step is training the rest of the organization in CASE methodologies and tools. This includes identifying appropriate training programs and seminars from outside the development organization. You should carefully consider establishing an *ongoing* training program for all new members entering the development organization. This is the surest way of institutionalizing CASE technology as part of your organization's standard practices.

The Construction Crew Approach

There are several different approaches to organizing and managing software development teams. Frederick Brooks in *The Mythical Man-Month* describes a proposal by Harlan Mills which advocates a surgical team approach. With this approach, the software development team is functionally organized much like a surgical team, with each team member holding a specific responsibility. The surgeon is the chief programmer, responsible for designing the program's requirements and design specifications. Everyone else on the programming team reports to the chief programmer, including administrative assistants and other software specialists, such as technical writers, user interface developers, and so on.

Other small teams, such as cockpit crews and baseball teams, work similarly. Implicitly, the entire team is signing up to work on the project for the duration of the "operation." Each individual is trained to work together as a team, and each is cross-trained to do several jobs.

The surgical team approach works well on small to moderately sized jobs where the goals are very well specified and turnover of the software development staff does not become a problem. In most moderate-to-large software efforts, however, this is not a practical constraint. Because of the fatigue and burn-out inherent in long-term projects, indenturing a programmer is rarely desirable. In many large defense contract software efforts and in large commercial applications, software development projects can last from three to five years. Few software engineers and programmers want to make or break their careers on just one software application.

An alternate approach is the *construction crew* approach. Constructing large buildings more closely approximates the problems associated with building large, multi-person, multi-year software projects. As with construction crews, large software efforts experience staff turnover, entertain a varied skill mix, and adjust to shifting development goals. There are many more people to manage, resulting in a necessarily more rigid, hierarchical management structure. In a surgical operation, much of what occurs depends on the previous actions—the context of the situation—making it difficult for a new surgical team member to enter the operating theater once the operation has started. If the chief software designer departs, a new one must be recruited and then "ramped up" on the current design. The new designer must become familiar with the "big picture."

Software teams, like construction crews, are best composed with discernible divisions of labor among the specialties. Houses and buildings are designed by architects who are never expected to wield a hammer. Once the blueprints have been approved by the building inspector, the local construction crews can proceed. Builders need never question the design, or blueprint, of a building. They simply follow the blueprint systematically, floor by floor, room by room, until the building is complete. If any members of the crew leave, new crew members can pick up the work almost immediately without understanding the architect's big picture.

Rarely, though, is software designed by software *architects* who only design but do not build as well. The fact that software designers must also build the software leads to several sociological consequences, such as the desire to begin coding prematurely and the tendency to ignore certain requisite features because they are difficult to code.

Just as members of construction trades have highly specialized tools, a similar trend is emerging in the software industry (Figure 13.4). Software development teams will consist of professionals specializing in such specific tools as Structured

Analysis tools, data modeling tools, and user interface tools. This specialization enables software professionals to make higher-leverage contributions to each application's development because they are able to do more in a shorter time span with fewer errors.

As in the construction crew analogy, separating the code inspectors (a.k.a. building inspectors) from the implementors (a.k.a. carpenters) is highly desirable. Code inspectors are not rushed by project schedules and therefore are more willing to spend the time necessary to do a thorough job. Code inspectors

Figure 13.4 Construction crew approach to software development.

BUILDING CONSTRUCTION	SOFTWARE CONSTRUCTION
Architect Works with developer to define requirements and develop blueprints.	**Software Architect/Designer** Works with end-user community to define requirements and develop specifications.
Carpenter Erects the building's framework structure.	**Internals Specialist** Creates data structures, procedure calling hierarchies, and encodes algorithms.
Electrician Installs electrical outlets. Connects building to electrical utility.	**Data Base Specialist** Writes access query calls to data base system.
Dry Wall and Trim Installs dry wall, paint, trim, and other interior work. Although small in bulk, this work entails 50% of a building's cost.	**User Interface Specialist** Designs and implements the human/machine interface. In interactive systems, the user interface consumes 40% to 60% of the total software.
Building Inspector Inspects building's quality during the phases of construction.	**Quality Assurance Group** Reviews the software for clarity, integrity, and efficiency.

rarely have their egos entwined with the design or code implementation. The code inspectors' function, however, must be organizationally mandated. They need the authority to pass or fail a software component during a quality inspection in order for their efforts to be successful.

Separate quality assurance groups are nothing new to software organizations. For years they have performed *acceptance testing* on *completed* software projects. The novel concept is having the quality assurance group judge the software at key points during the development cycle, such as after the requirements phase and the design phase. This role has traditionally been filled by the implementation team itself. Implementation teams are usually weary after completing a project phase, leaving them little energy or desire to thoroughly review their own work. Furthermore, implementation teams are frequently pressured to begin implementation without completing the requirements and design phases. A fresh perspective is always best, and a separate audit of these phases would substantially eliminate most of the design errors—the most difficult sort to correct during later implementation stages.

A fairly new concept in software engineering is the *software factory*. Software factories, like conventional factories, work in assembly line fashion with each group of workers specializing in one aspect of the manufacturing process. For software, this means specialized analysts, designers, implementors, and quality assurance professionals. The software factory concept also means having a set of software tools forming the backbone of the software production environment. Implementing the software factory concept is necessary to build *institutional success* in the software industry. We must be able to consistently produce high-quality, error-free software, accurately reflecting end-user requirements in a predictable amount of time—in short, a software assembly line.

The reader by now realizes that this book emphasizes tools designed for the software architect/designer, the information systems modeler, and the user interface specialist. It is only by conducting these requirements analysis and design specification tasks in a proper and logical manner that a project can be organized around the construction crew approach. Without this division of job responsibility, software development is destined to remain a fine art rather than an engineering discipline.

The following chapter discusses DOD-STD-2167, the Defense Department's documentation standard for specifying mission critical software systems. DOD-STD-2167 is important because it affects a large number of software development organizations involved in government and military systems work, and because it defines a software development cycle with an explicit set of reviews, walk-throughs, and deliverable documents. DOD-STD-2167 is one step in the software factory direction.

Chapter 14

DOD-STD-2167

Over the years, the Department of Defense has become very concerned with the quality, reliability, and maintainability of the software built by defense contracting organizations. After all, the nation's defense systems now largely rely on the integrity of these software systems. The DOD realized steps must be taken to sharply reduce the risk of hazard due to software defects. As a result, over the last decade, the DOD has assembled a set of DOD-STD and MIL-STD (Department of Defense Standard and Military Standard) documents governing the design and implementation of software components by both external defense contractors and by internal military software development organizations.

Spare no expense to make everything as economical as possible.
— Sam Goldwyn

Because of the characteristically large software systems implemented for military contracts, and because of the large number of *integrated* components, the Department of Defense recognized early the need for a *standardized* mechanism for developing requirements specifications. As many as 300 software engineers may produce a million or more lines of code for a major mission-critical project.

Also, because of the relationship between the Department of Defense and the military contracting community, the DOD must have a mechanism for specifying detailed defense system requirements that encourages fair and open bidding by all interested contractors. This need to accurately and completely specify a contract and its set of deliverables forces the DOD to develop and rely on straightforward, well-understood requirements standards such as DCD-STD-2167.

The DOD-STD-2167 specification format has, by mandate of the Department of Defense, become the standard methodology required for all military system contractors building *mission* critical software systems. Because of this directive, many of the CASE tools described in Part II of this book generate

DOD-STD-2167 documents, since compliance with DOD-STD-2167 is a necessity for most companies vying for military contracts.

Mission critical systems are data processing equipment, software, and services that involve:

- Intelligence activities.
- Command and control of military forces.
- Cryptologic systems relating to national security.
- Equipment or software forming an integral part of a weapons system.

How does DOD-STD-2167 fit in with CASE technology? Among other things, DOD-STD-2167 insists that all specified requirements for a software system be traceable to the software's design. That is, the contractor must develop traceability matrices to show the allocation of requirements from the system's specification to the individual software components and from the individual software components back to the system's specification. Building these traceability matrices is an onerous task at best, especially for large software systems with hundreds or thousands of individual requirements. This task becomes particularly complex as the requirements change and evolve during the course of the requirements analysis and design specification stages. Fortunately, many CASE tools have implemented mechanisms to automatically establish these traceability links between specification and design.

Software Development Process

DOD-STD-2167 requires a layered, top-down approach to design and development, emphasizing the requirements analysis and design specification project phases. DOD-STD-2167 also requires that well-documented, structured methodologies be employed during design and implementation and further specifies that requirements be traceable throughout all layers of the system. This means the system requirements documents must be written to allow the extraction of compliance information for the Department of Defense. The basis for this structured approach to system development is the Software and Hardware Development Life Cycle shown in Figure 14.1.

DOD-STD-2167's Software and Hardware Development Life Cycle is similar to the software development cycle presented in Chapters 1, 2, and 3. There are differences, of course, chiefly in the degree of design and reporting detail required for each development phase. Each phase in the life cycle concludes with the successful completion of a requirements, design, or test review. At each review point, documentation is produced according to a specified format. Many would argue that much of this work is unnecessary, but the requirement for this documentation forces software designers to thoroughly consider their designs during each development phase. This reduces the risk of error and greatly enhances reliability. The downside, of course, is slightly lengthened development cycles.

Figure 14.1 The DOD-STD-2167 software development cycle emphasizes requirements analysis and design specification. Design and coding reviews, conducted at the end of each project phase, must be successfully completed before the next phase can begin.

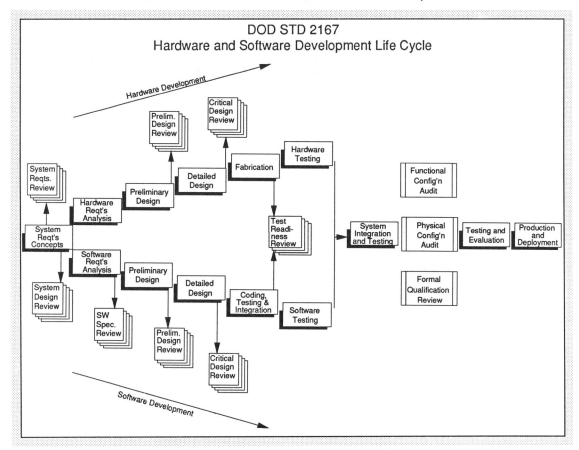

DOD-STD-2167 is primarily an overview document, focusing mainly on the requirements analysis and design specification phases of the development cycle. The amount of documentation that contractors must supply the contracting agencies is very large. In all, this documentation includes some 27 separate documents not counting source code and test suites! There is probably a small fortune awaiting the first company to develop and deliver a software development environment that automatically assembles and produces all 27 of these documents plus manages the source code base and test suites. These documents are specific deliverables required at the culmination of particular development phases, and their acceptance is governed by a formal review and audit process conducted by the contracting agency. Figure 14.2 shows each of these required documents, reviews, and audits.

For our purposes, the most important documents are generated during the software requirements analysis, preliminary design, and the detailed design development phases. These key documents are the Software Requirements Specification, the Interface Requirements Specification, the Software Top-Level Design Document, and the Software Detailed Design Document. Writing these documents requires analysis and design skills, areas where computer-aided software engineering can help.

DOD-STD-2167 splits the design specification phase into two separate components, the preliminary design phase and the detailed design phase. The preliminary design concentrates only on the higher-level software components, usually individual programs or large, separable modules. Once the contracting agency accepts the preliminary design architecture, the contractor assembles a detailed design, encompassing both the higher-level and the lower-level modules, as well as unit-level modules.

In addition to the specification, design, and review documents, other required documents include:

- Operational Concept Document.
- Software Development Plan.
- System Integration Test Plans.

Since these documents deal mostly with the management of the software project, they are not discussed here. This is not to imply a lack of automated software tools to assist in managing software projects; for the moment, however, computer-aided software engineering technology is only available for requirements analysis and design specification tasks. It would not be surprising to see the Defense Department push for the development of a standardized, integrated software development test bed (software factory environment) that covers all facets of software development, including project management. Realizing this ambitious goal is several years away, though.

Software Organization

DOD-STD-2167 specifies only the process for developing the software, not *how* the software is to be built or *what* tools the contractor can select for assistance. Section 4.2, "Software Engineering," of DOD-STD-2167 articulates the overall guidelines for software development. This section states that contractors shall use:

> *"systematic, well documented proven software development methods to perform software requirements analysis, design, coding, integration, and testing of the deliverable software."*

The methodologies selected by the contractor must be indicated in the Software Development Plan and the contractor must describe how those methodologies will support the formal reviews and audits required in the development contract.

Much of the development and review process centers around *Computer Software Configuration Items* (CSCIs). A software system built according to DOD-STD-2167 is organized into a set of Computer Software Configuration Components (CSCI). A CSCI is a program or major separable module that can be defined and specified separately from the others. DOD-STD-2167 defines CSCIs as:

> *"software which is designated by the contracting agency for configuration management."*

Figure 14.2 The DOD-STD-2167 standard requires 27 separate documents plus test suites and source code listings. These documents must be finalized and submitted to the contracting agency before the appropriate review cycles for each development phase can begin.

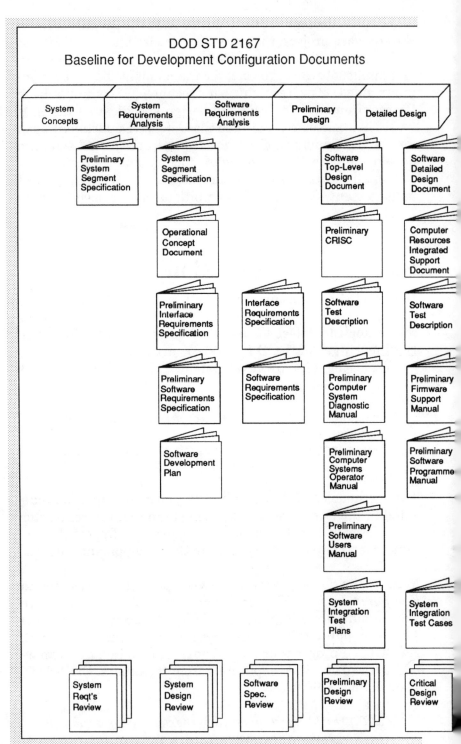

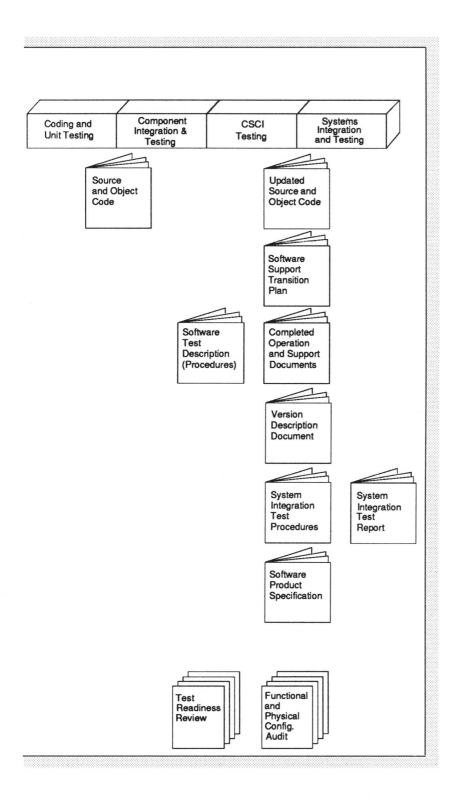

The contractor develops the top-level design of each CSCI by allocating requirements from the System Requirements Specification and the Interface Requirements Specification into Top-Level Computer Software Components (TLCSCs) and Low-Level Computer Software Components (LLCSCs) for each CSCI. Figure 14.3 is a less-confusing, visual description of this hierarchy.

Figure 14.3 Software systems built under contract for the Defense Department are organized into a set of Computer Software Configuration Items (CSCI). Each CSCI is composed of Top Level Computer Software Components which are themselves composed of lower-level components and units.

Of great importance to designers using CASE tools that support DOD-STD-2167 is the section on traceability of requirements to design:

4.2.8 Traceability of requirements to design. The contractor shall develop traceability matrices to show the allocation of requirements from the system specification to the CSCI, Top-Level Computer Software Components (TLCSCs), Lower-Level Computer Software Components (LLCSCs), and Units and from the Unit level back to the system

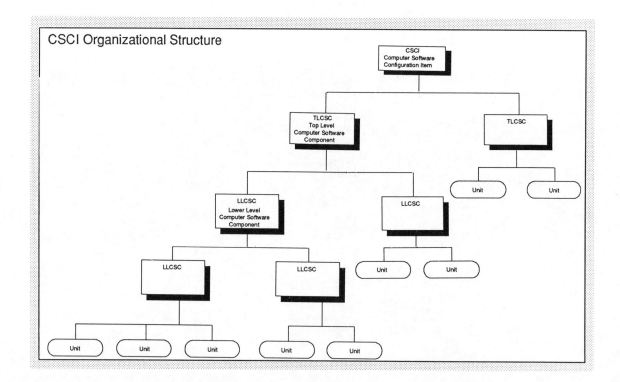

CSCI Organizational Structure

specification. The traceability matrices shall be documented in the Software Requirements Specification, Software Top-Level Design Document (STLDD), and the Software Detailed Design Document (SDDD).

This means that software developers must provide documentation indicating where each individual requirement is implemented. "Where" means the name of the software module containing the implementation. The reverse is also true; the documentation for each software module (top-level or lower-level) must indicate which particular requirements are implemented within that module. Furthermore, requirements must be traceable to tests and test cases built to verify the correct operation and performance of the individual components:

4.3.3 Requirements traceability to formal tests and test cases. The contractor shall develop a traceability matrix that shows, for each formal test case identified in the Software Test Description (STD), the requirements that are satisfied or partially satisfied from the Software Requirements Specification. The contractor shall document this matrix in the STD.

Requirements outlined in both the Software Requirements Specification and the Interface Requirements Specification documents must be traceable to higher-level specifications and must be *consistent* with other specification items; that is, two single requirements cannot contradict each other. Many of the requirements analysis and design specification tools described in Chapter 9, such as DesignAid from Nastec, automate (at least partially) these requirements and test case traceability procedures.

The traceability burdens imposed by DOD-STD-2167 demonstrate why computer-aided software engineering can assist with requirements analysis and design specification activities. Performing a full traceability audit by hand can be monumental, and even a simple design change can be upsetting. The only real solution is to automate this process, which is where CASE tools can help. Many analysis and design tool link the requirements specification documents directly to the code implementation. For example, the Nastec DesignAid tool provides requirements document editing facilities in addition to Structured Analysis and data modeling capabilities. Design components are tied directly to the design document and to their underlying implementation.

Even if your organization does not build defense systems, there are ample opportunities to apply computer-aided software engineering by following the spirit of the DOD-STD-2167 framework. The requirements traceability concept applies to all software systems, not just defense contracts.

The next, and final chapter of this book, *"Technological Trends in CASE,"* forecasts this technology's development over the next several years. It discusses the opportunities in the CASE field, the directions the industry is likely to pursue, and several of the technical hurdles which must be addressed before CASE is accepted by the majority of software developers.

Chapter 15

Technological Trends in CASE

This chapter discusses, as much as is realistically possible, the technological trends in computer-aided software engineering over the next five years. Fortune-telling is always a dangerous occupation, and in software technology, five years is about all one can expect to forecast with any reasonable degree of accuracy. The age of computer-aided software engineering is just beginning, and the tools and technologies described in this book form the basis from which new developments will grow. As this market expands and matures, the technology will undergo tremendous invention and innovation as we come to more fully appreciate the software development process. Undoubtedly, the computer-aided software engineering market will exhibit many of the growth and maturation processes seen with other software technologies as they grew from infant concepts to stable technologies and products.

Software technologies, as indicated in Figure 15.1, usually begin with a long and steady growth phase. Then they undergo a rapid acceleration in both technical growth and consumer interest. Finally, the innovation and invention processes stabilize as the technology becomes accepted throughout the industry. Most likely, a similar rapid expansion of both product vendors and CASE methodologies will occur before a market consolidation appears.

Where are we on the "technology growth curve" today? It is difficult to answer this question without the benefit of hindsight afforded by a fully matured market. However, there are several themes common among CASE tools and vendors, characteristics likely to be found in most of the newly developed methodologies. This chapter summarizes these characteristics and offers a few technological prophecies (wild guesses?) about what CASE will offer during the next five years.

When there are two bosses in town, there's money to be made!
— Clint Eastwood in
A Fist Full of Dollars

Figure 15.1 A developing technology is characterized by rapid growth, both in technological advancement and in the number of vendors supplying the technology. At this writing, CASE technology has just "rounded the knee" of the growth curve and is growing rapidly in both technological sophistication and the number of vendors entering the market.

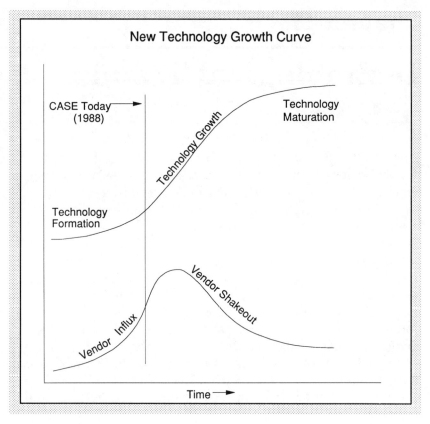

First though, we begin by describing what our development environment would look like if a magic genie could create the ideal CASE tool. From there, we can work backwards to today's state-of-the-art and interpolate what will come in-between.

The Ideal Development Environment

Let's face it. Ideally we would like to *never* write a single line of code! We might imagine a software development environment so powerful and robust that we simply input the application's requirements specification, push a magic button, and out comes the implemented code, ready for release to the end-user community. Testing would be unnecessary because this magic "application generator" produces perfectly correct software. If the application's requirements changed at some point, we would merely update the requirements specification, push the magic button again, and out would come fresh code implementing the new requirements (Figure 15.2).

Is such an ideal CASE environment possible? Will the current state-of-the-art advance to such a level of sophistication at which the application generator is entirely "specification driven" with no manual intervention? Unfortunately, the answer is probably "no"; we will never be able to keep pace with the demand for increasingly sophisticated software.

Our expectations will advance in tandem with the application generator's own technological capabilities. For instance, FORTRAN was devised during the 1960s as a simple, easy-to-use language for engineers and scientists so they would not have to learn assembly language. The goal was for the engineer to state the computational problem as a requirements specification in FORTRAN, and the compiler would translate it into an executable program. FORTRAN's development opened tremendous new frontiers in application programming and introduced thousands to computers, but many more still find the burden of learning the FORTRAN language too great. Likewise, the development of the spreadsheet (VisiCalc

Figure 15.2 In the ideal software development environment, the application developers merely input the requirements specifications and the environment generates the working application without fault, ready for distribution to the end-user community. Even the beta testing phase is bypassed because the generated code is "bug free."

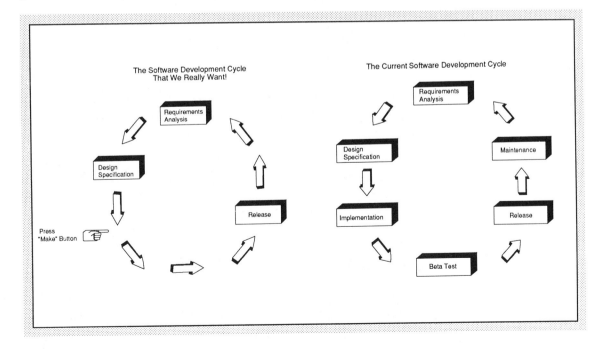

and Lotus 1-2-3) on the personal computer opened new frontiers in end-user computing for hundreds of thousands of new computer users. Yet there are many more who find spreadsheet "programming" with "formulas" too cumbersome.

The ideal software development environment is a code generator that transforms requirements specifications into releasable software.

With CASE technology, there will always be a point at which some level of software design expertise is required to complete the application development cycle, although we can build tools that help design and automatically generate major portions of applications. Over time, the percentage of the application automatically produced by CASE tools will increase. With current technology, CASE tools can automatically produce from 25% to 50% of an application's code. Over the next five years, this will increase to a range of 40% to 75%, depending on the application. In itemizing the functionality missing in most CASE environments, we find the list is fairly short:

- Better mini-specification technology.
- Automatic code generation from mini-specifications.
- Facilities to reuse existing software modules.
- Integration with other software packages (compilers, revision control systems, etc.).
- Code maintenance facilities.

Ideally, we hope to elevate the level at which the systems engineer or analyst interacts with the implementation process (Figure 15.3). Our goal is to refine the requirements analysis and design specification processes, making them rigorous enough so that most of the application's code—70% to 80%—can be automatically generated. Only very unique, well segregated, code modules should be implemented by hand.

The following sections examine these needed capabilities in light of our idealized CASE environment.

Automatic Code Generation

The framework for bridging the automatic code generation gap is already in place. There are many CASE tools that help the designer rapidly build data base applications, which in all

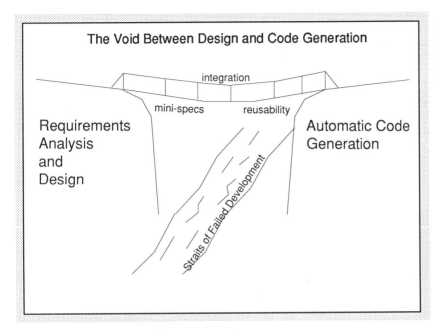

Figure 15.3 Automatically generating ready-to-work software directly from requirements specifications and design specifications is still a tenuous process. There are few formal "rigorous" procedures for automatically transforming design specifications into executable code.

fairness, constitute a substantial bulk of the applications being developed in commercial data processing shops today. Such tools contain screen painters, report layout editors, and code generators. The designer paints a set of data entry and data retrieval screens, lays out a set of reports, formulates the data base queries linking the screens and reports to the data base, presses the "generate code" button, and out spurts working COBOL code. Indeed, these CASE tools are firmly entrenched in the mainframe, large system environment where transaction oriented data base applications are prevalent. Unfortunately, these types of tools are insufficient for building more general purpose software—a Quick Schedule, for example (see Chapter 3).

Many Structured Analysis (Yourdon/DeMarco) and structured design tools pass design information from their data dictionaries to back-end code generators where appropriate data structures (logical data definitions) can be generated in a variety of languages ranging from C to COBOL. Most still lack, however, the ability to transfer the *program logic*, *algorithms*, and *program structure* information necessary to automatically generate 100 percent of the code. Several tools, such as ProMod and Iconix PowerTools, are more advanced than

Bold Prediction #1:
Generalized CASE tools for designing and building general purpose software programs will appear first on personal computers.

others in this respect, although this genre of CASE tools still lacks the "iterative development" capability of being able to edit a data flow diagram and its mini-specifications, produce the structure chart, generate executable (or compilable) code, and then return to re-edit the data flow diagram. Furthermore, these design tools are not yet integrated with user interface creation tools.

In fact, the mechanisms for automatically translating a requirements specification (i.e., data flow diagrams) into structure charts still lack rigorous definitions. The inherent problem is the diversity and imprecision of the mini-specification techniques used to describe primitive-level process bubbles in the data flow diagram. Obviously, the more precise mini-specification techniques, like the program design language and the decision table, fare better than the less precise techniques like Structured English.

Software design, especially the requirements analysis phase, is by nature a highly iterative process. After all, this is the flexibility we cherish so much in software—software's ease of modification. Next generation CASE tools must strive to meet these conflicting goals of ease of modification, reduced development time, and high quality, reliable implementations. Figure 15.4 illustrates such a next generation CASE environment where the entire design is created with a set of CASE tools, each linked into a centralized code generator and library of reusable modules.

The notion of a *central project design data base* is an expansion of today's data dictionary. Most CASE tools use a centralized data dictionary as the repository of data definitions, and this data dictionary serves as the unifying thread linking the different tool modules. More than just data structure definitions are required, however, in the next generation CASE environment. The data dictionary must be expanded to incorporate program structure and algorithms as well as data structure definitions before it can become a full-fledged project design data base.

The ability to facilitate "hand coding" of the generated software is the key to making the next generation CASE

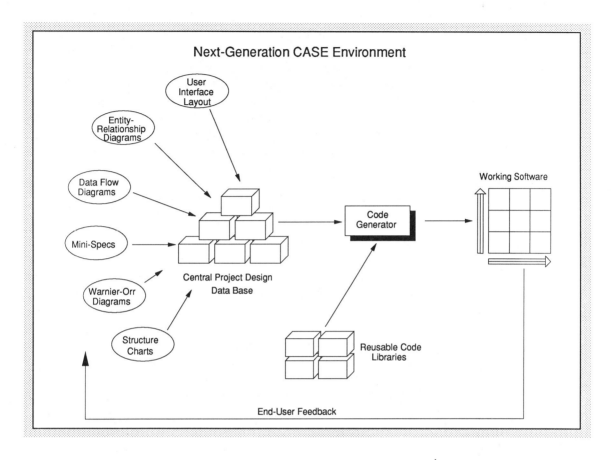

environment in Figure 15.4 a successful commercial reality. In our idealized CASE environment, human hands would rarely modify the computer generated code output by the code generator. The only exception is the necessity to expand the tool's scope when encountering an application with unique characteristics that demand custom coding. So if we accept the fact (resign ourselves to it?) that some amount of hand coding will be required on certain applications, then how can this custom work be incorporated into the specify/design/generate loop without losing synchronization with (or fouling up) the original design as it evolves?

Figure 15.4 includes a set of reusable software libraries comprised of useful functions and routines that may be cut and pasted into any software application being designed. These libraries may contain functions that cannot be designed (and code generated) using the standard CASE methodologies;

Figure 15.4 Computer-aided software engineering will evolve as bridges are built between the front-end requirements analysis and design specification tools and the back-end code generation and library maintenance tools. These bridges must be bidirectional to handle the iterative nature of software design and development.

that is, some routines may be hand coded and not machine produced. If the code generation facility is flexible enough to allow the insertion of these hand-coded routines, then the problem largely disappears, albeit with a slightly larger design cost and a larger programmer/engineer learning curve. After all, it is highly doubtful that computer-aided software engineering technology will ever completely remove the software engineer from the development cycle.

User Interface Generation

Until recently, the majority of the user interface generation tools focused on transaction oriented, form-filling screen design and report layout. In fact, most tool vendors refer to these facilities as "screen painters" or "report layout editors," indicative of their data base orientation. These facilities allow the application designer to lay out individual screens and specify the control sequence that moves the end-user from screen to screen. What these tools lack, however, is the ability to create interfaces that are more complex than forms.

In hypothesizing our ideal CASE tool environment, we might imagine an interface facility that allows the designer to select from a palette of different command and presentation structures: pull-down menus, dialog boxes, forms, tables, and so on. But in contrast to present generation interface design tools, we need a more precise control than simply specifying "when screen 27 is complete and validated, put up screen 28." We need an *interface erector set* much like Pinball Construction Set, the popular PC game program from Electronic Arts. The Pinball Construction Set allows users to interactively lay out a pinball game on-screen. Users can select flippers, buzzers, and other pinball "objects" from a menu and drag them to the desired location on the pinball machine. Once the desired configuration is obtained, the user places the program in "run" mode and the pinball layout becomes a working pinball game.

Envision a design tool that allows the software engineer to interactively lay out an interface (contrasted with a screen) by defining screen objects. These screen objects might be simple fields for string, currency, and date input; or, the objects might be more complex, such as menus, dialog boxes, scrollable tables, and even graphical objects. Our interface design tool would allow us, in erector set fashion, to select field validation routines, different types of push buttons, select text edit box characteristics, and specify control flow on a keystroke-by-keystroke basis. It would be versatile enough so, for example, we can specify that pushing the first "radio button" in a particular dialog box should disable the second button but not the third.

The Apple Macintosh HyperCard program is a step in this direction. Its user interface development facility is essentially "object oriented". Each screen object has a small program, usually one page in length, dictating the object's actions when appropriate events, like mouse clicks, occur. These small compartmentalized program fragments are essentially formal computer language mini-specifications. The HyperTalk language has high-level primitives for recognizing and acting on user interface events.

There are limitations to such a generalized design tool. For example, if we decided to create a new type of data entry field, the interface tool must be flexible enough for us to add the field validation routine to a reusable code library so this routine can be used on future projects as well as the current one. Similarly, if we created a new type of screen object, we should be able to define the object's implementation in the form of code generic enough to be used in other application designs.

User interface design tools will necessarily become more *object oriented*. (A more thorough description can be found in texts on the SmallTalk and C++ object oriented programming languages.) Object oriented programming has achieved considerable notoriety as a new programming style during the past several years. At its basic level, object oriented programming is a programming style focusing on data structures, called objects, rather than focusing on the algorithms that manipulate them. A program is a set of discrete objects and classes of objects from which new objects can be created during execution. Instead of passing data from routine to routine as in conventional software, each object has a set of *methods* describing how individual *messages* sent from a sending object changes the state of the receiving object.

Bold Prediction #2: Next generation CASE tools will encourage application designs built around the end-user interface.

Object oriented programming serves as an excellent user interface metaphor. Windows, menus, and graphical screen objects are the logical building blocks of any interface. Ideally, an interface design tool would allow the designer to specify interface objects at the level understood by the end-users: as forms, addresses, spreadsheets, or tables. Designers would write the "methods" delineating how the screen objects behave and interact with user input and with other screen objects.

Because clean, lucid user interfaces usually suggest simple underlying program organizations, algorithms, and data structures, much of the application's design will be driven by the user interface creation facility in next generation CASE tools. The ideal CASE environment would emphasize interface design during the requirements analysis phase.

Tool Set Integration

The underlying architecture of the next generation CASE environment shown in Figure 15.4—a variety of tools and methodologies cooperating through centralized design data base—raises two questions: Can this entire integrated CASE tool set (nee environment) be provided by a single vendor and can tool components from different vendors be integrated?

Bold Prediction #3: Applications will be designed in one environment (hardware platform and operating system) but generated for a host of other target environments.

Many vendors already offer the front-end components: data flow diagram editors, entity-relationship diagram editors, and screen layout editors, all tied into a central data dictionary. A smaller number of tools contain structure chart editors and some program design language mechanism for defining mini-specifications. These basic specification and design modules are not likely to require much additional technological investment (how many ways can you edit a data flow diagram?). If these vendors continue to invest in their technology and marketing programs, then it is entirely within the realm of possibility for one vendor to offer a completely integrated tool set. Of course, the fundamental technological constraint is the development of a central design data base structure that can integrate and synthesize the design components from the different tools.

The marketplace is likely to demand the capability to "plug" other design tools into the central design data base. For example, the current state of user interface design technology is far behind the more mature data flow and entity-relationship diagram technologies. As vendors introduce new functionality, it will be essential to integrate, via a standard interface, to another vendor's design data base.

The need for diverse front-end design tools is amplified by the trend toward designing on one hardware platform, usually the IBM PC or Apple Macintosh, and fielding the system on another platform, such as an IBM mainframe or a DEC VAX. Vendors are also likely to independently build back-end code generators for new languages and target machines as shown in Figure 15.5.

Fourth Generation Languages

Fourth generation languages such as FOCUS from Information Builders and 4GL from Informix, constitute an important

Figure 15.5 An appropriate standardized central design data base opens the door for vendors to offer back-end code generators for a variety of languages and hardware platforms.

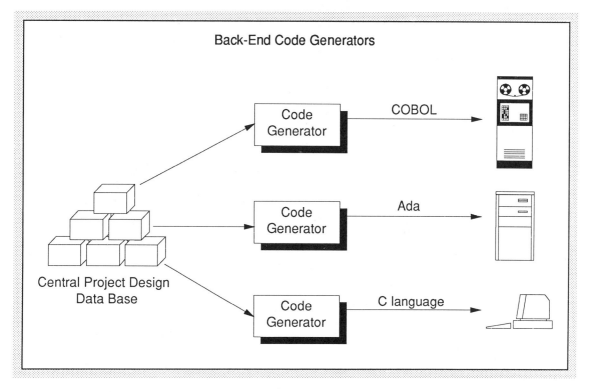

class of software development tools. They are higher-level, focused languages for writing programs that access data bases. Most strive to be nonprocedural and utilize a declarative syntax and semantics for describing such integral software components as screen and report layouts. This differs from conventional third generation languages (3GLs), such as C and PL/1, which provide very fine-grained data structure manipulation capabilities. Although convenient for doing complex data base manipulations in a minimum amount of code, 4GLs exact a performance penalty in order to achieve this sophisticated access. To their credit, all 4GL languages provide a more straightforward data base access mechanism than can be achieved by embedding data base access subroutine calls within a conventional language like C or COBOL.

Bold Prediction #4: 4GLs will provide greatly enhanced integration capabilities as vendors realize that 4GLs cannot be made the center of the universe.

However, most 4GLs serve two masters by being partly user interface layout and design languages and partly data base access languages. Consequently, they ignore the outside programming world, frequently making integration difficult. 4GLs can also be fairly rigid; if the application does not fit the 4GL declarative language, then the only alternative is to return to embedded data base access subroutine calls from within the conventional program. They also do not "degrade gracefully" in terms of functionality. As applications become increasingly more complicated, especially due to increasingly sophisticated user interfaces, 4GLs will probably become more limited in their application. They will be forced to provide robust data exchange and integration mechanisms.

Shoot-out at the CASE Corral?

If you are reading this section for predictions about which vendors will triumph in the CASE race, then you should skip to the next section. It is only human nature (and wise counsel) to want to select the "right" vendor: one whose products will not change drastically overnight, ruining a substantial training investment, and one who (heaven forbid!) will not go bankrupt.

Nevertheless, a quick scan of Appendix A reveals over 35 "design and analysis specification tool" vendors alone, and more are entering the market each year. Obviously, many of these companies will not succeed. A mature market will not tolerate 35 different, and incompatible, ways of doing roughly the same thing. There are over 15 vendors offering tools using the Yourdon/DeMarco Structured Analysis methodology. How many different (and innovative) ways can data flow diagram editors be implemented?

The attentive and insightful reader may have noticed that many of the CASE methodologies share the same underlying metaphors. All are graphical. All represent organizational hierarchy in some manner. Most represent relationships and structure by connecting boxes or bubbles with directed lines, and, many have mechanisms for selective detail hiding. Are there really many differences among the CASE methodologies?

For example, data flow diagrams, Warnier-Orr diagrams, Scandura FLOWforms (see Chapter 5), and many structure chart implementations utilize the "Outline Processor metaphor" of expanding the object to reveal additional detail and contracting the object to hide detail. Warnier-Orr diagrams and Jackson Structured Programming diagrams both represent hierarchical program structure. At a gross level, the only difference is that Warnier-Orr diagrams use an outline metaphor (brackets) and Jackson diagrams use an organization chart metaphor (boxes).

Several CASE tool vendors, such as Nastec, Visual Software, and Future Tech, are stressing their tools' ability to be customized and to incorporate new user-defined methodologies altogether. These tools provide facilities for creating new screen objects and for specifying the connectivity rules used for linking screen objects. These enhanced capabilities take advantage of the underlying data dictionary and consistency checking mechanisms for storing, tracking, and validating instances of these new objects as they are created during a design session. The ability to customize an existing methodology or to create an entirely new one gives developers the added flexibility needed to integrate new CASE methodologies and tools with their existing software development environments.

Bold Prediction #5: General purpose, design oriented CASE tools will become highly customizable, allowing developers to incorporate new methodologies.

The success of any particular vendor depends as much on marketing skill as on technological advantage, but look for vendors offering "open architectures" to be more successful than those that do not.

A Closing Word

I have had a tremendous amount of fun piecing together the computer-aided software engineering jigsaw puzzle during the course of researching and writing this book. With some trepidation in the previous few sections, I've offered my modest predictions about the future of CASE tools and the CASE marketplace. As I look out into the software development marketplace, I see a tremendous amount of innovation that will benefit those of us practicing software design and development for a living.

CASE is bringing vastly increased capabilities to the development process and is providing increased flexibility in fulfilling the needs of our individual end-user communities. What's more, as software projects continue to grow ever larger and more complex, CASE promises to restore much of the fun and excitement of software development by resurrecting the thrill of editing, compiling, and running that's kept so many of us working happily well into the early morning hours.

Appendix A

Compendium of CASE Tools

Specification, Design, and Data Modeling Tools

This compendium of specification, design, and data modeling tools is a reasonably complete inventory at the time of this writing. New vendors and tools, however, will appear as the CASE market expands and matures. Less fortunate ones will disappear. The quality of these tool descriptions varies considerably, largely as the result of the effort taken to research each tool, the author's interest in the tool, and the author's ability to acquire technical literature from the vendor. In all cases, an attempt has been made to be as accurate as possible, and as always, complete information is available from the respective vendors.

The astute reader will notice many of these tools support the Yourdon/DeMarco Structured Analysis methodology (data flow diagrams). By far, this is the most popular methodology implemented in today's CASE tools.

PRODUCT	DESCRIPTION
ACCOLADE Computer Corporation of America Four Cambridge Center Cambridge, MA 02142 (617) 492-8860	Accolade is a set of application development of tools, including a Screen Painter, an America Application Source Code Generator, a data base interface library, and a Project Management and Control System.
ANALYST Tektronix, Inc. (800) TEK-WIDE DEC VAX/VMS and Ultrix	The Tek/CASE Analyst provides support for creating Structured Analysis documents for real-time systems development. The Analyst supports Hatley and Ward/Mellor real-time extensions to the Yourdon/DeMarco Structured Analysis methodology. The Analyst supports five real-time tables for control specifications: decision tables, state transition matrices, action and transition tables, process activation tables, and decision/process activation tables. The Tek/CASE Designer, a companion tool, is a structured design tool that transforms Structured Analysis documents created with the Analyst into an initial system design. SA Tools/IBM PC, for the IBM PC environment, is an interactive Structured Analysis tool.

PRODUCT	DESCRIPTION
APS Development Center Sage Software, Inc. 3200 Monroe Street Rockville, MD 20852 (301) 230-3200	The APS Development Center is a set of integrated program design and screen layout facilities. The APS Generators read the APS Application Dictionary and translate the nonprocedural and semiprocedural specifications into compilable COBOL code for IMS, CICS, ISPF, and batch transactions.
ASA Verilog USA, Inc. Beauregard Square, 340 6303 Little River Turnpike Alexandria, VA 22312	ASA uses the LSA language to describe the organization of a system in terms of nested modules (the functions) and channels (the data flow). The resulting design is a representation of a state machine.
BRACKETS Optima, Inc. (formerly Ken Orr & Associates) 1725 Gage Blvd. Topeka, KS 66604-3379 (800) 255-2459 (913) 273-0653	(See Chapter 10 for a detailed description.) Brackets is an IBM PC-based tool for generating Warnier/Orr diagrams. Brackets functions much like an outline program, allowing the designer to expand or collapse all or part of a Warnier/Orr diagram with a single keystroke. Brackets can automatically generate COBOL procedure division code from detail program designs. Brackets files can also be imported from or exported to the STRUCTURE(S) COBOL Code generation program.
COINS Eclectic Solutions Corporation 5580 La Jolla Blvd., Suite 130 La Jolla, CA 92037 (619) 454-5781	COINS (Corporate/Office Information Network System) is a set of tools implementing the IDEF0/SADT (Structured Analysis and Design Technique) methodologies for requirements analysis and design specification.
CORVISION Cortex Corporation 138 Technology Drive Waltham, MA 02154 (617) 894-1669	CorVision uses a series of diagrams, screens, and pop-up menus to define an application's different components: files, file relationships and links, menus, screens, and reports. CorVision includes an entity-relationship diagrammer, a Data Set Attribute definition facility, and a Menu Diagrammer that visually represents the logical flow of the application from the user's perspective. Editing with the Menu Diagrammer restructures the application.
DESIGN/2.0 Meta Software Corporation 150 Cambridge Park Drive Cambridge, MA 02140 (800) 227-4106 (617) 576-6920 $350.00—IBM PC/XT, PC/AT PS/2, close compatibles $250.00—Apple Macintosh Plus, SE, II	Design/2.0 is a drawing package for manipulating graphics and text. Flow charts, systems designs, information networks, organizational charts, and presentation graphics can be designed. Built-in facilities allow the user to connect objects. Design/2.0 automatically recreates all associated text, connectors, and subordinate objects as the diagram is edited.

PRODUCT	DESCRIPTION
DESIGNAID Nastec Corporation 24681 Northwestern Highway Southfield, MI 48075 (313) 353-3300 (800) 872-8296 IBM XT/AT, DEC VAX	(See Chapter 9 for a detailed description.)
DESIGN MACHINE Optima, Inc. (formerly Ken Orr & Associates) 1725 Gage Blvd Topeka, KS 66604-3379 (800) 255-2459 (913) 273-0653	The DesignMachine is built on Optima's Data Structured Systems Development (DSSD) methodology for analyzing and designing systems. DesignMachine focuses on data modeling and generates systems development documentation such as entity diagrams and functional flows. Through a series of menus and lists, the designer defines objects and relationships between the objects in the system. With this data, DesignMachine produces entity diagrams and Warnier-Orr diagrams, including functional flows and data structures. DesignMachine interfaces with Optima's STRUCTURE(S) COBOL Code Generator for automatic COBOL source code generation based on designs created using DesignMachine.
DEVELOPMENT LIFE CYCLE METHODOLOGY DMR Group, Inc. 57 River Street Wellesley Hills, MA 02181 (617) 237-0087	The Development Life Cycle Methodology is a proprietary development method based on DMR's experience in building large systems for its consulting clients. The methodology is explained in a book of about 120 pages. Although not a software tool, it does use off-the-shelf design analysis tools such as Excelerator from Index Technology Corporation.
ENVISION Future Tech, Inc. 724 West Hi-Crest Drive Auburn, WA 98001 (206) 939-7552	Envision is a Microsoft Windows based tool implementing the Structured Analysis (data flow diagrams) and entity-relationship methodologies. Envision is highly configurable, allowing sophisticated users to define their own symbols and connection mechanisms. This capability enables users to incorporate new methodologies into the tool.
EXCELERATOR Index Technology Corporation 101 Main Street Cambridge, MA 02142 (617) 497-4473	(See Chapter 9 for a detailed description.)
ER-DESIGNER Chen & Associates 4884 Constitution Avenue #1-E Baton Rouge, LA 70808 P.O. Box 25130 Baton Rouge, LA 70894 (504) 928-5765	An entity-relationship diagramming tool.

PRODUCT	DESCRIPTION
FLOW CHARTING II+ Patton & Patton Software Corp 81 Great Oaks Boulevard San Jose, CA 95119 (408) 629-5376	Flow Charting II+ is an interactive IBM PC based flow charting tool.
FOUNDATION (DESIGN/1) Arthur Andersen & Co. 33 West Monroe Street Chicago, Il 60603 (312) 580-0033	The Foundation environment consists of three components: Method/1, for project management; Design/1, for planning and design; and Install/1, for implementation and support. Design/1 allows application designers to create relationships between design objects. A Design Dictionary maintains cross-reference indexes between objects. Design/1 also includes a screen painting facility, a data flow diagram editor, and a structure chart editor.
IDMS/Architect Cullinet Software, Inc. 400 Blue Hill Drive Westwood, MA 02090 (617) 329-7700	IDMS/Architect is a family of IBM PC based software engineering tools for designing data base and applications software. IDMS/Architect includes a PC-to-mainframe connection, allowing an application designer to create many of the components of a mainframe application on the personal computer.
INFORMATION ENGINEERING FACILITY Texas Instruments, Inc. (214) 575-4404 IBM MVS	The Information Engineering Facility is an integrated set of five software-development tools: A project Planning Toolset; an Analysis Toolset including an entity-relationship diagrammer; a Design Toolset including a process hierarchy diagrammer, a program design language facility, and a screen design editor; a Code Generation Toolset for producing COBOL program code based on the system definitions; and a Data Base Generation Toolset for generating control information needed for data storage and access.
INFORMATION ENGINEERING WORKBENCH KnowledgeWare, Inc. 3340 Peachtree Road, N.E. Atlanta, GA 30326 (404) 231-8575 Arthur Young International also distributes KnowledgeWare products in several countries outside the United States. IBM PC/AT	KnowledgeWare's Information Engineering Workbench is a set of CASE tools including the Entity-Relationship Diagrammer, the Data Flow Diagrammer, and the Action Diagrammer. The Data Flow Diagrammer tool allows the user to select between Yourdon/DeMarco, Gane and Sarson, and Martin symbols. The Action Diagrammer is a facility for creating process specifications. The Action Diagrammer uses a visual bracket notation to illustrate hierarchical structure, repetition, case structure, and subroutines, much like in Warnier-Orr diagrams.

PRODUCT	DESCRIPTION
INTERACTIVE EASYFLOW HavenTree Software Limited P.O. Box 2260 Kingston, Ontario Canada K7L 5J9 (613) 544-6035	Interactive EasyFlow is a flow-charting program which allows the software engineer to interactively flow chart a program on the screen using a number of predefined flow-charting symbols. When finished, the flow-chart can be printed on a variety of dot-matrix and graphics printers.
$149.00 IBM AT Color Graphics Adapter or Enhanced Graphics Adapter	Interactive EasyFlow is a reasonable tool for small-size and medium-sized flow-charting jobs, but it has no facilities for managing large systems. It provides no mechanism for hierarchically organizing flow charts and "exploding" higher-level diagrams into lower-level flow charts.
MACBUBBLES StarSys, Inc. 11113 Norlee Drive Silver Spring, MD 20902 (301) 946-0522	MacBubbles is a data flow diagram editor for the StarSys, Inc. Apple Macintosh.
NETRON/CAP DEVELOPMENT CENTER Netron Inc. 99 St. Regis Cres., N., Downsview, Ontario Canada M3J1Y9 (416) 636-8333 IBM PC IBM MVS/TSO	Netron/CAP is a COBOL application generator based on "frame" technology. A frame is a segment of reusable code that can be customized for each particular use. Netron/CAP includes a set of tools designed to manipulate frames and incorporate programmer customizations into them. The CAP Development Center components include: • CAPinput—a designer of interactive file maintenance programs • CAPscreen—a screen painter for interactive programs • CAPreport—a report painter • CAPframes—a library of reusable code components
PACBASE CGI Systems, Inc. One Blue Hill Plaza Pearl River, NY 10965 (800) 722-1866 (914) 735-5030	PACBASE is an application generator for creating data entry screens and output reports based on several popular IBM mainframe data bases. PACBASE provides an interactive screen and report layout editor and data definition facility. PACBASE emphasizes its requirements analysis and design specification capabilities based on its central data dictionary. PACDESIGN, for the IBM PC, will generate COBOL code directly from mainframe dictionary specifications.
POWERTOOLS **(formerly PRISM)** Iconix Software Engineering 1037 Third Street Suite 105 Santa Monica, CA 90403 (213) 458-0092 Apple Macintosh	(See Chapter 9 for a detailed description.)

PRODUCT	DESCRIPTION
PRODOC Scandura Intelligent Systems 1249 Greentree Lane Narbert, SPA 19072 (215) 898-7386 (213) 664-1207	PRODOC is a source code design and maintenance tool that, represents program structure graphically using visual programming techniques. PRO-DOC uses graphical symbols, called FLOWforms, to represent common programming constructs, such as case selection, repeat-until, for-do, and if-then-else. FLOWforms are independent of any particular programming language and are much like a graphical rendition of a program design language. Sections of code can be expanded or collapsed to reveal or hide program detail.
PROMOD ProMod, Inc. 23685 Birtcher Drive Lake Forest, CA 92630 (714) 855-3046 DEC VAX, IBM PC/XT/AT	(See Chapter 9 for a detailed description.)
PSCA Cadre Technologies, Inc. 222 Richmond Street Providence, RI 02903 (401) 351-5950	PSCA is an IBM AT based interactive data flow diagramming tool based on the Yourdon/DeMarco Structured Analysis methodology. PSCA was originally developed by StructSoft and now marketed by Cadre Technologies.
PSL/PSA STRUCTURED ARCHITECT Meta Systems, Inc. 315 Eisenhower Parkway #200 Ann Arbor, MI 48014 (313) 663-6027	PSL/PSA (Problem Statement Language/Problem Statement Analyzer) is Meta Systems' core product and serves as a central data base and data dictionary for other Meta Systems products. Structured Architect is an IBM PC based editor for data flow diagrams (Structured Analysis) and process specifications.
SOFTWARE THROUGH PICTURES Interactive Development Environments Inc. 150 Fourth Street Suite 210 San Francisco, CA 94103 (415) 543-0900	Software Through Pictures is a family of editors and tools that provide facilities for Structured Analysis (Yourdon/DeMarco data flow diagrams), structured design (Yourdon/Constantine), entity-relationship diagrams, and Data Structure Design (Jackson). IDE stresses the open architecture and integration aspects of their tools. Each tool has well-defined input and output ASCII file formats, allowing software engineers to "tap in" to the design process at any point.
STATEMATE1 Ad Cad, Inc. University Place, Suite 200 124 Mt. Auburn Street Harvard Square Cambridge, MA 02138 (617) 576-5732	Statemate1 is a tool for requirements analysis and design specification. It contains modules for describing application systems from three perspectives: the behavioral, functional, and structural views. For example, the behavioral view describes the system as a set of states and provides a precise description of the system's dynamic responses to internal and external stimuli.

PRODUCT	DESCRIPTION
STRADIS/DRAW DFDdraw SCdraw PROKIT WORKBENCH PROKIT ANALYST McDonnell Douglas Professional Services Company P.O. Box 516 St. Louis, MO 63166 (800) 325-1087	STRADIS/DRAW is an interactive editor for structure charts, data flow diagrams (Structured Analysis), and data models available on IBM mainframes. DFDdraw is a data flow diagram editor for the IBM PC. SCdraw is an editor for creating structure charts on the IBM PC. Professional STRADIS/DRAW and DFDdraw use a common file format, allowing data flow diagram designs to be transferred between the IBM PC and IBM mainframe environments. PROKIT ANALYST includes facilities for structure chart creation and project management.
TAGS/IORL Teledyne Brown Engineering Cummings Research Park Huntsville, AL 35807 (205) 532-1613	(See Chapter 10 for a detailed description.)
TEAMWORK Cadre Technologies, Inc. 222 Richmond Street Providence, RI 02903 (401) 351-5950 Apollo, Hewlett-Packard, IBM PC, Sun.	(See Chapter 9 for a detailed description.)
VISIBLE ANALYST WORKBENCH Visible Systems Corporation 49 Lexington Street Newton, MA 02165 (617) 969-4100 IBM PC	The Visible Analyst Workbench is an IBM PC based charting and diagramming tool that will create the system life cycle diagrams required by any methodology. Users can define custom symbols and store them in a symbol library, and text can be interspersed with graphics on the same page. The Visible Analyst consists of three modules. The first, the Visible Analyst, is the foundation diagramming tool. The second, Visible Rules, is an add-on module that supports Yourdon/DeMarco or Gane and Sarson rules. The third tool, the Visible Dictionary, adds a central repository for information related to a project.
VS-DESIGNER VS-OBJECT MAKER Visual Software, Inc. 3945 Freedom Circle Suite 540 Santa Clara, CA 95054 (408) 988-7575	VS-Designer is an integrated set of CASE tools implementing the Yourdon/DeMarco Structured Analysis, Information Engineering (Martin), Entity-Relationship, Warnier-Orr, and Jackson design methodologies. Visual Software stresses VS-Designer's adaptation and customization capabilities that allow custom methodologies to be implemented within VS-Designer's framework. VS-Designer includes a Drawing Editor, configurable word processor, Symbol Editor, and display system to help users customize the VS-Designer system. The VS-Object Maker is used to

PRODUCT	DESCRIPTION
	modify existing or create new symbols.
X-TOOLS Software Design Tools 6290 Sunset Blvd. #1126 Los Angeles, CA 90028 (213) 463-6102	X-Tools implements the Nassi-Shneiderman diagramming conventions for code structuring.
YOURDON ANALYST/ **DESIGNER TOOLKIT** Yourdon, Inc. 1501 Broadway New York, NY 10036 (212) 391-2828 IBM PC/XT/AT	The Yourdon Software Engineering Workbench implements the Yourdon/DeMarco Structured Analysis methodology (data flow diagrams) with Ward's real-time extensions, including state transition diagrams. A structure chart facility is an integral part of the tool kit, as is an entity-relationship diagrams modeler which supports Chen's conventions.

User Interface Design Tools

Only a small selection of user interface design tools is presented here. By far, the IBM PC is the most popular computing environment for these products because of its convenience and low cost. The IBM mainframe is probably the second most popular platform because of the large number of data entry, inventory, data base, and other types of transaction applications. These mainframe applications almost exclusively use form-filling interfaces, which is a relatively easy interface style for which to create interface design and layout tools. Many of the mainframe design specification tools listed previously in this Appendix contain screen design and report layout capabilities, and several are integrated with code generation tools.

Many of the interface design tools for the IBM PC are screen generators for creating dBASE data entry and help screens. dBASE II and dBASE III, the popular data base programs from Ashton-Tate, have a data base programming language that allows application developers to write custom data base applications on top of dBASE. Since many small businesses use dBASE for customized inventory and order entry applications, a substantial number of programers specialize in dBASE language software. This user base supports a large number of dBASE aids, including application screen generators.

Attempting to create an exhaustive list of these screen generators would be futile given the rapidly changing pace of the personal computer software market. However, the tools described in the following list and in Chapter 11 provide a fair indication of the capabilities of this class of CASE tools.

PRODUCT	DESCRIPTION
APS DEVELOPMENT CENTER Sage Software, Inc. 3200 Monroe Street Rockville, MD 20852 (301) 230-3200	The APS Development Center is an integrated set of programming tools including the APS Screen Painters. The APS Screen Painters allow developers to interactively layout and edit IBM 3270 data entry screens and reports.
CHARM WorldWide Data Corporation 39 Broadway New York, NY 10006 (718) 438-2807	Charm is an interactive interface generator for building data entry and reporting screens and menus. Charm interfaces with several different data bases including Oracle, Unify, and Ingres.
CLARION Barrington Systems, Inc. 150 East Sample Road Pompano Beach, FL 33064 (305) 785-4555	Clarion is an IBM PC based application interface generator. Clarion uses a fourth generation-like language to specify screen interfaces.
C-SCAPE Oakland Group, Inc. 675 Massachusetts Avenue Cambridge, MA 02139 (617) 491-7311 $199.00	C-SCAPE is a source code generation facility that works in conjunction with Dan Bricklin's Demo Program by converting Demo's output to C code. C-SCAPE contains a subroutine library of input and output functions that allow the creation of menus, input fields, and text, based on the screen composed using Demo. See Chapter 11 for a description of Dan Bricklin's Demo Program.
DAN BRICKLIN'S DEMO PROGRAM Software Garden, Inc. P.O. Box 238 West Newton, MA 02165 Version 1A $79.95 BM PC, XT, AT Monochrome card, Color Graphics Adapter, or Enhanced Graphics Adapter 256KB or more DOS 2.0 or later	(See Chapter 11 for detailed description.)
JYACC FORMAKER and APPLICATION MANAGER JYACC, Inc. 116 John Street New York, NY 10038 (212) 267-7722 (800) 458-3313 (outside New York State)	(See Chapter 11 for a detailed description.)

PRODUCT	DESCRIPTION
SAYWHAT! The Research Group 88 South Linden Avenue South San Francisco, CA 94080 (415) 571-5019	SayWhat! is a tool for interactively creating and editing display screens to be used with the dBASE III database program. These screens are typically used for data entry and data display. SayWhat! is not designed to be a general purpose interface design tool, but it does have capabilities for creating menus and windows.
Version 3.0 $49.95 IBM PC/XT/AT or compatible 128 KB memory Monochrome or Color Graphics Adapter PC-DOS 2.0 or later	SayWhat! screens for an application are saved in a file and then "called up" by a memory resident utility whenever a GET or SAY command is issued in dBASE III. SayWhat! screens can also be hooked to Pascal, BASIC, and C programs, and are accessed through the normal data read and write functions.
SKYLIGHTS Ergosyst Associates, Inc. 900 Massachusetts Street Lawrence, KS 66044 (913) 842-7334	Skylights is a software package that enables developers of C-language applications for IBM PCs to implement user interfaces. Skylights has two components: a set of routines linked with applications to provide run-time user interface management, and an interactive screen editor for developing and maintaining user interfaces. With the interactive screen editor, screens are stored in window "catalogs" and are invoked from the application program.
	Skylights will convert screens and images created with other programs, such as Dan Bricklin's Demo Program, AutoCAD (from Autodesk), and Dr. Halo (from Media Cybernetics).
SQL/MENU Kolinar 3064 Scott Boulevard Santa Clara, CA 95054-3301 (408) 980-9411	SQL/MENU generates full screen SQL/DS applications to display, update, delete, and insert data from the SQL/DS data base. The XMENU/E screen editing facility is used to create a control file of screen definitions used by SQL/MENU during operation.
IBM 370 architectures, VM/CMS	

Appendix B

CASE Training Organizations

The following list of organizations offering training courses or seminars in CASE technology is relatively short. However, as CASE grows in popularity during the next several years, a much larger group of educational organizations will enter the market. Indeed, it is likely that the number of training companies offering at least one CASE course will grow tenfold in the next three years. Nevertheless, the following list is a reasonable starting point for readers interested in hands-on instruction.

Obviously, the syllabuses for the following courses and the course offerings themselves are bound to change as the technology matures, more tool vendors enter the market, and new methodologies are implemented in CASE tools. This list does *not* contain tool-specific courses because most CASE tool vendors offer training and support for their products. However, tool vendors that offer courses not specific to their own tool products are included.

CASE Training Organizations

Digital Consulting, Inc. 8 Windsor Street Andover, MA 01801 (617) 470-3880	**Software Engineering and CASE Technology.** • Software Engineering Methods and Procedures • Human Factors for Successful Software Engineering • CASE Systems and Environments • Planning and Measuring Productivity Improvement • Checklists for Method and Tool Evaluations
Integrated Computer Systems Integrated Computer Systems 5800 Hannum Avenue P.O. Box 3614 Culver City, CA 90231-3164 (800) 421-8166 (213) 417-8888	**Computer-Aided Tools for Software Analysis and Design.** • Producing data flow diagrams, hierarchy charts, and data dictionaries using graphical design aids • Rapid prototyping tools to speed design • Tools for the prevention and early detection of errors • Text/graphics documentation tools for project visibility and management control **Structured Design and Programming.** • Basic Design Principals • Software Engineering Principals • A Data View of the System • Physical Design • Designing Congruent Structures • Modular Program Design • Real-Time Design

Case Training Organizations

Ken Orr & Associates 1725 Gage Blvd. Topeka, KS 66604--3379 (800) 562-8000 (913) 273-0653	**Data Structured Systems Development.** **Structured Requirements Definition.** **Computer-Aided Program Design.** **Project Planning and Control.** Ken Orr & Associates provides training and consulting services in structured software design and in CASE tools, including Brackets and DesignMachine.
KnowledgeWare, Inc. and Pacific Information Management, Inc. 2121 Cloverfield Blvd., Suite 203 Santa Monica, CA 90404	**Information Engineering Conference.**
McDonnell Douglas P.O. Box 516 St. Louis, MO 63166-1516 (800) 325-1087 (314) 232-0232	**Structured Systems Analysis and Design.** **Advanced Structured Analysis and Design.** • Structured Systems Analysis Tools • Development of Logical Data Flow Diagrams • Development and Use of Data Dictionaries • Static and Dynamic Data Modeling • Mini-specification tools • Principles of Structured Program Design
Nastec Corporation 24681 Northwestern Highway Southfield, MI 48075 (800) 872-8296 (313) 353-3300	**The CASE Project Management Seminar.** • Methods for defining work to be performed • Estimating, scheduling, and assigning tasks • Measuring project progress and productivity **The CASE Estimating Seminar.** Reviews problems associated with estimating and suggests helpful procedures to improve future estimates. **Computer-Aided Structured Analysis & Design.** Instructs participants in the principles of Structured Analysis and design using Yourdon/DeMarco techniques.
Technology Transfer Institute 741 Tenth Street Santa Monica, CA 90402 (213) 394-8305	**The James Martin Seminar.** • Joint application design (IE-JAD) • Joint Requirements Planning (JRP) • CASE tools and techniques • CASE tools linked to code generators • Fourth-generation methodologies for application creation • Automated DP methodologies
Wang Institute Tyngsboro, MA (617) 649-7371	**Data Structured Systems Development.**
Washington University St. Louis, MO	**Computer-Aided Program Design.**

Appendix C

CASE Related Conferences, Symposia, and Newsletters

At this writing, there are very few conferences and newsletters devoted exclusively to computer-aided software engineering. Increasingly common, though, are sessions dedicated to CASE at software engineering conferences and seminars sponsored by the IEEE (Institute of Electrical and Electronic Engineers) and the ACM (Association for Computing Machinery).

CASE Conferences, Symposia, and Newsletters

CASE	International Workshop on Computer-Aided Software Engineering. Sponsored by Index Technology Corporation in conjunction with Purdue University, Northeastern University, and the Greater Boston Chapter of the ACM.
CASE: Commercial Strategies. Ovum, Inc. Princeton Professional Park Suite C-9 601 Ewing Street Princeton, NJ 08540 (609) 921-6886 $595.00	A market research report containing: • Management Summary • Users and Markets • Tools and Technologies • The CASE Industry • User Profiles • Research Profiles
CASE Outlook. Gene Forte, Executive Director 224 S.W. First Avenue Portland, OR 97204 (503) 226-0420 $495.00/year	Monthly newsletter featuring: • CASE tool evaluations • New product announcements • Event and trade show listings • New book, course, and training announcements
The CASE Report. Nastec Corporation 24681 Northwestern Highway Southfield, MI 48075-2325 (313) 353-3300	A monthly eight page report devoted to CASE technology. Distributed free of charge by Nastec, a major CASE tool vendor, the CASE Report features detailed and interesting articles on major software engineering issues.

CASE Conferences, Symposia, and Newsletters

Computer-Assisted Software Engineering: Vendor and User Issues in an Emerging Market Schubert Associates, Inc. 10 Winthrop Square Boston, MA 02110 (617) 338-0930	Market research report.
International Conference on Software Engineering	Sponsored by the Computer Society of the IEEE and the ACM Special Interest Group on Software Engineering Approximately 30 CASE tool vendors were present at the ninth annual conference in 1987.
International Data Corporation	Market research study on CASE.

Appendix D

DOD-STD-2167

DOD-STD-2167A (April 1, 1987), superseded DOD-STD-2167 (June 4, 1985), which in turn suiperseded DOD-STD-1679A (NAVY, October 22, 1983) and MIL-STD-1644B (March 2, 1984). Although largely the same, there are differences between DOD-STD-2167A and DOD-STD-2167. Copies of these and other DOD-STD documents referenced in this book can be obtained from the Navy Publications Office, 5801 Tabor Avenue, Philadelphia, PA 19120-5099. Order Line (215) 697-2179.

Other DOD and MIL-STD documents, such as those listed in the following table, describe in greater detail the review, auditing, and configuration management activities. These standards are referenced throughout DOD-STD-2167.

Related DOD and MIL Standard Documents

DOD-STD-480	Configuration Control—Engineering Changes, Deviations, and Waivers
DOD-STD-2168	Defense System Software Quality Program
MIL-STD-483	Configuration Management Practices for Systems, Equipment, Munitions, and Computer Software
MIL-STD-490	Specification Practices
MIL-STD-881	Work Breakdown Structures for Defense Material Items
MIL-STD-882	System Safety Program Requirements
MIL-STD-1521	Technical Reviews and Audits for Systems, Equipment, and Computer Software
MIL-STD-1535	Supplier Quality Assurance Program Requirements

Glossary

Algorithm. A procedure or process that describes how to perform a specified function or action.

Analysis. The study and modeling of a process, business area, or operation prior to implementing a software system.

Analyst. The data processing professional who serves as a bridge between the end-user community and the software development team. An analyst works with the end-users to formulate a requirements specification. Structured Analysis is one frequently used requirements specification technique.

Application generator. These tools take design specifications and generate compilable code, usually COBOL. Most application generator tools are used for building data base applications.

Application program. A software program written for end-users to solve a commercial, business, or industrial need. Examples of application programs are payroll accounting packages (commercial) and real-time control software for factory control (industrial). See *system software*.

Application programmer. A software engineer or programmer who writes application programs. Application programmers typically have detailed knowledge of specialized business functions, such as accounting, order processing, or process control, in addition to computer programming expertise.

Automatic code generation. The capability of a software design tool to automatically generate compilable or executable code directly from the software design.

Balancing. The relationship between a parent data flow diagram and a child data flow diagram with respect to input and output data flows. Data flows existing in a parent data flow diagram (process node) should also exist in the child data flow diagram.

Baseline. A configuration identification document fixed at a specific time during a software system's life cycle specifying the composition—the component modules—of the software system.

Beta test. A software development cycle phase where prerelease copies of the software are sent to actual end-users. Beta test releases identify trouble spots, performance problems, and bugs. Active end-user polling is conducted to provide maximum feedback to the development team.

BNF (Backus-Naur form). A formal method for specifying the production rules used to parse a formal computer language such as C or COBOL. BNF descriptions can be used to formally define and specify a wide range of computer languages including command line languages.

CASE. An acronym for Computer-Aided Software Engineering. The purpose of CASE is to provide software engineers and programmers with software-based tools that help specify functional requirements and architect designs for software applications. A long-range goal of CASE technology is to automatically generate software based on designs built with CASE tools.

Cohesion. Cohesion is a measure of how well a particular software module's components—its code and local data structures—belong together. High cohesion, a strong measure of locality, is good.

Context diagram. A context diagram is the top-level diagram of a data flow diagram. The context diagram depicts all of the net inputs and outputs of a system, but shows none of the underlying process node (bubble) decomposition in the data flow diagram. Context diagrams are useful when viewing the system as a black box and only the input and output data flows need be displayed.

Control flow diagram.   A control flow diagram shows the flow of control signals between processes and between processes and control specification sheets.

Control specifications.   Control specifications convert input control signals into output control signals or control process activations.

Coupling.   Coupling is an indication of how tightly program modules are interconnected. High coupling, which means a large number of connections, is generally bad.

CSCI (computer software configuration item).   A term used in DOD-STD-2167 indicating a hardware or software component which is designated by the contracting agency for configuration managment.

Data dictionary.   A collection of data dictionary entries including the names of all data items used in a software system, together with relevant properties of those systems; a set of definitions of data flows, data elements, files, data bases, and processes in a data flow diagram.

Data flow.   A piece of data, which may have subcomponents (substructures), that passes along vectors between process nodes (bubbles) on a data flow diagram.

Data flow diagram.   A graphic depiction of the different data items in a system and their movement from process to process. Data flow diagrams depict a system from the data's viewpoint rather than the control flow's viewpoint. Data flow diagrams, however, reveal only data flow, not control flow. The data flow diagram represents a partitioning of a system.

Data modeling.   Data modeling is the process of identifying an application's data elements, data structures, and file format structures. This includes delineating the relationships between data elements, generally with entity-relationship diagrams.

Data structure diagram.   A graphic diagram illustrating the relationships between different elements in a data or file structure. Generally, these diagrams depict the decomposition of higher-level data structures into lower-level data structures.

Decision table.   A decision table shows the transformation between a set of inputs and a set of outputs. Decision tables map input control signals into output control signals. Decision tables are a useful mini-specification technique when the control processing is better expressed as a "look-up table" than as an algorithmic procedure.

Decision tree.   The decision tree is a variant of the decision table that depicts a graphical view of the conditional selection process used to determine a set of actions from a set of inputs. The decision points are the nodes in the tree; the actions are found at the leaves.

Design specification.   The process of composing a software "blueprint," showing how to build what is required by the requirements specification document. Design specifications include module decompositions, data structure definitions, file format definitions, and important algorithm descriptions.

DOD-STD-2167.   The standard structured systems methodology for defense contractors. DOD-STD-2167 specifies that Structured Analysis and design be used, and dictates that requirements be traceable throughout all layers of the system. Also called MIL-STD-2167.

End-user.   An individual who uses a software application program. The "customer" of the analyst (systems engineer) who specifies the application program's functionality and the software designer who architects the program's implementation.

Entity-relationship diagram.   A diagram depicting entities (objects and data elements) and the relationships between those entities. Entity-relationship diagrams are used to model information and data in an organization or system.

Flow charts.   Flow charts are graphical representations of low-level program control flow. Flow charts consist of graphical symbols connected by arrows depicting the program's control flow. Generally, each flow chart symbol directly corresponds to a line of code in the underlying program.

Formal computer languages.   Formal computer languages are languages such as COBOL, FORTRAN, and C. Formal programming languages are sometimes used as a Structured Analysis mini-specification technique because such mini-specifications force the analyst to focus on very low level details and because the mini-specifications can be directly compiled to generate working software.

Fourth Generation Languages.   Fourth generation languages (4GLs) are high-level languages which provide data base access facilities. 4GLs are much easier to use than languages traditionally used for programmatic data base access such as COBOL and C. Many 4GLs provide form layout and data input capabilities.

Functional decomposition.   The process of designing a system by breaking it into its functional component parts. The components correspond directly to system functions and subfunctions.

Functional requirements.   The specification of a proposed system. A functional requirements document defines, to the greatest detail possible, the interactions between the software system and its environment (end-users, etc.).

Functional specification.   A detailed description of the software system to be implemented, itemizing each feature and function. Functional specifications can be written delineations of the required software features or they can be generated from formal specification methodologies like Structured Analysis.

Gane and Sarson diagrams.   Gane and Sarson diagrams are equivalent to data flow diagrams, except that "square bubbles" with rounded edges are used for processes and "pipes" for data flows. These diagrams can be considered a different notation for data flow diagrams.

Hierarchical decomposition.   A method of breaking a system down into its components in a top-down manner.

HIPO (hierarchy plus input-output).   HIPO charts represent modules of a software system as a hierarchy and explicitly depict data flow—the inputs and outputs—between modules. Data can only flow between parent and child modules.

Information model.   An information model depicts the data and information used by an organization, usually a business function, in a graphical form. The information model highlights the relationships between the data as well as the data elements themselves. The entity-relationship diagram is an information modeling technique.

JAD (joint application design).   JAD is a requirements analysis technique pioneered by IBM. In JAD, a design workshop is held where end-users are the main participants. Systems engineers are present to assist the end-users in creating report designs, screen designs, and information flow models.

Jackson structured design.   A structure charting methodology for explicitly specifying sequence, selection, and iteration between program modules.

Leveling.   The process of successively partitioning data flow diagram parent processes into child processes in order to construct an hierarchically structured system. The result presents the system as a top-down partitioning of data flow diagrams.

Leveled set. The data flow diagram depicting all the lowest-level, or primitive, process nodes. The leveled set may contain process nodes from several different levels in the whole data flow diagram because not all levels can be decomposed to the same depth.

MIL-STD-2167. (See *DOD-STD-2167*.)

Mini-specifications (also called mini-specs). Mini-specifications describe the algorithm, or process, inside a process node on a data flow diagram. Mini-specifications detail how input data flows (data elements) are processed and output data flows are generated. There are a variety of mini-specification techniques, including flow charts, decision tables, and program design languages.

Module. A collection of program functions. Typically, program modules contain a set of routines with well-defined inputs and outputs for performing the module's assigned tasks.

Nassi-Shneiderman diagrams. A visual program design language for blocking out code. Nassi-Shneiderman diagrams have visual constructs for *if-then, iteration*, and other program language control structures.

Process specification. A description of the transformation performed on the input data flows to produce the output data flows in a data flow diagram. Also called a mini-spec or mini-specification.

Program design language. A language with a set of formal constructs and syntax but whose structure resembles loosely structured pseudocode. Program design languages are one mini-specification technique used to describe processes in a data flow diagram. (See *visual program design languages*.)

Pseudocode. A loose form of structured English used to represent an algorithm for a low-level process. Pseudocode is one mini-specification technique used to define processes in a data flow diagram.

Real-time processing. Real-time systems interact directly with a changing physical environment. A requirement of real-time software is that must keep pace with the changes in the external environment.

Requirements analysis. Requirements analysis is the first stage of the software development process, the goal of which is to write a complete requirements specification itemizing the required features and functionality needed in the application program. The requirements analysis process is performed by an analyst or a systems engineer and involves much interviewing and interaction with the application's intended end-users.

SADT (Structured Analysis Design Technique). A proprietary variation of Structured Analysis and data flow diagramming created by Softech, Inc.

Sink. A receiver of a data element or data input residing outside of the software system. A sink typically is a person, an organization, or a device.

Source. An originator of a data element or data input residing outside the software system. A source typically is a person, an organization, or a device.

State transition diagram. A state transition diagram is a graphical representation of the states in a system and the events that cause transitions between the various states. State transition diagrams are used to specify control flow in a control flow diagram.

Stepwise refinement. The process of breaking a process into its component parts in a hierarchical fashion. Stepwise refinement is a synonym for functional decomposition.

Structure chart. A graphic tool that depicts the partitioning of a system into modules, showing the hierarchy and organization of those modules and the communication interfaces among them.

Structured Analysis. In terms of structured methodology, analysis is a clearly defined series of steps that produces a requirements specification. Structured Analysis focuses on the "what" of a system: what a system does and how data items (data flows) move between processes. Structured Analysis, developed by Edward Yourdon and Tom DeMarco, is used to build data flow diagrams and process mini-specifications.

Structured design. Structured design focuses on the "how" of a system: how a system is constructed. Structured design's main tool is the structure chart that integrates a specified set of rules to produce a top-down, modular design.

Structured English. (See *pseudocode*.)

Structured specification. A structured specification is a functional requirements document built using the Structured Analysis methodology. Structured specifications are largely graphics-based, relying on data flow diagrams to communicate the software's operation.

System software. A computer program written to control the computing resources of a given computer. Examples of system software are operating systems and operating system utilities. Systems software is typically written in lower-level languages such as assembly language or C. (See also *application program*.)

Systems engineer. Similar to an analyst, but typically working with engineering, military, or real-time applications instead of commercial data processing applications. Like the data processing analyst, the systems engineer is responsible for building the requirements specification. The systems engineer may also be responsible for verifying that the implemented software system adheres to the requirements specification.

Top-down design. The process of system design that identifies major components and decomposes them into lower-level components until the desired level of detail is reached.

Unit test. Unit testing involves testing each individual module built during the implementation phase, then integrating the modules into a single program structure. The program as a whole is then tested to ensure the modules fit together and perform as designed.

User interface. The end-user communicates with the application program through its user interface. User interfaces allow end-users to perform operations (commands) and view their results.

Visual program design languages. The visual program design language, a mini-specification technique for data flow diagram processes, is a convenient way to express both pseudocode and compilable source code. Each basic programming construct is represented as a visual template which is filled in by the designer. Program segments can be expanded and contracted to reveal and hide successive levels of detail.

Warnier-Orr diagrams. A data structure and file format definition methodology used during the design specification stage of the software development cycle. Warnier-Orr diagrams show the hierarchical structuring of substructures within larger structures in an outline style format. Warnier-Orr diagrams also indicate the sorting order of data structures within files.

Bibliography

Chapter 1

Brooks, Frederick. *The Mythical Man-Month*. Reading: Addison-Wesley Publishing Company, Inc., 1985.

> This book is a classic in software engineering project management. It is chock full of pointed, pithy, bits of wisdom, based on the author's years of experience at IBM managing the OS/360 project. Every software development manager, software engineer, and programmer should read this often quoted work.

"CASE Makes Strides Toward Automated Software Development," *Computer Design*, (January 1, 1987).

Chapter 2

Boehm, Harry. *Software Engineering Economics*. New York: McGraw-Hill, 1981.

> This is the definitive tome on analyzing, sizing, and estimating software project costs. *Software Engineering Economics* is indispensable for project managers responsible for providing detailed cost and scheduling estimates to their management.

Chapter 3

Software Engineering Standards. ANSI/IEEE Standard 830-1984: IEEE Guild for Software Requirements Specifications. Piscataway: The Computer Society of the IEEE, 1984.

> This book is a collected set of ten ANSI/IEEE standards for software engineering. A glossary of software engineering terminology is also included. *Software Engineering Standards* is recommended reading for those charged with managing and controlling large software projects.

Freedman, Daniel P. and Weinberg, Gerald M. *Handbook of Walkthroughs, Inspections, and Technical Reviews*. Boston: Little, Brown and Company, Inc., 1982.

> Freedman and Weinberg present an excellent, meaty, and highly detailed treatment of this otherwise fuzzy and ill-defined subject. This is one of the few worthwhile software methodology books. It describes exactly how to conduct code walkthroughs and reviews including descriptions of the walkthrough's format, who should attend, and the attendees' individual roles.

Pressman, Roger. *Software Engineering: A Practitioner's Approach*. 2d ed. New York: McGraw-Hill, 1987.

> Pressman's book is an excellent text book covering the fundamentals of software design and project management. For learning about software engineering practices, this is the best place to start.

Chapter 4

DeMarco, Tom. *Structured Analysis and System Specification*. Englewood Cliffs: Yourdon Press, 1979.

This is the Bible upon which Structured Analysis is based. This book is extremely lucid and well written, and replete with examples. If you don't already own a copy, go out and buy it! *Structured Analysis and System Specification* is an undisputed software engineering classic.

Gane, Chris and Sarson, Trish. *Structured Systems Analysis: Tools & Techniques*. Englewood Cliffs: Prentice-Hall, 1977.

Gane and Sarson data flow diagrams are virtually identical to Yourdon's and DeMarco's. This book is very thorough and contains many examples. It covers data flow diagrams, Structured English, decision trees, and other mini-specification techniques. *Structured Systems Analysis: Tools and Techniques* is for the "hands-on" software engineer. The text includes example exercises at the end of each chapter and is suitable as a text book.

Weaver, Audrey M. *Using the Structured Techniques: A Case Study*. Englewood Cliffs: Yourdon Press, 1987.

This book is a breezy way to learn Structured Analysis and information modeling techniques. The author uses a set of characters working in a commercial data processing environment to introduce structured systems concepts. Full of examples, the book traces the development of a single project from start to finish. The narrative is fun to read, and the hero wins by finishing the project on schedule using structured techniques.

Chapter 5

Hatley, Derek J. and Pirbhai, Imtiaz A. *Strategies for Real Time and General Systems Development*. New York: Dorset House, June 1987.

Raeder, Georg. "A Survey of Current Graphical Programming Techniques." *IEEE Computer* (August 1985).

Scandura, Joseph M. "A Cognitive Approach to Software Development: The PRODOC Environment and Associated Methodology." *The Journal of Pascal, Ada, and Modula-2*. 6 (1987) no. 4.

Ward, Paul T. and Mellor, Stephen J. *Structured Development for Real-Time Systems*. Englewood Cliffs: Prentice-Hall, 1985.

Chapter 6

Constantine, L and E. Yourdon. *Structured Design*. Englewood Cliffs: Yourdon Press, 1975.

The original structured design text espousing the principles of cohesion and coupling. Although now difficult to find in bookstores, the structured design principles outlined in *Structured Design* are incorporated in the currently popular software engineering texts.

Sanden, Bo. "Systems Programming with JSP: Example—A VDU Controller." *Communications of the ACM*. 28 (October 1986) no. 10.

Chapter 7

Orr, Kenneth. *Structured Systems Development*. Englewood Cliffs: Yourdon Press, 1977.

This is the basic reference on Warnier-Orr diagrams. It is replete with examples, usually one to a page, sometimes two. You can almost learn the concepts just from studying the diagrams and reading the captions.

Higgins, David A. "Structured Programming with Warnier-Orr Diagrams, Part I: Methodology." *Byte Magazine* (December 1977).

Higgins, David A. "Structured Programming with Warnier-Orr Diagrams, Part II: Coding the Program". *Byte Magazine* (January 1978).

Chapter 8

Badre, Albert and Shneiderman, Ben, eds. *Directions in Human Computer Interaction*. Norwood: Ablex Publishing Corporation, 1982.

Shneiderman, Ben. *Software Psychology: Human Factors in Computer and Information Systems*. Boston: Little Brown & Co., 1980.

Shneiderman, Ben. *Designing the User Interface: Strategies for Effective Human-Computer Interaction*. Reading: Addison-Wesley Publishing Company, Inc., 1987.

Ben Shneiderman is one of the gurus of user interface design. This recent work covers many of the interface innovations brought by the personal computer revolution. For a first reading on user interface principles, this book is an excellent choice.

Chapter 9

Nastec Corporation. *DesignAid Tutorial*. Southfield: Nastec Corporation, 1986.

————. *Getting Started with DesignAid*. Southfield: Nastec Corporation, 1986.

Index Technology Corporation. *Excelerator Tutorial*. Cambridge: Index Corp., 1986.

PRISM Toolset User's Guide: FreeFlow, SmartChart and PRISM Design Language. Santa Monica: Iconix Software Engineering, Inc., 1987.

This reference presents a fairly good tutorial on the Structured Analysis methodology as it coaches the reader through the rudiments of using FreeFlow, PRISM's data flow diagram editing module. It explains the rudiments of functional decomposition, leveling, balancing, and data dictionary definition.

Chapter 10

Ken Orr and Associates, Inc. *Brackets Demonstration Diskette*. Topeka: Ken Orr and Associates, Inc., 1986.

Seivert, G.E. and Mizell, T.A. "Specification-Based Software Engineering with TAGS." *IEEE Computer*, 18, (April 1985) no. 4.

Teledyne Brown Engineering. *IORL, Input / Output Requirements Language—Reference Manual*. Huntsville: Teledyne Brown Engineering, 1984.

TAGS, Technology for the Automated Generation of Systems—Reference Manual. Huntsville: Teledyne Brown Engineering, January, 1986.

Chapter 11

Software Garden. *Dan Bricklin's Demo Program Reference Manual*. Cambridge: Software Garden, Inc., 1986.

Microsoft Corporation. *Microsoft Windows Software Development Kit: Programmer's Utility Guide*. Version 1.03. Bellevue: Microsoft Corporation, 1986.

JYACC Corporation. *JYACC FORMaker and JAM Demonstration Diskettes*. New York: JYACC Corp., 1986.

Chapter 12

Grzanka, Len. "CASE Plays Major Role in DEC's Engineering Market Impact." *Digital News*. (November 30, 1987).

Chapter 13

Evans, Michael W. *The Software Factory: Concepts and the Environment*. New York: John Wiley & Sons, Inc., 1987.

The Software Factory is a good text for experienced software developers wanting a higher-level perspective on the software engineering and development process. It focuses on the issues and components of a "software factory," an environment for producing well-built, high-quality software packages in a repeatable, assembly line fashion.

Yourdon, Edward. *Managing the Structured Techniques*. Englewood Cliffs: Yourdon Press, 1986.

Chapter 14

Department of Defense. *DOD-STD-2167A*. Washington D.C.: The United States Department of Defense, April 1, 1987.

This document is a must for defense software contractors. Other relevant DOD-STD and MIL-STD documents governing software engineering practices such as specification practices, technical reviews and audits, and configuration management are referenced in DOD-STD-2167, Section 2.8.

Ingram, Dr. Douglas S. "DOD-STD 2167: Requirements Will Accelerate CASE Development." *The CASE Report*. Southfield: Nastec Corporation, June 1987.

Index